PROMOTING INNOVATION AND CHANGE IN ORGANIZATIONS AND COMMUNITIES

PROMOTING INNOVATION AND CHANGE IN ORGANIZATIONS AND COMMUNITIES

A Planning Manual

JACK ROTHMAN
University of Michigan

JOHN L. ERLICH
California State University, Sacramento

JOSEPH G. TERESA
University of Michigan

John Wiley & Sons, Inc.
New York London Sydney Toronto

Library of Congress Cataloging in Publication Data:

Rothman, Jack.
Promoting innovation and change in organizations and communities.

Includes index.
1. Community organization—Handbooks, manuals, etc. 2. Community development—Handbooks, manuals, etc. 3. Diffusion of innovations—Handbooks, manuals, etc. 4. Evaluation research (Social action programs)——United States—Handbooks, manuals, etc.

I. Erlich, John, joint author. II. Teresa, Joseph, 1941- joint author. III. Title.
H62.R675 658.4'06 75-19454
ISBN 0-471-73967-7

Printed in the United States of America

10 9 8 7 6 5 4 3 2 1

ACKNOWLEDGMENTS

There is no way to thank adequately all of the people who participated in the making of this book. It is a collective product of many individuals who were engaged in diverse roles in a complex social experiment. In fact, there were so many participants and contributors that it is not feasible to list all of their names here.

Nevertheless, because of the scope of the assistance we received, we must express our appreciation. First, without the continuing financial support and professional confidence of the National Institute of Mental Health, the series of studies, of which this project is a part, would not have been remotely possible.* The School of Social Work at the University of Michigan made the work easier by providing institutional sponsorship, including a congenial intellectual atmosphere and administrative support.

At the heart of the study were the professional practitioners who carried out the guidelines in human service agency settings. These thirty professionals, eight who participated in the pilot study, and twenty-two in the full field study, provided the experience and data that we have synthesized in this volume. Their intelligence, patience, and dedication in a difficult task is commendable, but it also points to as yet unattained potentialities of the collaboration between researchers and practitioners in the field. Betty Deshler, Charles Chomet, and Angie Current merit special mention for continuing and varied roles, both as field staff and supervisors of other practitioners.

A corps of secretarial and clerical staff members, research assistants, graduate students in field work internships, and special studies courses, as well as undergraduate students in work-study assignments all contributed a great deal of effort and technical assistance to the undertaking. Singular contributions were made by Sue Rasher, Sue Martin, John Ferguson, Karen Kirkhart, Vivian Roeder, Judy Hartoog, and Alan Gordon.

Colleagues at the University of Michigan and elsewhere aided us as critics and consultants. We especially thank Bruce Francis, Eugene Litwak, Jesse Gordon, Edwin Thomas, and

*This investigation was supported by National Institute of Mental Health Research Grant Number MH 161125-05.

Tony Tripodi. Bruce Francis particularly helped us to conceptualize the design and analysis procedures. Jan Eckstein extended valuable editorial consultation and assistance.

This version of the manual emerged from the thoughtful attention of the many reviewers of earlier draft versions, including practitioners in agencies, faculty from numerous universities and disciplines, and students in classroom situations at the University of Michigan and the California State University at Sacramento. Their varying perspectives have improved the utility of the book.

This cross-discipline collaboration among people from differing professions, those theoretically oriented as well as those practice oriented, was essential to the effort. Anyone attempting a similar undertaking should be aware of the need to blend differing orientations and competencies. This is extremely difficult. With perserverance, mutual respect, and dedication to a common purpose the effort can be successful. We believe such collaborative projects should be increased. The hazards and strains should not be ignored by anyone contemplating similar work; nor should the fruits and satisfactions be underestimated.

Jack Rothman

John L. Erlich

Joseph G. Teresa

June 1975

Table of Contents

INTRODUCTION

There are growing frustrations over the failures and limitations of human service programs and projects geared to social action. The titles of two recent books on community change are significant: *Why Organizers Fail* and *Community Organization: Studies in Constraint.*[1] Both books provide vivid illustrations of how grass roots organizers and social planners in a wide range of situations are utterly frustrated and defeated in their efforts to accomplish their goals. One of the authors observes: "Community programs directed to significant social change have probably failed more often than they have succeeded. Community phenomena have proven inordinately complex and intractable to planned intervention."[2]

The task of the community worker or human service professional is formidable. Often goals are broad, idealistic, and unpopular (welfare rights, affirmative action, improved mental health). There may be strong community resistance to innovative approaches or to increased service budgets. Even more opposition may be engendered to programs involving shifts in social status, established ideology, or power relationships. But part of the problem may lie with the practitioner himself and the tools he brings to the job. Many human service workers, for example, are not able to take advantage of available social science knowledge.

[1]Harry Brill, *Why Organizers Fail: The Story of a Rent Strike* (Berkeley: University of California Press, 1971); Irving A. Spergel, ed., *Community Organization: Studies in Constraint* (Beverly Hills, Cal.: Sage Publications, 1972).

[2]Spergel, *op. cit.*, p. 9.

This book is a preliminary effort to confront that issue. The difficulty with "do-gooders" (a mixed category composed variously of human service workers, community volunteers, liberals, radicals, and other socially concerned individuals) is not lthat their goals are wrong or that they meddle where they shouldn't, but that they don't meddle very well. The fundamental purpose of this book is to provide effective theories and strategies that will enable the "doing of good" in execution as well as in intent.

A criticism often heard from people who work in the community is that academic courses on social change are usually too abstract or "irrelevant." For their part, people who spend most of their time in the academic world are inclined to criticize practitioners for their conceptual and theoretical "illiteracy." The traditional approach to bridging the gap between theory and practice has usually been to present one or more case studies demonstrating how a theoretical design served in some way to help the practitioner improve his or her performance. While these studies have made the academicians who contributed to them feel in touch with real problems, for the most part they did not do enough to assist the practitioner in the community or the student who would soon be in the field.

We have gone one step farther in the attempt to achieve a meaningful synthesis of theory and practice. Appropriate research findings from the social science literature were retrieved and codified, and generalizations were developed in areas pertinent to community and organizational change, such as participation and diffusion of innovations. These generalizations were then converted into their applied form. The resulting "action guidelines" were field-tested, retested, and refined.[3] They were finally set down in this practice manual in a form that allows them to be widely disseminated and easily replicated. (We will expand on the project design shortly.) The general method is analogous to the research-development-diffusion model employed in the physical sciences and, particularly, in industry.

In this book we have not only offered specific strategies or action guidelines for people who work in human service agencies but have also suggested some tactical steps for effectively carrying out these strategies. At the same time, detailed attention is given to *personal, client, organizational,* and *community* factors that bear on a practitioner's attempts to achieve a specified objective with a particular strategy. Examples given by practitioners themselves demonstrate the specific ways in which the guidelines were actually carried out in settings that ranged from neighborhood centers to statewide mental health organizations.

[3]"Field testing" implies examining the feasibility and specifications of a new method or product, not statistically validating a hypothesis.

Although this book is meant to be useful to practitioners in the field, it is formulated particularly for students training in human service professions. The illustrations and the frame of reference have come from the field of social work, but the book will also be useful to action-oriented sociology and psychology students, as well as to students in professional fields such as public health, city planning, public administration, community mental health, and adult education. The organizations and agencies in which the action guidelines were field-tested included such disparate settings as an urban planning council, community mental health center, social welfare workers union, family service agency, a health department, YMCA, Model Cities, intermediate school district, juvenile court, and a drug abuse planning council. (A full listing of sites used for field testing will be found at the end of this chapter.)

The approach we have taken to social intervention in this presentation is broad and eclectic. The action guidelines were derived from basic social science research findings; they are general principles that may be used by a variety of people concerned with organizational and community change, for a variety of purposes.

The subject matter has been called community planning organizational change, community work, diffusion of innovations, service delivery, social action, and the like. Under whatever name, we will be dealing with interventions that are oriented toward influencing social services and institutions and solving community welfare problems. This activity is performed by human service professionals from several disciplines as well as by citizen volunteers in civic associations and political action groups. Most of these activities have multiple but related purposes such as establishing and improving human service programs, directing and coordinating such programs, maintaining community organizations and relationships, modifying or reforming community institutions and practices, and conducting programs of community relations and public eduation.[4]

There is a conception of the social change process that influences the general approach taken in the manual. We assume that change, particularly in the human service fields, takes place in a series of incremental steps. Even revolutionary change must be viewed in terms of sequential tactical actions and reactions, building up to a culminating event that radically transforms a society.

From this point of view, a practitioner should proceed by setting a sequence of goals that are specific, realistic, and *proximate*—that is,

[4]We have been guided by the conceptual orientation to social intervention in Jack Rothman, "Three Models of Community Organization Practice," *Strategies of Community Organization*, Second Edition, Fred Cox, John L. Erlich, Jack Rothman, and John E. Tropman (Itasca, Illinois: F.E. Peacock, 1974).

short-run and tangible. A general objective is approached by moving through incremental stages; the attainment of one stage leads to the sighting and definition of the goal for the next one.

To employ the manual effectively, then, one must scale down a given purpose to a goal of limited size and time dimensions, so that it can be achieved within approximately five to 12 weeks. The setting of such limited goals is crucial to the entire enterprise. The practitioner then can be sure of what he or she is attempting and can be clear about whether it has been achieved. Both rational strategy and meaningful evaluation grow out of this.

There is a common tendency in the human services to speak of our goals in such grand terms as building a better community, improving social functioning, making institutions more responsive to people, or eliminating poverty or racism. It is sometimes difficult to move from these emotionally satisfying big objectives to ones that are finite and feasible. It may be uncomfortable to shift to "thinking small," but it is also necessary. This kind of specification and delimitation has permitted many of the strategies illustrated in this manual to be achieved in about two or three months. While as teachers we will continue to challenge our students to confront problems of major importance, we will also caution them to chisel off pieces that are small enough to handle. In reality short- and long-run efforts often go hand-in-hand (i.e., organizing a neighborhood on a block-by-block basis).

This approach to goals has the added benefit of permitting greater accountability. When goals are formulated in such global generalizations as "promoting community self-help," it is difficult to be responsible for failure or clear about success. Certainly in some situations, for political and organizational reasons, it is necessary for practitioners to be somewhat vague about their objectives. Our aims are high and our practice environment incredibly complex and unpredictable. Protection, through obscuring intentions, may be necessary. However, for many of us (and the authors include themselves, because they have been involved in a variety of community change efforts over the past 20 years), this fuzziness has become a habit rather than a necessary defense against potential detractors. Recognizing this shortcoming, we have tried to lay out a much more deliberate approach to intervention than may be found in most of the literature on social change. We need to say *specifically* what it is that we are trying to do, and to be held responsible when things do not turn out as we hoped. This kind of rigorous goal definition permits what we have always said is elusive: evaluation. And certainly accountability is important in keeping faith with the people we serve. At the same time, as a by-product, the chances of increased learning and competence are enhanced; if we set more precise goals, we can analyze much more systematically what we've done—our weaknesses and strengths, both conceptual and practical.

HOW THE ACTION GUIDELINES WERE DEVELOPED

The action strategies described in the manual were developed from an extensive six-year research project, which we can only outline briefly here.[5] Basically, the project represented an effort to yield research-derived *substantive knowledge* concerning approaches to affecting social policies and programs, provide *practical aids* for operators in the field, and contribute *methodological designs and tools* for further research activity relevant to systematic innovation and change.

The initial three years of the project consisted of a wide-ranging search of social science and professional literature to retrieve research studies related to social intervention.[6] Over 900 research studies were abstracted, codified, and synthesized. Studies were treated in the following practice issue areas:

Practitioners' roles

Participation

Organizational behavior

Political and legislative behavior

Adoption of innovations

Movement of populations

[5]The project was sponsored by NIMH, through a grant to the University of Michigan School of Social Work. A book, *Planning and Organizing for Social Change: Action Principles from Social Science Research,* Jack Rothman, contains the full set of generalizations and intervention principles (Columbia University Press, 1974). A preliminary report, by Jack Rothman on this activity will be found in Henry S. Maas, *Research in the Social Sciences: A Five Year Review* (New York, National Association of Social Workers, 1971), pp. 70-107. Details of the methodology are presented in a forthcoming book, *Research and Development in The Human Services: Constructing Effective Systems Intervention Strategies* by the authors, tentatively scheduled for publication by the University of Michigan Press.

[6]Journals in the following fields were thoroughly surveyed: in the disciplines: sociology, political science, social psychology, applied anthropology, psychology; in the professions: city planning, public health, adult and community education, social work, and public administration.

As a consequence of this effort, over 200 consensus generalizations and 400 subgeneralizations based on empirical research and related to social intervention, were developed. These generalizations were converted to their applied form in order to produce a series of "action guidelines." In other words, inferences concerning the use of the generalizations for practical purposes were made in each instance.

Subsequently, a limited number of action guidelines were selected for implementation in a field test. Criteria for selection included: (1) commonality- -relevance for a wide range of settings; (2) implementability—relative ease of execution; and (3) quantifiability—tangibility and measureability of outcome. The purpose of this facet of the project was to field test the feasibility and to operationalize the action guidelines in actual practice situations and to develop a manual that would set down specific steps, stages, and resources needed to implement these guidelines in real agency and organization settings.

In a preliminary pilot study (1971-72) conducted in the southeast Michigan area, eight professionals participated as staff, implementing 10 selected guidelines in the context of normal agency problems and main objectives.7 In the larger field test (1972-73), 22 administrators, line practitioners, and policymakers were selected to execute four guidelines that represented a spectrum of tasks and situations and were considered to be the most promising of the original set. This phase of field testing was conducted in the same Michigan area.

Field staff implemented the guidelines in terms of problems and circumstances found in their regular agency situations. Outside of agency time they recorded their experience with the guidelines in structured log forms, participated in staff-seminar meetings, and consulted with project field supervisors. An initial log was completed before beginning an implementation, biweekly periodic logs were filled out during the course of executing the guideline, and a final summary log was made out at the conclusion of the implementation.

Practitioners were asked to provide data concerning the results of the intervention in "hard" empirical terms — the increase in dollars devoted to service programs, the percentage increase in participation at meetings, the number of new clients engaged in an innovative program. Through this outcome data, and by using outside raters, it was possible to assess the degree of success in implementing guidelines. The log entries, augmented by supplementary information (personal traits and attitudes of practitioners, their agency structure,

[7]Sites for field testing and data collection on practitioners were encompassed in an arc including the following southeast Michigan and neighboring cities: Detroit, Ann Arbor, Ypsilanti, Jackson, Toledo, and Lansing.

community features, and characteristics of the client population), constitute the primary research instruments and data on the basis of which action guidelines were studied and the manual was composed.

RESEARCH AND COMMON SENSE

Four principles of intervention, or action guidelines, will be considered in the book:

Promoting an Innovative Service or Program:

By demonstrating it first with a smaller portion of the target population, then expanding to the larger group.

Changing the Goals of an Organization:

By introducing new groups into the organization who support those goals *or*

By increasing the influence of those groups within the organization who support those goals.

Increasing Participation in Organizations and Groups:

By offering benefits associated with participation.

Increasing Effectiveness in Role Performance:

By clarifying the role and obtaining agreement about it among relevant superiors and influentials.

Now, it is clear that these principles do not state startling, unusually sophisticated, or esoteric ideas. Indeed, they appear to be quite commonplace and, as our field staff has informed us, they are typically used by practitioners in their everyday work. The criterion of "commonality" employed in selecting guidelines for the field test no doubt contributed to this. In our view, these strategies are basic to social intervention. Although the guidelines were derived independently, from research studies, virtually all of the practitioners who participated in the field-testing noted the familiar and fundamental character of such strategies.

What, then, is the virtue of the extensive research process that preceded formulation of the guidelines? Is this nothing but another example of social scientists rediscovering the obvious?

Wisdom gleaned from tried-and-true experience in the front lines of community action and agency practice is probably the best source of practical strategies and techniques. As former full-time (and currently "sometime") practitioners, the authors are aware, however, that rational considerations related to goal attainment do not always dictate practice choices. The need simply to survive in a turbulent, unpredictable environment sometimes guides our actions. Trends in practice modes also enter. Behavior modification, enabling, open classrooms, participatory democracy, program budgeting, the War on Poverty, systems analysis; all rise and fall on the winds of professional fashion. Public relations needs and organizational pressures also play their part: Can we come up with a large enough number of clients served, or sufficient use of facilities to justify the continued support of multifarious benefactors? Calculating a head count sometimes substitutes for calculating an effective strategy.

Research has demonstrated that many commonly accepted and widely used approaches are wrong. Urban renewal programs, instead of aiding intended beneficiaries, increase their misery; approaches to juvenile delinquency prevention falter and fail; mental health practices are found to be wanting; and the selection of clients penalizes the people most in need of service. Planners muddle community programs by inappropriate types of coordination or misguided approaches to involvement of participants.[8] This listing could be expanded manyfold.

When research supports a given initiative, this is a genuine "finding"—because the opposite result was just as likely. When systematic research *and* practice common sense jointly sustain a strategy or technique, as they do with these guidelines, this is strong authentication that should not be taken lightly.

What are the implications of this authentication? There are two. First, the cross-validation suggests increased emphasis on using these approaches. Among the many tools in the practitioner's kit these should be drawn upon frequently—perhaps in preference to some others—with a reasonable degree of confidence that they will do an effective job.

[8]Eleanor P. Wolf and Charles N. Lebeaux, "On the Destruction of Poor Neighborhoods by Urban Renewal," *Social Problems, 15,* (1) (Summer 1967), 3-8. Walter B. Miller, "Inter-Institutional Conflict as a Major Impediment to Delinquency Prevention," *Human Organization, 17,* (3) (Fall 1958), 20-30. Edna E. Raphael, Kenneth I. Howard, and David T.A. Vernon, "Social Process and Readmission to the Mental Hospital," *Social Problems, 13,* (4) (Spring 1966), 436-441. David Wallace, "The Chemung County Evaluation of Casework Service to Dependent Multiproblem Families," *Social Service Review, 41,* (4) (December 1967), 379-389. Robert A. Scott, "The Selection of Clients by Social Welfare Agencies: The Case of the Blind," *Social Problems, 14,* (3) (Winter 1967), 248-257. Donnell M. Pappenfort and Dee Morgan Kilpatrick, "Opportunities for Physically Handicapped Children: A Study of Attitudes and Practice in Settlements and Community Center," *Social Service Review, 41,* (2) (June 1967), 179-188. Frances Fox Piven, "Dilemmas in Social Planning: A Case Inquiry," *Social Service Review, 42,* (2) (June 1968), 197-206. Robert W. Janes and Samuel W. Byuarm, "The Effect of Voluntary Community Improvement Program on Local Race Relations," *Phylon, 26* (1) (September 1965), 25-33.

Second, the application of these approaches can be more highly systematized. It should be possible for them to be repeated by a given practitioner in new situations with greater ease and impact. And they should be capable of being replicated readily—although not mechanically—by other practitioners, especially those new to the field or students in training. One purpose of the manual is to facilitate such systematization and replication.[9]

While the listed guidelines have been derived from social science research, and field experience with them in operating agencies has given the authors confidence in their utility, they are not presented as a panacea or a routine prescription. The particular strategy or action principle embodied in the guideline is not the only or necessarily the best option for attaining the given goal in a particular practice situation. We did not conduct comparative research to test the effectiveness of alternative avenues to a given goal. Rather, we selected and operationalized a particular approach that was reasonably supported by the research literature. Thus we offer here an *available* strategy, not an optimal strategy, chosen from a range of alternatives.

The reader will have to rely on his judgment in the application: Does this initiative fit my practice situation? Am I comfortable with it organizationally or ideologically? Does it seem as good as or better than alternative approaches that come to mind? For example, in the case of use of benefits (or rewards) to promote participation, some readers may differ ideologically with the behavior-modification cast of the guideline. Perhaps "issue organizing" around particular critical situations in the community might better promote a social action posture requiring participation. Or encouraging participation on the basis of an altruistic "public-regarding" ethos might be more consistent with certain educational goals or personal values favored by a particular practitioner. Our suggestions have to be assessed and utilized in the context of such general considerations.

The effort to tighten up practice has ramifications. Opportunities for practitioners have been reduced since the "golden era" of social programs (the early and middle 1960s). It is all too tempting to orient our concerns toward the arenas to which the money seems to be going. In our judgment, this is short-sighted. The rapid ex-

[9]Practitioners in our study repeatedly told us of the importance of this. Some representative comments were: "The guideline provides a systematic model for trying to change an agency role. I think it clearly states the steps to be taken in such a way as to make its success possible and probable." "I have used this action principle on several occasions and find that it almost always works. It can be helpful and should be of use to other practitioners. It conceptualizes, and therefore permits an orderly sequencing of planning and implementing, rather than just intuition, for the practitioner engaged in a task where the guideline has utility."

pansion of the human services field in the 1960s did not allow for the serious and systematic attention to the components of social intervention that could have led to further systematic development; indeed, there were very few attempts to get at the "basics" of intervention. We went with the fads and the fashions, and now we are paying the price: We are blamed for the failures of programs designed by others primarily for cosmetic purposes. It is high time to rebuild from a more solid base of knowledge. Common and uncommon sense, both practice wisdom and research findings, are necessary for that task.

THE STRUCTURE OF THE MANUAL

Each of the next four chapters presents and analyzes one of the four action guidelines described earlier. A final chapter will draw some conclusions and suggest further steps, including ways of sequencing use of the different guidelines.

The general format of the four guideline chapters is similar:

Introduction to the practice problem

Action principles derived from research on the problem

Illustrations of implementation—patterns and operations

Quantitative findings from practitioner logs

Practitioners' view of problems and prospects

Getting started: thoughts for initiating action, and an initial log for listing first steps

Slight variations will be made in several chapters because specifics in the subject matter suggest different emphases in the presentation.

In the short introductory section we will consider why this problem is important, how it affects practitioners, their organizations, and their clients, and various other dimensions of the problem.

The next section cites and briefly reviews important research on the problem, and makes a generalization from this research. The principle or action guideline derived from the generalization is then stated, and its important conceptual, definitional, and practical aspects are described.[10]

[10]These sections are developed from relevant portions of *Planning and Organizing for Social Change, op. cit.*

We next illustrate the action principle as it was actually carried out by the practitioners in the field study. A number of different patterns of implementation are given when variations were found. These indicate specific steps and stages the practitioners followed in executing the guideline. We will also indicate how each of the elements of the guidelines was operationalized. (Operationalization pertains to the way *concepts* in the action guideline statement are converted into *real world actions, provisions, materials, etc.*) This section of the chapter draws heavily on case narratives prepared by practitioners.

We follow with a section based on more quantitative findings from the standard checklists in the logs that were filled out by practitioners, both during the course of carrying out a guideline (periodic logs), and at the end (final summary logs). These findings cover such matters as groups and individuals involved in implementation as well as facilitating and limiting factors. The data presented and discussed are taken from final summary log reports. In addition, tables in Appendix C present data from periodic logs, which may be of interest for purposes of comparison. These findings suggest, for example, what types of community groups to involve, whether to stress community, client, or agency factors in planning an implementation, and what aspects of the practitioner's personal resources to mobilize or discipline in carrying out an intervention. The presentation will emphasize the results of "successful" practice, those instances where intended outcomes were substantially attained, although we will also discuss differences between the more and the less successful implementations. (Appendix B contains a complete recording of an implementation, against which to compare the statistical summary.) A more complete discussion of the methodology of the study will be found in Appendix A. A full treatment of the design and rationale is forthcoming.[11]

Next, the practitioners speak of their experiences in their own words: techniques tried, resistances, confusions, successes, as well as advice they would give to others about how to maneuver. For the most part these are short statements taken from comments made in the concluding section of the final summary log.

Each chapter concludes with a section on *Getting Started.* Here questions are asked to help the practitioner through the thinking process needed to initiate action with the guideline. This is followed by a *Guide to Action* initial log form, on which preliminary reflections about beginning action steps can be set down. Here the emphasis is on specifying a goal that is proximate — moderate in size and concrete.

[11] "Research and Development in the Human Services: Construction effective Systems Intervention Strategies," University of Michigan Press (tentative).

(Again we feel obligated to underscore the importance of this step.) The initial log also calls for preliminary thoughts about how each of the elements of the guideline might be operationalized, as well as about which key groups and individuals might be involved. Examples from the field experience are given in order to aid in filling out the form. In a discussion below we will underline the prominence of the log in using the manual.

The Appendix B contains the periodic log, on which may be recorded some of the main factors included as an implementation proceeds, and the final summary log, which is for recapping the experience and evaluating the degree to which an intended goal was attained, what was learned in the process, and how future implementation might be improved. All the log forms are meant to be aids to both implementation and assessment, and can be used to record the full process of implementation, from thinking through and planning initial steps to evaluating the results.[12] Appendix B contains an example of recording of a full guideline implementation by a practitioner. This shows details of the flow of the process, difficulties encountered, etc.

More action-oriented readers may prefer to start with practice principles and practitioner comments on the field test, or to eliminate the research materials and conceptual content altogether. They have the option of following that course in their individual reading. The order we have chosen reflects the process actually followed in the project: moving from research to action principles to field trial and experience. This order also allows an interpenetration of research and action, the intellectual and practical, the concept and its operational form. Our agenda includes improving the impact of practice; we also hope to contribute to practitioners' knowledge and to increase their sensitivity to the theoretical undergirdings of their work.

HOW TO USE THE MANUAL

Different readers will use the manual in different ways. It is possible to start from one's practice situation and then look through the manual to see if any of the guidelines fit. The other way is to start with a guideline that is of interest and then to search one's practice situation for an appropriate problem to which to apply it. It will not be difficult, based on our experience, to find a match between practice

[12]The initial log is not a narrative record of events as with a ship's log or military log. Instead, it *records* initial planning and serves as an *analytic tool* to facilitate planning.

and the guidelines. The order of presentation of guidelines in the book is somewhat arbitrary. Users should not feel limited to this sequence in their study or application. (We will discuss patterns of sequencing further in the concluding chapter.)

After reading the contents of a chapter, filling out the initial log in the Guide to Action is the crucial mobilizing step. To reiterate, *selecting a well-defined and short-term goal is of the highest importance.*[13] A word of warning: the action principles look very simple, but this is deceptive; their implementation is very complex and demands patience and perseverance. The requirements for integration of concepts and actions, and for clarity and specification in designing strategy are alien to most practice behavior in this field.

Our use of the manual, both with graduate students and practitioners in in-service training programs, has suggested several emphases and options. Students should be encouraged to apply the initial log to a live practice situation as soon as possible. The manual is not meant to be a textbook in the usual sense — as a vehicle for the acquisition of abstract concepts through illustration and discussion. Rather, learning the concepts will take place most effectively in an attempt to apply them. There are important benefits to be gained from working back to the text from the application experience, along the lines of John Dewey's principle of "learning by doing."[14]

Although the initial log form is short and placed toward the end of a given chapter, its size and location should not obscure its saliency in using this manual. A proportionately much longer period of time should be anticipated for working with the initial log than for reading and digesting the concepts and data in the chapter itself. The instructor will find it useful to formally introduce and review the initial log form early in a particular training situation. We have found it beneficial for the instructor to use the log form personally beforehand in an example from his own experience. This serves to acquaint him with the process and the demands of application, and enables him to better answer questions and provide guidance. (Some instructors or students may also decide to selectively review the original studies footnoted in the text as a way of making the theoretical considerations more concrete.)

We have discovered that a real practice situation should be ad-

[13]An extremely valuable aid in facilitating this line of thinking is Robert Mager,- *Preparing Instructional Objectives,* (Belmont, Calif.: Fearon, 1962).

[14]We have found it particularly helpful to use the quantitative findings section retrospectively after the initial log has been filled out. This permits the reader to check his initial thinking against general tendencies of successful practitioners. But keep in mind that these findings summarize the full experience of implementation, not the beginning steps.

dressed, instead of a simulation. Simulations require the artificial concocting of endless contingencies to deal with the many factors involved in implementation. The introduction of a live practice situation serves an additional purpose. Students have sometimes initially felt that the content of the chapters was obvious or simplistic. Working with the log under real-life circumstances conveys the complexity and difficulty involved in effectively intervening in most organizational and community contexts.

Student use of the log offers a diagnostic tool for the instructor regarding where the student is in his learning of concepts and techniques. "Perfect" application should not be expected in the first attempt. Instead, this first endeavor should be seen as an application exercise that will reveal where students need further help—for example, in understanding the principle underlying the action guideline, in being able to sufficiently delimit goals, and in linking action steps appropriately to the action principle or to the goal. The first attempt at application serves as a trial and an orienting experience. Like the first pancake in the batch, it can be viewed as expendable. One way of dealing with this common experience in the first attempt is to provide two assignments in applying the log to the specific guideline, the first of which is seen basically as a practice trial, and the second as a more serious application.

In our use of the manual we have found it helpful initially for students to work in teams of two to four members. In this way they may collaborate in developing the initial log, applying it to a practice situation that one or two of them experience. Therefore, not every user needs to have a pertinent practice circumstance immediately available; those available may be shared. Groups have found it of interest to summarize their deliberations on newsprint and place these on the wall for others to see. This conveys the essence of each of the application cases to the entire body. Newsprint summaries may include answers to each of the items on the initial log, specific examples of each of the four types of benefits involved in the participation guideline, or any other idea that it would be useful to make evident to everyone.

While this book is termed a planning manual," by now it should be clear that it is not analogous to a technical blueprint. It offers a general strategic direction (such as partializing or providing benefits) to achieve a specific desired practice objective (such as promoting an innovation or fostering participation). Some typical steps or possible alternative steps are suggested, as well as factors to consider in planning, and obstacles that may be anticipated. One cannot expect to proceed step by step in cookbook fashion. The user's intelligence, sensitivity, judgement, creativity, and moral choice are essential, and are in no way mitigated by the relevant social science knowledge that is offered to facilitate implementation.

Use of these guidelines and the procedures associated with them has two additional benefits. First, the approach encourages more self-conscious, deliberate planning in promoting social change. It also offers a useful tool for diagnosing a practice situation and developing a systematic problem-solving style. Our experience with the practitioners who field-tested these guidelines has given us a very strong belief that this approach can help students (and practitioners) to examine in a much more deliberate way the dynamic interplay of variables during an intervention and the effect of each one. The usual case study or point-by-point illustrations are at best haphazard vehicles for examining the process of practice; to find even two case studies that can be compared is often regarded as a minor miracle.[15]

Second, use of a guideline forces one's professional attention to be focused on a problem. The minutes of a unit meeting of practitioners showed that applying guidelines in this systematic way seemed to change the practitioners' characteristic way of functioning:

> Our discussion reached the following conclusions about the effects of the guideline on practice behavior:
>
> 1 *Concentration and organization of time and effort:* The guidelines required practitioners to focus their energy, set deadlines, and move expeditiously in dealing with delimited tasks. Usually, things slide with less control.
>
> 2 *Concentration of thought:* The guidelines required practitioners to think a problem through in a focused way. Usually a pragmatic "muddling through" thought process is used.

With regard to the manual as a diagnostic tool, the practitioners often found factors associated with the organizations that employed them and with their own particular styles of operating that they completely took for granted. They therefore had failed to take account of them in much of their strategic planning. From this perspective, this book will be useful to the student who wants to take a hard look at basic practice components. The illustrative logs may well serve (per-

[15]Several practitioners commented on the way planfulness was facilitated: "It helped me clearly define the problem and develop alternative solutions or approaches to solving it. I found it most helpful in plotting out a plan and analyzing what was happening." "This guideline can be used as a means of analyzing one's situation and clarifying one's position. It requires the practitioner to think in specific terms and to clearly understand his/her role and role expectations."

haps in amended form) as a device for both planning a strategic intervention and looking carefully at the various forces and factors playing on the practitioner as he or she attempts to carry out the chosen strategy. The social-psychological components of practice—community, client population, organizational, and personal—are laid out in such a way that they may be compared across widely varying situations. For example, a number of practitioners found important variations in the way the agency structured affected their ability to carry out different interventions. This diagnostic feature may be particularly useful to human service practitioners who lack formal training or background in community and organizational change. At the same time, the manual is not intended as an all-inclusive diagnostic and problem-solving tool. It needs to be supplemented by other approaches and materials.[16]

THE RIGHT TO DECIDE AND ACT

In an early experience in using this manual, some students asked, "What right does the practitioner have to change the goals of an organization?" The same question is often posed in terms of manipulation vs. self-determination, or imposition vs. participation.[17] A community psychologist stated the matter somewhat differently in correspondence concerning the manuscript:

> *It seems to me that you've provided an excellent technology for social action. Technologies are badly needed in this area, but of course they only provide part of what is needed. To use a metaphor, your manual tells us how to operate the car, and this*

[16]For the purposes of diagnosis, a variety of sources may be used in conjunction with the manual. We have found the following especially helpful: in community analysis — Fred Cox, John L. Erlich, Jack Rothman, and John E. Tropman, *Strategies of Community Organization, op. cit.;* Ralph Kramer and Harry Specht, *Readings in Community Organization Practice* (Englewood Cliffs, N.J.: Prentice-Hall, 1969); O.M. Collective, *The Organizer's Manual* (New York: Bantam, 1971); Robert Perlman and Arnold Gurin, *Community Organization and Social Planning* (New York: Wiley, 1972). In organizational analysis — Yeheskel Hasenfeld and Richard English, eds., *Human Service Organizations,* (Ann Arbor, Michigan: University of Michigan Press, 1974); Mayer N. Zald, ed., *Social Welfare Institutions,* (New York: Wiley, 1965); Amitai Etzioni, ed., *Complex Organizations: A Sociological Reader,* (New York: Holt Rinehart and Winston, 1964); Warren G. Bennis, *Changing Organizations,* (New York: McGraw-Hill, 1966).

[17]Some of the discussion in this section has already appeared, in different form, in an earlier work, Jack Rothman, *Organizing and Planning for Social Change: Action Principles from Social Science Research* (New York: Columbia University Press, 1974).

is obviously necessary and useful. However, we also must decide upon the best destination.

Value questions of various kinds are brought to the surface by these comments: What are proper goals? Who should select them and by what process? What are the parameters of ethical behavior by practitioners regarding the pursuit of social ends?

This book is written to provide knowledge that will enhance the competence of people concerned with human betterment by assisting them to become more precise and effective in attaining their goals. It is assumed that agents for professional change do indeed seek to produce specific ends and that they hold the responsibility and should enhance their capability to achieve such ends. These goals are of course mediated through the interplay of various constituencies and interested parties such as clients, board members, organizational supervisors, and political elites. Frequently the community practitioner sees his fundamental role as facilitating the decision-making capacity of these relevant actors. Nevertheless, as Morris[18] has suggested, "...the exercise of professional leadership requires us to select our goals for action... our concern with helping others to make up their minds does not excuse us from the obligation of making up our own."

Many practitioners in the human service fields cripple their effectiveness through a muddy engagement with terms such as "self-determination," "participatory democracy," and "manipulation." This does not imply that such concepts are unimportant or meaningless. But their application is highly complex, and not particularly aided by philosophical sloganeering. In making a study of the self-determination notion, one observer points out several contingencies that shape its applicability: clients may be ambivalent or contradictory concerning their true desires; reality factors such as legal restrictions, conditions of health, or financial insufficiencies may limit certain wishes; one man's desires may impinge on the prerogatives of others, and may even destroy the people closest to him or oppress those further away. Human worth, the author concludes, is of greater utility as a concept in giving value direction to professional behavior. "If what the client wants will result in the exploitation of others or the degradation of himself, the worker should try to help him change his desires."[19]

Studies of community processes have found that broad public at-

[18]Robert Morris, "Community Planning for Health — The Social Welfare Experience," in Public Health Concepts in Social Work Education (New York: Council on Social Work Education, 1962), pp. 168-169.

[19]Saul Bernstein, "Self-Determination: King or Citizen in the Realm of Values?," *Social Work*, *5*, (1) (January 1960), 3-8.

tention and participation may have deleterious effects on such social goals as desegregation of school systems, fluoridation of drinking water, and the passage of millage proposals to improve public education. A change agent seeking to promote such goals would do well to ponder relative values and social benefits attached to generating a great deal of public awareness and activity or proceeding in a more private manner. The well-known political tactic of keeping the situation "quiet" while getting your own supporters out is one not to be dismissed lightly.

Contrary to much rhetorical posturing, "enabling," or "participation," is not the method of choice in all situations. If a community change agent is to be only a docile, automatic expeditor of whatever decisions are made by others, then human service professional schools are greatly overtraining their students. If the practitioner does not stand ready to thwart wishes that promote racism, hatred, or exploitation, his function is tarnished.

While there are limits on the self-determination concept, there are also constraints on professional intervention. We do not imply that a practitioner needs to be assertive in all his activities; although that is certainly his option, and on occasion, his requirement. Surely, while oriented toward particular social objectives, the practitioner needs to be guided also by the outlook and wishes of others, to be highly sensitive regarding when to hold back or to defer to other affected or interested publics. Cheating, lying, bullying, and brutalizing are all incompatible with human values. Enhancing the opportunity for choice is an objective that should be optimized whenever feasible; and if the practitioner's reasoned intention is to increase participation, research-based strategies to support that aim will be found in this volume.

The strategies offered are meant to be used by practitioners or change agents in planning their work. But other people may also be consulted and involved in determining if and how to apply the guidelines. Groups of citizens or community professionals can use the guidelines themselves directly in analyzing a problem, or the practitioner may make the information or approach available to various community and agency groups as a resource to them to guide their deliberations.

It might make life easier if there were a single, invariant prescribed role, such as dominating all decisions on the one hand or being accommodating on the other. Actually the practitioner may be at either of these extremes from time to time, or (most of the time) somewhere in the middle. Simple, unidimensional formulas are comforting, but they reflect neither what occurs in the real world of action nor the imperatives for making an impact on a complicated human fabric of interacting individuals and social structures.

Important as they are, such value questions are not given prominence in this volume;[20] the function of the book is to make change agents more knowledgeable from a "scientific" standpoint. This should enable them to better *manipulate* their relevant world. That evocative term is deliberately used because, frowned upon as it is, *manipulation* is the business of the professional – acting on or changing the social or physical environment in some valued direction (architects aim to create more beautiful or functional buildings; doctors to improve health; and teachers to develop better informed citizens). Being calculating in goal-oriented activity needs to be distinguished from engaging in dishonest, illegal, arrogant, or despotic behavior.

In some of the human service fields, in particular social work, value considerations have dominated discourse in a disproportionate way. This book aims to counterbalance such valid concern by shifting attention to such equally critical matters as competence, incisiveness, accountability and predictability in performance. Allowing that change agents and those they work with have goals, we focus on what social science research literature has to say about potentially effectatious means for reaching them. We present here the actual practice behavior reported by the practitioners themselves as they carried out these interventions. The presentation vividly depicts the choices and actions of sensitive and committed practitioners as they go about the job. In general, our staff accepts the need and appropriateness of affirmative, purposive moves on the part of practitioners. The particularities and nuances are subject to scrutiny and debate, just as are the general directions taken by the workers. The behaviors reported here are not meant to convey exemplary moral choices; they may be viewed as a vehicle through which readers can further examine and sharpen their own value positions.

The authors cannot offer a formula for resolving the complex ethical and moral issues involved in taking responsibility for social outcomes. The reader, with his fellow students and teachers, will have to make assessments along these lines in reviewing and appraising the various illustrations of practice found throughout the manual. He will have to consider these matters in an even deeper and more critical way when he begins to design actual intervention strategies for himself based on the action principles that are outlined. A sensitivity that is humane and just, without being also crippling to affirmative confrontation with social ills, is the goal.

[20]These matters are discussed at greater length by one of the authors in "An Analysis of Roles and Goals in Community Practice" in Ralph M. Kramer and Harry Specht, eds., *Readings in Community Organization Practice* (Englewood Cliffs, N.J.: Prentice-Hall, 1969), pp. 260-268.

CONCLUSION

We conclude this chapter by pointing out an integrating feature of using the manual. We have found it to facilitate a clearer interface between academic work and field work and between teacher and student.

Relatively few materials can be used not only in the classroom but also in student field work and internships. This book can bring the classroom and the field closer together, because the particular strategies, the tactics necessary to carry them out, and the instruments needed to record the entire process can be shared meaningfully by both classroom and field instructors.

In addition, this material can engage teachers and students-in-training in a mutual experience. That is, our past effort suggests that the best approach to this material is for students and teachers to join together in figuring out the best way to use it. It is definitely not the sort of material to be crammed down anyone's throat.

The process of participating in the development of this material has brought the authors, as academicians and researchers, closer to people who are deeply concerned about social problems and vitally engaged in community problem solving. It has served as a vehicle for joining together individuals with different perspectives and different professional resources who have unique but mutually reinforcing contributions to make toward the creation of a more humane and just community. In a similar fashion it has increased communication between a graduate school and operating social agencies.

No manual in this field could possibly cover all of the contingencies and ambiguities of practice, even in the mobilization of the simplest strategies. There is not now, nor in all probability will there ever be, an "ultimate" guide to social intervention or politics. But practice can be made less mysterious, less conceived in vague generalizations, and less clothed in an aura of an art that you either "have or haven't got." The authors are prepared to be called to account for what is contained in this volume. Theory has been put to the acid test in the application and operationalized to a considerable extent. The student who is training for practice in the community should find little that is obscure about he material. Either it can be made to work in the turbulent cross-currents that are always part of practice or we will have failed. Our experience with more than 200 practitioners and students over a period of three years suggests that the material can indeed be used and that it can bring about successful outcomes. Not inevitably, but if the guidelines are applied with care, and if the limiting conditions are taken into account, a reasonable, acceptable degree of success may be anticipated in the pursuit of humanistic ends.

AGENCY AND ORGANIZATION SETTINGS FOR FIELD STUDIES

Area Health Planning Council
Area Service and Planning Council for Families
Catholic Youth Organization
Catholic Social Services
Community Psychiatry Department, State Mental Hospital
County Child Care Planning Federation
County Health Department
Department of Social Welfare, Regional Office
Elementary School (School Community Agent)
Family Service Agency
Human Relations Office, School District
Intermediate School District (School Social Worker)
Juvenile Court
Mental Health Association for Children
Model Cities Program
Neighborhood Community Center
Neighborhood Multi-Service Center
Regional Council for Urban Planning
Social Welfare Workers Union
Student Counseling Office, University
Y.M.C.A.
Youth Service Bureau, Regional Office for the State

The names of agencies and of practitioners are not specified in order to preserve a reasonable amount of confidentiality. In some cases, more than one practitioner was from that type of setting. Sites were drawn from the following set of cities in the southeast Michigan area: Ann Arbor, Detroit, Jackson, Lansing, Ypsilanti; and in Toledo, Ohio.

2

PROMOTING AN INNOVATION

The human service professions generally, and the area of community organization in particular, have often been characterized as change-oriented fields. For this reason the process of the diffusion and adoption of innovations invites our attention. Practitioners are constantly involved in promoting new programs, new techniques, new tactics and new ideas that they wish to propagate in working with target and client systems of various kinds. In many cases these new programs are already well-established elsewhere and are only "new" in terms of being transposed to that particular situation. On the other hand the innovation is sometimes an entirely unique creation of the practitioner and the people he is associated with (for example, the "teach-in" as a tactic or Mobilization for Youth as a program). In either case, the process followed in promoting the idea and the problems to be encountered is apt to be similar.

Often a practitioner is overwhelmed or immobilized in introducing an innovation because the task seems so large, the obstacles so disarming, and the time available so restrictive. One of the participants in the field study discussed her situation in the following terms:

> *I had been working on an individual basis with a number of pregnant girls who attended programs at our community center. Because of this activity I was asked to serve on the advisory committee of the board of education School-Age Parent Program. It became obvious to me that the girls were having a very limited educational experience. I saw the need to help them think through what they intended to do and what alter-*

natives were available to them. Many seem to have given up on the idea of any kind of future after high school. Not only would they need help in planning for themselves, but they would need special skills that would help them proceed with their intentions.

After analyzing all this, I became convinced a more substantial guidance program was necessary for them. However, taking into account the usual kinds of attitudes that prevail in the public schools I knew that I would be facing a lot of resistances to an intensive high quality service. Because of all the time I knew would be involved in trying to set up such a program—while still performing all my other duties—I merely thought about this from time to time but took no specific steps.

RESEARCH ON INNOVATION

Fortunately, a fairly comprehensive and systematic literature exists on the subject of diffusion of innovations. Much of the early research was conducted by rural sociologists interested in agricultural extension problems—how new farming methods and materials came to be adopted by farmers. Other fields that have contributed to this area include anthropology, medical sociology, education, and industry. The planned parenthood and public health areas have also stimulated a great deal of interest in recent years.

From a number of these studies by different disciplines and professions we have drawn the following generalization:

Innovations that are amenable to trial on a partial basis will have a higher adoption rate than innovations that necessitate total adoption without an anticipatory trial.[1]

[1]Everett Rogers of the University of Michigan has codified much of the research on innovation in his two books, *The Diffusion of Innovations,* (New York: The Free Press, 1962); and the revised edition with F. Floyd Shoemaker, *The Communication of Innovations,* (New York: The Free Press, 1971). Pertinent research in this area includes: Johan Arnt, "A Test of the Two Step Flow in Diffusion of a New Product," *Journalism Quarterly, 45,* 457-465 (1968); Marshall H. Becker, *Patterns of Interpersonal Influence and Sources of Information in the Diffusion of Two Public Health Innovations.* Ann Arbor: University of Michigan, Pub. Health Practice Res. Program, Rept., 1968; James Coleman et al., *Medical Innovation: A Diffusion Study* (New York: Bobbs-Merrill, 1966); Frederick C. Fliegel and Joseph E. Kivlin, "Farm Practice Attributes and Adoption Rates," *Social forces, 40,* 364-370 (1962); Frederick C. Fliegel and Joseph E. Kivlin, "Attributes of Innovations as Factors in Diffusion," *American Journal of Sociology, 72,* 235-248 (1966); Eugene A. Havens and Everett M. Rogers, "Adoption of Hybrid Corn:

Generally, an innovation is any program, technique, or activity perceived as new by a population group or organization. An innovation, as the term is most often used in the research literature, refers to new technical, professional, and commercial ideas and practices, such as contraceptive devices, new medical equipment, and farming techniques. These are typically legitimate, conventional, and within the normative consensus of a community and its elites. The promotion of broad and radical political change is not usually defined in the diffusion literature, though it seems likely that some applications can be made to this area.

This concept of partialization can be applied in two ways, for which Everett Rogers uses the terms "observability" and "trialability." That is, an innovation is more likely to be adopted by an individual or group if there is an opportunity, first, to see the innovation in action and witness its results ("observability") or, second, to employ a portion of an innovation before having to employ the total innovation ("trialability"). In observability one typically divides the target population; in trialability one divides the innovation itself. Both approaches may be combined in a given episode. Studies also emphasize the importance of "opinion leadership." According to research, the likelihood that an innovation will be adopted by a larger population is increased if the innovation is first utilized by a smaller group of opinion leaders. This smaller initiating group may be characterized as style setters, information disseminators, key communicators, sparkplugs, or gatekeepers, among other descriptions. Thus innovations frequently take place in a two-step sequence, from a small subsystem of early adopters and opinion leaders to adoption by a larger population or system. The subsystem may use only part of the innovation at the outset.

A useful illustration of these findings is provided by Carlson's study of how the new math became part of the curriculum of schools in

---

Profitability and the Interaction Effect," *Rural Sociology, 26,* 409-414 (1961); E. Hruschka and H. Rheinwald, "The Effectiveness of German Pilot Farms," *Sociologia Ruralis, 5,* 101-111 (1965); Elihu Katz and Paul F. Lazarsfeld, *Personal Influence: The Part Played by People in the Flow of Mass Communications* (New York: The Free Press, 1955); Joseph E. Kivlin and Frederick CC. Fliegel, "Differential Perceptions of Innovations and Rate of Adoption," *Rural Sociology, 32,* 78-91 (1967); Edwin Mansfield, "Technical Change and the Rate of Imitation," *Econometrica, 29,* 741-766 (1961); Herbert Menzel and Elihu Katz, "Social Relations and Innovation in the Medical Profession: The Epidemiology of a New Drug," *Public Opinion Quarterly, 19,* 337-352 (1955); Stephen Polgar, et al., "Diffusion and Farming Advice: A Test of Some Current Notions," *Social Forces, 41,* 104-111 (1963); Everett M. Rogers, and George M. Beal, "Community Norms, Opinion Leadership and Innovativeness among Truck Growers," *Wooster: Ohio Agri. Exp. Sta., Res. Bul.,* 912 (1962); Everett M. Rogers with Lynne Svenning, *Modernization among Peasants: the Impact of Communication* (New York: Holt, Rinehart and Winston, 1969).

Allegheny County, Pennsylvania.[2] Five superintendents who were closely associated with one another introduced the new approach in 1959. As a result of their example and their contacts with other superintendents, an additional 10 shcools adopted it in 1960. Then 12 more schools tried it in 1961. By the end of 1963, 38 schools were employing this altogether different method of teaching mathematics. This is a good example of the sequential, snowballing pattern that is found in the dissemination of many innovations.

From this concept of partialization found in the research, we have derived the following action guideline:

> **PRACTITIONERS WISHING TO PROMOTE AN INNOVATION IN A GENERAL TARGET SYSTEM SHOULD DEVELOP IT INITIALLY IN A PARTIAL SEGMENT OF THAT TARGET SYSTEM.**

Although the generalization permits partializing either the target population or the innovation, for purposes of systematic and consistent treatment the guideline focuses on the target population. A target system is defined as a particular group, organization, community, or society toward which an innovation is directed. In the context of our guideline we are dealing largely with the organizational and subcommunity level. Adoption of the guideline implies an incremental, stepping-stone process; success on a small scale with a limited group is used as the basis for promoting a new idea, or having it spread spontaneously, across a wider population. There are many familiar analogues: the demonstration project, the pilot program, the modeling of new roles or behavior, and the free sample. In their book on innovations in organizations Zaltman and his associates support this action principle: "The more obvious the innovation is, the more likely it is to be adopted. This suggests still another factor. The more amenable to *demonstration* the innovation is, the more visible its advantages are, and thus the more likely it is to be adopted."[3]

Rogers' writings contain concepts from which we can infer some attributes of a partial target system that are conducive to communication and linkage. Communication appears to be facilitated when two groups possess similar outlooks, values, social status, or education. There is more comfort and trust when people are similar; messages are more likely to be sent and received accurately. For some

[2]Richard O. Carlson, "School Superintendents and Adoption of Modern Math: A Social Structure Profile," in Matthew B. Miles, ed., *Innovation in Education* (New York: Teachers College, Columbia University, 1964).

[3]Gerald Zaltman, Robert Duncan, and Jonny Holbek, *Innovations and Organizations* (New York: Wiley-Interscience, 1973), p. 39.

types of situations, then, similarity of the partial and general target systems may be advisable.

On the other hand, Rogers notes that this similarity may also serve as a barrier to communication. New ideas usually enter a system by way of higher-status, more cosmopolitan opinion leaders. Characteristics of opinion leaders as determined in mass communications and diffusion studies include higher social status, more education, greater media exposure, more contact with the change agent, and more openness to innovative ideas. Typically, opinion leaders have slightly more of these traits than other individuals at the same social level. These characteristics suggest attributes to be sought in selecting target populations for some types of innovations, particularly those using mass communications as the medium of transmittal.

As we noted earlier, radical ideas, or a context of intense political conflict, would not provide a suitable setting for this guideline. The strategy is most useful when the innovation is reasonably legitimate and conventional, and when the following conditions are present:

> The cost of large-scale application is high while the cost of a limited demonstration is small.
>
> There is little or no information about the value or cost of a large-scale application.
>
> The process is not easily reversible once it is begun.
>
> A large-scale application might alert and mobilize opposition, but a small-scale one would not.
>
> The larger system has little or no receptivity to the innovation.

This incremental, partialization notion can be connected with the idea of *proximate* goals. These are moderate, tangible objectives that can be attained in the short term. Looking at the new math illustration, a partial target system of five superintendents initiated the innovation. A proximate general target system of 10 additional schools had accepted this method in the next year. A practitioner who was attempting ultimately to reach the 38 schools that adopted the innovation by the end of the study as a general target system, would have performed in a reasoned way by starting out with the 5 $\longrightarrow$ 10 formulation as a lead-in to implementing the guideline. This 15 now constitutes a new *aggregate* partial target group that can be used as the basis for impacting the next stage proximate general target system. One can visualize a rippling effect resulting from casting a pebble into the water. A given proximate general target system is intermediate to where the pebble lands (partial target system) and the farthest out ripple (general target system). The implementation of this guideline, then, may usefully be conceptualized as a series of *incremental stages.*

OPERATIONALIZING THE GUIDELINE

The selection of an appropriate, facilitative partial target system is crucial in carrying out the guideline. That is, the partial system chosen should enhance the probability of the innovation's success on a limited scale. An organizer in a welfare workers union, for example, wanted to introduce a system of implementing the union's programs at the individual building level. He took into account many factors in selecting an initial target building:

> *The basic consideration for the successful application of this guideline, at least in my case, was the selection of the target subpopulation. I was able to employ the following factors: Geographic location, history of organizational activity leading to cohesiveness (how long had the folks been relating to each other organizationally), leadership (both actual and potential) within the partial target population, level of skill and experience within the target population.*

Figure 2.1 illustrates other instances of innovation promotion in order to show the range of innovations to which this guideline has been applied, as well as to demonstrate how other practitioners have applied the concepts of a general target system and partial target system. The chart also indicates the mechanisms by which the transfer was made from the smaller to the larger target system.

PATTERNS OF IMPLEMENTATION

There were two important variations in the patterns of implementation of the guideline in the field test. In the first pattern, which we call a "spontaneous" contagion model, the action proceeds from the practitioner (P) to the partial target system to the general target system. This pattern is typical of the agricultural extension approach in which one farmer uses a new seed and is successful; his

Setting	Innovation	General Target	Proximate (short run) Target	Partial Target	Transfer Mechanism
A community mental health center in a semi-rural county.	Stimulate local unions to accept the function of community care givers for their members.	All 200 local unions in the county.	Fifty unions from around the county.	A limited number of union members and leaders participated in a workshop on community care giving — including ten unions.	The country-wide (all-inclusive) AFL-CIO Labor Educationa Committee voted sponsorship of a follow-up workshop to be offered to all county locals.
Traditional settlement house serving a largely black population.	Introducing an intensive educational focus into a program that had been essentially recreational.	Entire school age membership of the settlement house.	The same as general target.	A group of 20 teen members were involved in two educational counseling sessions.	Board of Directors voted an allocation for hiring an educational director to serve the membership.
A regional planning council serving several counties.	Have the planning council gain responsibility for advising HUD on housing applications from all regional municipalities.	All 30 municipalities in the region.	12 municipalities with whom practitioners have had positive previous contact.	With HUD approval, reviewed and assessed trial applications from four municipalities.	HUD approved review procedure for all municipality applications.
A social welfare employees union in a metroplolitan community.	Decentralize program implementation through building level unit committees.	All 25 building level units in the union: the total membership.	Six units in a contiguous area.	Shop stewards at a single building location were involved successfully in union program implementation functions.	The union executive board instituted a policy of building level program implementation.

Figure 2.1 Elements of the Innovation Guideline Operationalized

neighbors see the results and then plant the same seed. It can be depicted as follows:

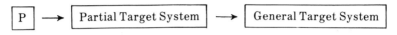

P → Partial Target System → General Target System

"Spontaneous" Contagion Model

In the second pattern, the action moves from the practitioner to the partial target system, and then to a relevant decision-making unit and from there to the general target system. In other words, a decision-making unit intrudes as a necessary pass-through point between the partial and general target systems. This process typically is used in organizational situations.

P → Partial Target System → Decision-Making Unit → General Target System

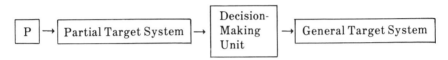

Decision-Making Unit Model

In the spontaneous contagion process the general target system accepts the innovation directly. In the decision-making unit arrangement a transfer mechanism or agent authorizes the carryover from the smaller to the larger group. The authorization may involve carrying out the program either with or without the prior explicit acceptance of the general target system.

Variations on the pattern of practitioner → Partial Target → Decision-Making Unit → General Target are many. Sometimes the practitioner needs initial approval from a supervisor or the agency director. Occasionally he first receives approval from the Decision-Making Unit to carry out the demonstrations, completes it, and returns to the Decision-Making Unit for authorization to spread to the general target. In some instances there are two Decision-Making Units involved. Some practitioners arrange to have the Decision-Making Unit experience the demonstration directly as, for example, attending a conference at which a new technique or medium is employed.

Practitioners in the field study followed both of the basic patterns. An illustration of the spontaneous contagion model is taken from the experience of a president of a social workers union who wished to institute a training program for his executive board, using a method by which case examples and sharing personal experiences are used to enhance effectiveness in dealing with grievance problems. He obtained approval from the board before he began the process.

> *I then contacted a select group of four board members, requesting them to participate on the committee. I asked them to present a case example for the meeting and scheduled a committee time with them.*
>
> *I chaired the committee meeting, suggested the rationale for the model to be used, and assumed responsibility for following up on specific tasks. The committee decided to conduct the training session in front of the board following the format of the committee meeting. Individual contacts were made to publicize the training session. The model was used at the training session, and the response was most favorable as the board had directly seen and experienced what I was trying to get across.*
>
> *The general target system, the executive board, participated with interest in the training session with positive evaluative comments ("we were really able to share problems in a new way"; "it was really helpful to know that other people had some of the same problems"; etc.).*
>
> *The key suggestion — at the training session — was that a next target system, for the future, could be the general membership with the same model being applied.*

The decision-making unit pattern was followed by a community worker in a traditional family service agency who was attempting to develop the concept of outreach services. She believed the agency should work directly with clients in a low-income housing project, rather than expecting them or, more likely, middle-class substitutes—to come to the agency offices. The problem was to convince the agency board to provide this type of service and the housing manager to clear the way for it to operate within the project.

> *My use of the guideline involved a small group of residents living on a court in a low-cost housing project. We were able to convince the Housing Authority that social work intervention could make a difference in the social problems in the housing project; reduce the social causes for eviction. A sub-goal was the introduction and sustaining of an out-reach program by our agency to housing project residents. We selected one court (5 families) out of the entire project as a demonstration; set up a time limit for evaluative purposes; promised progress reports at specific intervals; and met with the residents regularly as well as just "dropping in." This plan was submitted in writing to the board along with my periodic progress reports.*
>
> *The plan worked almost too well in that it was constantly referred to in agency Board meetings; the out-reach idea was*

new here but it really impressed the Board and the Housing Director, and was accepted as a legitimate and appropriate agency program. The results with the residents were not as spectacular, but represented at least a beginning, and we gradually expanded to other courts.

In the great majority of cases in our study a formal decision-making unit was necessary to foster or legitimize the transfer and broadening of the innovation. This is of particular importance because in much of the diffusion literature such mechanisms are not acknowledged. This may be partly true because many diffusion studies deal with agricultural extension and similar enterprises, in which a single practitioner or change agent deals with a geographically limited and homogeneous population of individuals or families. In such work diffusion can take place more informally, either through a demonstration by the change agent followed by social contagion throughout the target population, or by means of opinion leaders who are encouraged to adopt the innovation and through the examples they set to influence others to try some new approach or procedure. Clearly, most human service practitioners are organizationally based, and this means that they require more formal and structured procedures in order to execute processes similar to those carried out by extension agents.[4]

Another difference in implementation concerned the amount of effort expended by the practitioner in diffusing the innovation from the partial to the general targets. In some instances the practitioner was very active in promoting the diffusion. For example, the community center worker quoted earlier demonstrated an intensive guidance program for unwed mothers in one high school. She then set out to have the same format introduced throughout the school system:

I now had to involve additional individuals and groups. I proceeded to develop a proposal and arrange for meetings with the following: my Center's Board of Directors, School Age Parents Advisory Board, Episcopal officials (for funds), school administrators, teachers and students. After a number of meetings and a month and a half, we were able to gain administrative approval and a verbal commitment for funding of the program so all relevant students might benefit.

In other instances, such as with the social work union training program, the partial group did the "selling."

[4]In his revised book with Shoemaker, Rogers includes a section on "Authority Innovation Decisions," which considers the effects of decision-making units in organizational settings.

These patterns might be identified as a spontaneous process on the one hand and a directed process on the other. In the spontaneous process, the practitioner is active in securing the adoption of the innovation by the partial target, but leaves the diffusion of the innovation to the general target in the hands of the partial target. The diffusion is thus carried out by the partial target, either by active promotion or by "inactive" modeling or example. Looked at another way, the spontaneous process might be the result of a naive practitioner's belief that upon reaching the partial goal he could sit back and allow the guideline to do the work, or it might be the result of a not-so-naive practitioner's recognition of the isomorphism between the practice problem and population on which the research on diffusion of innovations was based.

By contrast, the directed process involves the practitioner both in the adoption phase of the partial target and in the diffusion phase to the general target system. It may involve the practitioner's "supervision" or encouragement of the partial target system in the diffusion to the general target system, or it may involve the practitioner as the sole "line of communication" between the partial and general target system. Again, viewed another way, it may be the act of a skeptical practitioner, doubting the validity of the guideline, or it may be the act of a practitioner who recognizes a lack of exact correspondence between the practice problem and the population on which the research was based.

The innovations being promoted by the practitioners fell into two categories. First, some of the practitioners had a fairly concrete detailed "product" to promote—a policy or program for adoption:

> *The development of a policy statement calling for an increase in the number of psychiatric beds for children in the metropolitan area.*
>
> *To establish the Poverty and Social Problems Curriculum in six schools in the tri-county area.*
>
> *A rotating toy library for use by six child care facilities.*

Second, some practitioners had a more fluid "process" of participation or involvement as an innovation to be promoted:

> A subcommittee or task force of the eight private agencies in Wayne and Oakland Counties involved in institutional work with children to work cooperatively with three representatives of the public sector.
>
> Small groups of black and white students who will meet together in one junior high school.

There were also differences in the practitioner's attitudes toward the innovation. Some practitioners were convinced of the validity of the new program. Others, however, were less certain and saw the guideline as a basis for "testing" rather than "selling." We have seen the first attitude expressed in several of the previous examples. In this illustration a mental health worker describes what can be considered a feasibility study:

> *My first experience involved a program designed for mentally retarded adults to prove that such services could be delivered with volunteer help, and that response from volunteers would be forthcoming. Up until that time the agency had resisted using volunteers to any extent. Two small groups of adults were selected initially by using some Department of Social Services community care homes and their residents. Eventually we had other home operators asking that their residents be allowed to participate, and ultimately we used our experiences in this program to write a proposal to the public school's Adult Education Department for a weekly socialization program for 200 mentally retarded adults. All of this took planning in great detail initially because we could not afford for those first few programs to fail.*
>
> *We recruited and trained volunteers; we selected the initial group with some care; and tried to monitor everything constantly.*
>
> *Through demonstrating with a small portion of the target population, we could then open up the program to the larger target population—which we did. If we had not limited the group initially we would have had disaster, because we did not have the volunteers, the space, the equipment nor the "know how" to handle a large group. In addition we did not have the acceptance of the agency that this was a viable way to proceed in this program.*

In the discussion thus far we have spoken of dichotomous categories—for example, a decision-making unit or the lack of one, spontaneous or directed diffusion—but the processes of social change are more complex. If we trace the steps of a practitioner in action, we may correct any tendency to oversimplify. Here the director of a mental health association lists the steps he followed in getting the county mental health board (the general target) to endorse a policy statement calling for the provision of more psychiatric beds for emotionally disturbed children (the partial target was the Children and Youth Committee of the board):

1. *Collect basic data identifying the scope of the problem;*
2. *Renew active support of my own organization by presenting the problem to the Board of Directors at its December 2nd meeting;*
3. *Discuss the problem informally with Mental Health Act staff;*
4. *Discuss the problem informally with selected members of the Children and Youth Committee;*
5. *Present the issue formally to the Children and Youth Committee;*
6. *Discuss the problem informally with representatives of the State Department of Mental Health;*
7. *Encourage suggestions to meet the problem from members of the Children and Youth Committee, and from Mental Health Act and State Department staff;*
8. *Encourage site visits to prospective facilities;*
9. *Elicit a formal recommendation from the Children and Youth Committee to the full Mental Health Act Board;*
10. *Move to secure support of the full Mental Health Act Board.*

Excerpts from his final report convey some of the flavor of this activity:

> *I first discussed the need for additional beds informally with several Committee members and with the Committee staff person. These contacts were with people whom I did not feel were resistive on doctrinaire grounds. These people encouraged me to bring the issue to the Committee for general discussion.*
>
> *During the following two weeks, I again talked informally with several Committee members, and also spent some time meeting personally with mental health board staff in an effort to help them understand the nature of the need and the more desirable options available. The key staff person agreed that it would be helpful for me to present basic information to the Committee at its next meeting, and informed the Committee Chairman that I was going to prepare some helpful information.*
>
> *With staff assistance from my own agency, I researched some of the issues related to in-patient care.... It was possible to prepare materials that provided valid answers... .*
>
> *Prior to the actual Committee meeting, I again discussed the matter informally with several Committee members. I*

discussed the data I was collecting and asked them for their thoughts and suggestions.

At the December 15 meeting I presented the information that had been collected. Surprisingly (to me) there was general agreement about the validity of the data, and little support for the notion that there were alternatives to hospital care for the children in question. Inasmuch as the time seemed right to suggest a formal policy statement, I did so. After some discussion, the policy statement was adopted.

The Committee, through its chairman (a member of the full Board) made its recommendation to the Mental Health Board at its late December meeting. The Board adopted the policy statement and directed the Committee to work for its implementation.

QUANTITATIVE FINDINGS FROM PRACTITIONER'S LOGS

Of the staff of 22 practitioners who participated at the onset of the second-year main field test, 20 actually implemented the action principle of the guideline (that is, developed the innovation in a partial target system). Fifteen practitioners were judged by our panel of raters to have completely or almost completely attained their stated goal, and our discussion below of individuals and groups contacted and facilitating and limiting factors in implementation is based on the experiences of this group.[5]

The experience of practitioners in contacting important community groups and individuals while implementing this guideline is summarized in Tables 2-1 and 2-2. Forty-seven percent of the practitioners contacted between 1 and 5 important community groups, while 27 percent contacted none. The largest number contacted was 20. Fifty-three percent indicated public agencies as important mainly for legitimation and participation. One-third indicated private agencies, generally to seek immediate participation. Forty percent in-

[5]We will not attempt a full summary of field-test findings here. We have found that such a summary in all its detail and complexity has impeded the use of the manual for specific intervention purposes. Some highlights and tendencies will be presented in a highly succinct fashion. The methodology note in the Appendix A spells out limitations of these data. Any reader wishing a detailed treatment of the research design and findings will find it in the forthcoming publication cited earlier: *Research and Development in The Human Services: Constructing Effective Systems Intervention Strategies.*

Table 2-1
Key Community Groups Contacted[a,b]

Type of Group	Percent of Practitioners Who Considered This Group Important	Major Reasons Contact
Public agency	53	Legitimation Participation, immediate and future
Private agency	33	Immediate participation
Voluntary association	40	Information and guidance Public relations

[a]For Tables 2-1 and 2-2 refer to the logs in Appendix B for full range of variables from which those cited here are reported.

[b]Number of groups considered important: Range was 0-20. Between 1 and 5 groups were indicated by 47 percent of the practitioners, with 27 percent indicating none.

dicated voluntary associations most frequently for public relations or information and guidance.

Practitioners considered from 1 to over 30 individuals important, with twenty-seven percent indicating over 30.

Agency executives were most frequently considered important by the successful practitioners (67%). The following types of individuals, although not considered important by a large percentage of practitioners, were contacted in large numbers by those who so viewed these categories: board members ($\overline{7.6}$) (line over figures in-

Table 2-2
Key Individuals Contacted[a]

Types Most Frequently Considered Important	Major Reasons for Contact
Agency executives	Future participation Immediate participation Legitimation
Board members	Legitimation
Board committee members	No trends
Agency peers	No trends
Community people	Immediate participation
Clients	No trends

[a]Number of individuals considered important: Range was 1-over 30; mode (27%) over 30.

dicates mean score) and committee members ($\overline{8.3}$), agency peers ($\overline{6.2}$), community people ($\overline{6.7}$) and clients ($\overline{14.8}$).

Key agency executives were contacted primarily to obtain future participation (10%), immediate participation (17%), or legitimation (17%). In addition, legitimation was sought from key board members (17%), and immediate participation from relevant community people (10%).

Certain tentative practice implications may be inferred from this information. Probably a moderate number of important community groups will be contacted during implementation of this guideline (perhaps between 1 and 5) depending on the nature of the particular situation. We found that less successful practitioners tended to contact a larger number of groups. The time and energy required to work with very many groups may not be efficient in relation to your objectives. Contacts with different types of organizations (public, private, voluntary) are likely to be useful. Such organizations will probably be contacted for a variety of reasons, public agencies in particular for legitimation and immediate participation.

More contacts with important individuals than with groups may be anticipated. While some readers may not make *any important organizational* contacts, at least minimal contact with such *individuals* is necessary. Approximately a quarter of the contacts are with fairly large numbers of these individuals (30 or more).

There are many different reasons for making such contacts; obtaining an individual's participation was the most common. Participation is likely to be sought from agency executives and community people. Agency executives are also a logical source of legitimation or formal approval. The use of much time in soliciting participation of various types of individuals may be expected. Not much effort in the field test went into seeking financial or other material resources. This suggests that it may be efficacious to select an innovation for which there are already existing resources (especially in short-run situations).

When practitioners listed the factors that facilitated and limited their progress, they tended to put greater stress on the facilitating factors. (The facilitating and limiting factors, and the practitioners' evaluation of their importance, are listed in Table 2-3). Personal sources of facilitation were particularly emphasized by practitioners, perhaps because these are the most accessible and subject to immediate practitioner control.

Certain tentative practice advice may be inferred from this information gathered from practitioners in the field study. First, there are several ways in which you may use personal resources. For example, (1) develop and rely upon good relationships within the agency; (2) select a program to which you are committed and which is logically

Table 2-3

Facilitating and Limiting Factors–Scores from Intensity Scale (0=None, 4=Great Deal)

	Facilitating Factors (General Intensity $\overline{3.2}$)		Limiting Factors (General Intensity $\overline{1.2}$)
	<u>Personal</u> ($\overline{3.6}$)[a]		<u>Personal</u> ($\overline{1.6}$)
1	Good relationships with agency, staff, board members, administrators	1	Lack of time
2	Commitment to program	2	Overinvolvement
3	Position or role	3	Lack of commitment to agency
4	Prior experience		
5	Commitment to agency and guideline		
6	Knowledge of community, clients, programs, and ideology		
7	Good reputation, self-confidence		
	<u>Client</u> ($\overline{2.5}$)		<u>Client</u> ($\overline{1.1}$)
1	Participation	1	Lack of knowledge of organization
2	Interest in program	2	Competition from other activities
3	Receptivity	3	Lack knowledge and skills
	<u>Agency</u> ($\overline{2.7}$)		<u>Agency</u> ($\overline{1.8}$)
1	Administration support and involvement	1	Hindering structure
2	Staff support	2	Lack of power
3	Supervisor support and involvement	3	Lack of funds and resources
4	Board support	4	Unclear or shifting goals, programs, assignments
5	Staff involvement	5	Lack of staff
6	Assignments and tasks consistent with effort		
	<u>Community</u> ($\overline{2.7}$)		<u>Community</u> ($\overline{1.1}$)
1	Support of organization	1	Competition from other activities
2	Support of practitioner	2	Lack of knowledge of organization
		3	Lack of knowledge or skills

[a]These figures represent mean scores.

related to your position or role in the agency; (3) take advantage of your prior experiences in a deliberate way—select a program and setting in which your experience will be an asset.

In addition, you should consider fostering support for the program at all levels within the agency, particularly at upper levels of the agency, as this was reported to be an important facilitating condition. If the program is consistent with your other assignments and tasks in the organization, this can serve to legitimize the activity and allow a concentration of energy as well as an interpenetration of contacts, resources, and other factors.

Both community and client factors may be of assistance. Community participation and community support of your organization and yourself may be significant—build such support or select groups to work with in which such support already exists. Client participation may be important. Their interest in and receptivity to the program or organization are also considerations. Select a program in which clients are interested, or work hard to develop such interest.

You are likely to experience limiting forces most intensely within your own agency situation. Such agency limitations frequently result from lack of clarity or instability, so that the clarification of goals, programs, and assignments may be a useful tactic. Since internal lack of funds or staff may be a problem, it would be advisable to plan a program realistically within the means of the agency, or think of tapping available external resources. To a lesser extent, the agency's structure may be hindering, or its lack of power or authority may be limiting. Both of these factors suggest strategic considerations in the choice of a program.

The need to manage time and energy efficiently was emphasized in the field study by the frequent mention of lack of time and overinvolvement as major personal limitations. Within the client population and the larger community, the biggest limitations are likely to be competition from other activities and lack of knowledge. This calls attention to the educational functions of the practitioner's job (interpretation, communication, public relations) and the need to formulate programs that are meaningful and interesting enough to compete with the many other forces that demand the attention of clients and community people.

We have attempted to put the findings to use in a variety of ways. The implications, however, are no stronger than the data upon which they are based. Like many prescriptions, the material above should be labeled, *Caution, Use with Care.* The findings are tentative and suggestive. Your own good judgment should influence your evaluation and use of them. Some of the more narrative, direct comments by practitioners that follow amplify and qualify the data that were reported.

PRACTITIONERS' VIEWS OF PROBLEMS AND PROSPECTS

General support for the principle underlying the guideline was expressed by a number of practitioners. As two of them noted:

> *There is a universality about the application of the principle of spreading innovation from a small group of "converts" to a wider clientele. The key to it is the "experiencing" of the innovation by the small group. The guideline works because it reflects truth about the way people learn anything.*
>
> *I feel the guideline itself is sound. If meetings of black and white students are ever to become a regular part of the curriculum in my school the worth and feasibility of the innovation will first have to be demonstrated with a small group. It would be too risky to the system to initially implement on a large scale without any demonstration of the innovation's worth.*[6]

Several practitioners commented that the guideline helped them to be more systematic in their work, and some of them found the guideline easy to understand and apply. For example:

> *The guideline serves the purpose of breaking down in concrete terms a specific method for initiating and implementing change. I think it is useful to be specific, purposeful, and sequential in pursuing a goal. This guideline suggests such an orientation.*
>
> *Given some clarity as to support for its use, the guideline is sensible, practical, do-able, and realistic.*
>
> *It is one that I can put into use in a number of situations with little or no difficulty on my part.*

Other practitioners noted that it is useful for long (and medium) range planning because operational problems can be seen on a small

[6]Because this was the first guideline that was implemented in our field test, unfamiliarity with approaches and procedures may have influenced the practitioners' reactions. Half of the practitioners rated the guideline 5 (most useful) on the 1 to 5 continuum of usefulness; the average rating was 4.0.

scale before the innovation is attempted on a large scale. They also felt that the initial experience by a limited portion of the target system was helpful in determining the potential success or failure of the innovation itself.

> *You do have an opportunity to work out problems of the innovation and to test its value before trying it on the total target system.*
>
> *It allows for a test of the idea or change for the practitioner as well as a strategy for gaining acceptance.*

While the practitioners expressed enthusiasm for the ideas behind this mode of action, they also pointed out a wide range of problems related to its execution.

1 The perennial problem of time was noted (already indicated also on the quantitative checklist), as was the related factor of the need to select a feasible, moderate-sized proximate goal.

> *I had little time to do the implementation of the guideline.*
>
> *I guess it was having to be patient before things started happening. Assessment had to constantly take place along with the incredible amount of public relations. At first the pay off is small but it makes the professional more credible.*
>
> *The guideline is still valid but there has to be a caution of thinking small and clearly—and limiting the goal sufficiently.*
>
> *I would not advise one person to try to work in as many communities as I have attempted to do. It's too much of a workload if responsibilities are not delegated to other leaders and organizations.*

2 The selection of the partial target system was described as both a very important and a difficult task.

> *The most difficult thing is defining the appropriate "limited portion" of the target population.*
>
> *It is important to choose a partial target system that will carry the innovation out with the total target.*
>
> *I found the most problematic aspect to be getting the larger community involved in the effort.*

The experience of a health planner who attempted to establish a preventive patient education program by working first with part of the agency staff illustrates some hazards involved in selecting the partial group:

> *In some ways, the partialization of staff "backfired" in this situation. In that there was little experience of staff being involved in planning and carrying out such a piece of agency work, those involved became extremely ego-involved and those not directly involved developed a real we-they attitude as though they had no role whatsoever, even though they were needed to help carry out contacts. Apparently in this particular situation, this type of partialization in relation to this particular staff grouping did not work, given the previous experience, attitudes, and total situation.*

Another practitioner, a particularly sophisticated and skilled professional, experienced success even in a political and controversial setting, because he had successfully chosen the partial target:

> *I believe that the guideline's use produced a favorable result in that the organizations represented in the partial target system were not able to block the Planning Council's housing review system. I think that had we confronted all elements of the target system simultaneously—particularly if we had dealt with all the local governments without first gaining agreements with HUD—we would have been defeated before we were even ready to begin.*

Two general recommendations regarding the selection of a partial target group can be drawn from the experiences of the field test. First, the group should be so constituted as to insure the success of the limited demonstration. That is, it should have some of the following characteristics: receptive to the innovation, generally accepting of change, good relationship with or willingness to work with the practitioner, good motivation, special qualifications such as education, and skills or experiences that would facilitate a successful demonstration.

Second, the partial group should be respected by the general target population (or least not be a deviant, disapproved segment). There should be strong linkages and good means of communication between the partial and general targets. (This second recommendation would not apply when one wanted the demonstrated to be a *fait accompli* before diffusing, so as not to arouse a known opposition.)

The size of the partial target, and its *proportional* size relative to the general target should have a bearing on both these matters. In our limited study we were not able to find any discernable patterns regarding proportional size and outcome.

3 Action implications are suggested from other practitioner comments:

GIVE ATTENTION TO INTERPERSONAL FACTORS.

The narrative comments reinforced the high intensity rating given to personal factors.

Practitioners stressed the degree to which this guideline called for the exercise of interpersonal skills with board members, clients, the agency executive, and other people.

> *One needs to be clear about the nature and quality of interpersonal relationships involved in the process of trying to reach the goal.*

This suggests that the guideline entails modes of influence such as persuasion, example, and communication. It does not typically involve manipulation of power or the use of conflict and contention. (In the familiar French and Raven[7] terminology, referent and expert power receive emphasis; coercive power is in low key.) As one practitioner puts it, "This approach is useful for getting new ideas accepted that do not have major implications for the existing power relationships."

DETERMINE THE AMOUNT OF ENVIRONMENTAL SUPPORT–OPPOSITION AND OBSTACLES.

> *Nothing in the guideline itself would automatically alert you to consider very strong influences in the environment. It seems to me that the successful implementation of any innovation would generally require a substantial support in the environment.*
>
> *The most problematic aspects was for me securing the resources to conduct the demonstration properly in the first place.*
>
> *The guideline is a natural approach to innovations which have some support by those who control resources enough to conduct the demonstration. In my situation there are generally enough*

[7] J.R.P. French, Jr., and B. Raven, "The Bases of Social Power," in D. Cartwright, ed., *Studies in Social Power* (Ann Arbor: University of Michigan, 1959), pp. 150-167.

actors that support can be found for most anything if the timing is right.

My mistake was that I overestimated the need for a program without assessing whether parents really wanted it before having some other needs met.

It may, in some ways, presume an administrative structure predisposed to giving sanction to experimentation and trying out new ideas. It requires that the practitioner trying to use it must be very clear about the realities of his authority to effect change, or even do his basic every-day job.

The guideline did not help achieve my goals. The following events occurred that prevented this from happening:

The board president resigned and delayed appointment of board members to committee.

The board was delayed for over a two month period in electing a new president.

Some board members disagreed with the person selected as the new president.

Conflict between board members over the goals of the agency began to come into the open.

Some board members began to work toward a change in staffing of the agency.

TRY THE STRATEGY FIRST ON A LESS IMPORTANT ISSUE: AFTER THIS EXPERIENCE EXPAND TO A LARGER SCALE OR TO MORE SIGNIFICANT INNOVATION.

I feel that working through the goal formulation and operationalizing elements aspects on the initial log was the most problematic of the guideline. Although the examples given were of great value, I still feel one had to have the experience of working it through before it could be understood and of future use.

Perhaps a good way to end this general discussion of the guideline, and to form a bridge with its actual implementation in the field, is to heed the words of one practitioner:

Once one determines how the innovation can be experienced initially by the partial group there is little problem in carrying it out.

GETTING STARTED

In attempting to use this guideline for the first time you might follow this thought-action process:

1 Think of some new program, technique, or other activity that you have been planning to carry out, or that ties in with general tasks and objectives of your current position or assignment.

2 Attempt to set this down as a goal, but of moderate scope and of short-range time dimension—something that could be completed in a minimum of about five and a maximum of 23 weeks.

3 Conceptualize the general or "total" target system at which this innovation is directed: Who are the people collectively who would be benefiting from utilizing or participating in this innovation?

4 Think through a smaller segment of that target system, a more delimited subgroup:

   (a) Who might relatively easily be drawn into a trial or demonstration of the innovation.

   (b) With whom there is high likelihood of success in an initial trial.

   (c) Whose success would be likely to have an impact on the larger target system, or on a relevant Decision-Making Unit that could legitimate or authorize transfer of the innovation to the larger target system.

5 Our review of patterns of implementation suggests that early in the game, authorization or legitimation is often needed in order to proceed. This may be obtained from an administrative superordinate (supervisor, agency director, etc.) or from the agency board. Also quite early in the process, persons or organizations may need to be approached who can provide resources to carry through the small-scale demonstration, or can offer access to the smaller target system. Make a determination of the individuals, groups, or organizations whose acceptance needs to be gained.

6 When you have worked the issue through in your mind to this point, begin to fill out the Initial Log. This is meant to assist you to formulate (put down on paper) some tentative early

steps that you might take in starting to carry out this guideline.

INITIAL LOG FORM

As a further step toward getting started, we suggest that you put down your tentative thoughts regarding implementation of the guideline. The Initial Log Form we developed for the field test was helpful to practitioners in that connection. The Initial Log is a tool for organizing your thinking in a systematic way. It is geared especially to helping you think about your goal, ways of operationalizing the guideline, the key individual and community groups to involve, and the facilitating and limiting factors in the situation (personal, agency, client, community).

Following the Log Form you will find illustrations of key sections that were completed by project practitioners.

INITIAL LOG

A Preliminary Guide for Action

1 Date of Preparation of Guide for Action ____________.

2 In relation to using the guideline, what is your goal (i.e., the innovation)? Be as specific and concrete as possible. Keep a short-term time perspective (five to 12 weeks).

3 Describe the circumstances (conditions, events, assignments, requests, etc.) that led you to use this guideline to achieve the goal above.

4 Look back at the intervention guideline. How would you begin to define or concretize *each* element of the guideline in your immediate practice situation (i.e., how might you operationalize these components)? Keep in mind the delimited innovation goal stated in question 2.

(a) What is the *General Target System:*

The Proximate Target:

(b) What is the *Partial Target System* (specifically):

(c) Is a Decision-Making Unit involved? Describe it. How will its members be encouraged to accept the innovation?

(d) How will you foster diffusion from the partial to the larger target—for example, forms of linkage, communication, promotion?

5 List the *major* steps you anticipate going through to utilize this guideline. Describe specific behaviors in the order in which you expect they will occur.

6 Whay *key* community groups will you probably involve (if any)?

Group	Reason for Contact

7 What *key* individuals will you probably involve (if any)?

Individual(s)	Title and/ or Affiliation	Reason for Contact

8 Facilitating and limiting factors in guideline implementation.

As an aid to implementation you should consider factors that will affect your progress. We have provided checklists of common *facilitating factors*, those that will assist you to carry out the guideline, and typical *limiting factors*, those that may inhibit your success. In the checklists we have included conditions that were frequently indicated by practitioners in the field study. Others may be important in your own situation, and space is provided for you to note these.

Following the itemized checklists, you are asked to estimate the relative importance of various facilitating and limiting factors.

Personal Factors

Facilitating

- ☐ Good personal relationship with administrator.
- ☐ Good personal relationship with supervisor.
- ☐ Good personal relationships with staff.
- ☐ Personal commitment to the agency.
- ☐ Personal knowledge of clients.
- ☐ Personal position or role.
- ☐ Good personal reputation.
- ☐ Self-confidence.
- ☐ Other: ______________________________

  ____

Limiting

- ☐ Poor personal relationships with board (members).
- ☐ Lack of personal knowledge of the community.
- ☐ Poor personal reputation.
- ☐ Personal loss (demotion, job title, etc.)
- ☐ Overinvolvement.
- ☐ Fatigue.
- ☐ Lack of time.
- ☐ Other: ______________________________

  ____

Agency Factors

Facilitating

- ☐ External authority requires your organization to support your effort.
- ☐ Affiliated organizational support.
- ☐ Board involvement.
- ☐ Administration support or involvement.
- ☐ Administration disinterest.
- ☐ Supervisor involvement.
- ☐ Supervisor disinterest.
- ☐ Physical facilities aid the effort.
- ☐ Other: ______________________________

____

Limiting

- ☐ Lack of power or authority of your organization.
- ☐ Unclear or shifting goals, programs, or assignments.
- ☐ Lack of agency knowledge of clients or community.
- ☐ Lack of agency support, or hindering action of affiliated organizations.
- ☐ Lack of agency support, or hindering action of supervisor.
- ☐ Other: ______________________________

____

Client Factors

Facilitating

- ☐ Voluntary client participation in your organization or program.
- ☐ Client participation in your organization or program through a legal or administrative ruling.
- ☐ Client is generally interested in your organization.
- ☐ Client shows receptivity to your organization or program.
- ☐ Other: ______________________________

____

Limiting

- ☐ Client shows a general negative response to your organization.
- ☐ Client is disinterested or dissatisfied with your organization or program.
- ☐ Client lack of knowledge of your organization, its purposes, programs, or activities.
- ☐ Other: ______________________________

____

Community Factors

Facilitating

- ☐ Voluntary community participation in your organization or program.
- ☐ Community support of clients.
- ☐ Other: ______________________________

____

Limiting

- ☐ Community disinterest or dissatisfaction with your organization or program.
- ☐ Community lack of knowledge of your organization, its purposes, programs, or activities.
- ☐ External influences make the community unsupportive of your organization or program.
- ☐ Community residents are specifically disinterested in your program.
- ☐ Other: ______________________________

9 Facilitating factors—relative importance.

In general, to what degree do you think *personal factors related to yourself* may be facilitating in implementing this guideline? (These factors might include good relationships with staff, good relationships with community people, personal knowledge of community, and positive effects of skill.)

Rate the degree of facilitation:

None ______ ______ ______ ______ ______ Great Deal
0 1 2 3 4

In general, to what degree do you think *agency* factors may be facilitating in implementing this guideline? (These factors might include administration support, supervisor support, staff support, and physical facilities aid effort.)

Rate the degree of facilitation:

None ______ ______ ______ ______ ______ Great Deal
0 1 2 3 4

In general, to what degree do you think *client* factors may be facilitating in implementing this guideline? (These factors might include client participation in organization or program receptivity to organization of program, client receptivity to organization or program, and client support of practitioner.)

Rate the degree of facilitation:

None ______ ______ ______ ______ ______ Great Deal
0 1 2 3 4

In general, to what degree do you think *community* factory may be facilitating in implementing this guideline? (These factors might include community support organization generally, influential and other community groups support organization or program, changes in community tend to support organization or program, and community support of practitioner.)

Rate the degree of facilitation:

None ______ ______ ______ ______ ______ Great Deal
0 1 2 3 4

10 Limiting—relative importance.

In general, to what degree do you think *personal factors related to yourself* may be limiting in implementing this guideline? (These factors might include poor relationships with staff, poor relationships with community people, lack of personal knowledge of community, and negative effects of insufficient skills.)

Rate the degree of limitation:

None ______ ______ ______ ______ ______ Great Deal
0 1 2 3 4

In general, to what degree do you think *agency* factors may be limiting in implementing this guideline? (These factors might include unclear or shifting goals, programs, and/or assignments; lack of funds, facilities, and other resources; lack of support or hindering action of supervisor; and lack of support or hindering action of staff.)

Rate the degree of limitation:

None ______ ______ ______ ______ ______ Great Deal
0 1 2 3 4

In general, to what degree do you think *client* factors may be limiting in implementing this guideline? (These factors might include negative response to organization generally, clients interference with organization activities, and dissensus among clients.)

Rate the degree of limitation:

None ______ ______ ______ ______ ______ Great Deal
0 1 2 3 4

In general, to what degree do you think *community* factors may be limiting in implementing this guideline? (These factors might include negative response to organization generally; lack of knowledge of organization purposes, programs, or activities; influential community groups or leaders that do not support organization or program; and competition by other activities with community residents' time and interests.)

Rate the degree of limitation:

None ______ ______ ______ ______ ______ Great Deal
0 1 2 3 4

ILLUSTRATIONS OF INITIAL LOGS COMPLETED BY PRACTITIONERS

I. EXAMPLE OF OUTREACH PROGRAMS IN HOUSING PROJECT

A. Goal Statement

To establish outreach services for tenants in a housing project served by a traditional family service agency. (A broader goal, beyond the application to the guideline in this particular instance, is related to a desire for the agency to establish outreach services in the community generally.)

B. Concretization (Operationalization) of Guideline Elements

General Target System: All tenants of the housing project (20 courts)

The Proximate Target: tenants in six courts

Partial Target System: One court made up of six families. This court will be selected fairly randomly, because there is little basis for knowing which court offers the best potential for successful initial implementation.

II. EXAMPLE OF SOCIAL WELFARE EMPLOYEES UNION

A. Goal Statement

To establish a pattern of implementation of union programs at the building level through building committees at each work location.

B. Concretization (Operationalization) of Guideline Elements

General Target System: All building units (25 in all)

> *The Proximate Target:* Six units contiguous to one another and to the partial system.

Partial Target System: One building-level committee structure where staff has already expressed an interest in operating in this way. (This interest can be built on to bring about an initial successful trial.)

3

CHANGING AN ORGANIZATION'S GOALS

The overwhelming majority of human service practitioners spend their entire professional careers working in one or another organization, and they often work at least in part on behalf of (or in relation to) still other organizations. It is clear that organizational factors set parameters for practice and shape available strategies and programs. Meyer Zald has succinctly stated the practitioner's situation: "'Needs' and 'problems'...are defined and shaped by the employing agency. The techniques selected to deal with them also depend upon requirements of the organization. Whether the practitioner facilitates, fund raises, or foments, whether he plans, serves as a resource expert, counsels, or agitates is determined by the structure, aims, and operating procedures of the organization that pays the bill."[1] The collective welfare of practitioners' clients and constituents is profoundly affected by the organizational structures and goals of social agencies. Changing an organization's goals thus becomes a key task for many practitioners, and failure to accomplish this objective is frequently a great hindrance to effective practice.

The chairman of a welfare workers union took on this task when he decided to move his organization toward more "radical" or working class goals:

> *What I wanted to do was to further develop the working class orientation and efforts of the union. Not that the constitution did not permit such a direction. It's just that the way the organization actually operated, its goals were more along a*

[1]Meyer N. Zald, "Sociology and Community Organization Practice," in Meyer N. Zald, ed., *Organizing for Community Welfare* (Chicago: Quadrangle, 1967), pp. 33, 35.

> *trade union model than a working class one. The trade union approach emphasizes strictly bread and butter issues such as wages, workload, work speed-up, and the like. I wanted to incorporate the notion of working class interests that went beyond the local job situation. For example, finding solidarity with clients as fellow workers and with other peoples' movements. This means that sure we would be concerned about bread and butter issues, but would also go beyond them—link up with clients' rights groups and other grassroots organizations, take a more pro-client position, protect workers who engage in protest actions with clients, etc.*

Unfortunately, organizations usually are less than enthusiastic about intervention overtures directed at them. Morris and Binstock have described the problem this way:

> *For a number of reasons, organizations are predisposed to resist changes embodied in social planning goals....The propensity of organizations to resist...poses important practical questions for the planner. Is it possible to predict or anticipate which target agencies are especially likely to resist? How extensively?*
>
> *No classification has yet been developed which provides systematic guidance for predictions as to which organization, under what circumstances, will resist certain types of planning goals....For the present, social planners must rely upon a sensitive reading of each new situation against an extensive backdrop of relatively intimate knowledge of the pertinent organizations.*[2]

In this chapter, we want to help the practitioner to move beyond intuitive, *ad hoc* engagements with organizations by spelling out at least one potentially effective means of influencing an organization's goals.

RESEARCH ON ORGANIZATIONS' GOALS

Our review of the existing research on organizations' goals has yielded the following useful generalization:

[2]Robert Morris and Robert H. Binstock, *Feasible Planning for Social Change* (New York: Columbia University Press, 1966), pp. 94, 102.

An organization's dominant goals reflect the influences of the most powerful individuals or groups in the organization and their vested interests.[3]

For example, in a university setting described by Gross[4] goals such as academic freedom, developing student intellect and creativity, preserving the cultural heritage, and pure research are emphasized in organizations where the faculty has more power than other groups. However, in universities controlled by legislatures or the state government, emphasis is placed on goals such as service to the community and vocational or technical training.

From this generalization relating goals to interests and values of power groups we have derived the action guideline:

PRACTITIONERS WISHING TO CHANGE AN ORGANIZATIONS GOALS MAY APPROACH THIS PROBLEM BY ALTERING THE STRUCTURE OF INFLUENCE WITHIN THE ORGANIZATION BY EITHER: (A) INCREASING THE POWER OF THOSE GROUPS WITHIN THE ORGANIZATION THAT HOLD GOALS COMPATIBLE WITH THE PRACTITIONER'S OR (B) INTRODUCING NEW GROUPS INTO THE ORGANIZATION THAT HOLD GOALS COMPATIBLE WITH THE PRACTITIONER'S.

This guideline embodies a structural and "political" orientation to organizational change. The supposition in applying this guideline is that the "powers that be"—agency director, board, supervisors—are not in sympathy with the goal change. This is not uniformly so. In some instances the executive may be highly innovative and a major resource for change. Occasionally the practitioner may become allied with the executive in promoting goals that are opposed at higher policy levels. Other types of initiatives may be taken—for example, persuasion, sensitivity training, use of outside consultants—when

[3]Edward Gross, "Universities as Organizations: A Research Approach," *American Sociological Review, 33,* (4) (1968), 518-544; J. Gusfield, "Social Structure and Moral Reform: A Study of the Women's Christian Temperance Union," *American Journal of Sociology, 61,* (3) (1955), 221-239; J. Gusfield, "The Problem of Generations in Organizational Structure," *Social Forces, 35* (4) (1957), 323-330; J. Mehina and C. Perrow, "The Reluctant Organizations and the Aggressive Environment," *Administrative Science Quarterly, 10* (2) (1965), 229-257.

[4]Edward Gross, "Universities as Organizations: A Research Approach," *American Sociological Review, 33* (4) (1968), 518-544.

there is a reasonable amount of common purpose and consensus on values among the various actors and interests in the situation. This basic strategy is thus only one of several available alternatives.

An illustration of the generalization may be found in Gusfield's study of the Women's Christian Temperance Union.[5] In this case, a change in the leadership of the movement led to a shift from an emphasis on humanitarian reform of the underpriviledged to a stance of moral indignation toward the middle-class moderate drinker.

Another example is contained in Mehina and Perrow's study of a youth commission in a local midwestern city.[6] This commission had been established to recommend new programs to deal with the city's youth problems, but it actually performed as a clearing house and was devoid of activity or programs. The study indicated that the commission's inactivity stemmed from overlapping memberships; that is, most of its members belonged to other youth organizations that were not interested in the development of new, competitive efforts in this field. Only after citizens without ties to existing youth organizations were added to the commission did it begin to initiate specific programs.

In addition to offering strategies for action, the guideline also provides a diagnostic tool. That is, practitioners may be aided in identifying dominant goals at any given time if they assess the interests of the most powerful groups in the organization.

Parsons has observed that a task-related, primary orientation toward the attainment of specific goals is "the defining characteristic of an organization which distinguishes it from other types of social systems."[7] In this sense, an organization cannot be understood, or worked with, without reference to its goals. Two observations should be useful in analyzing organizations and their goals.

First, *most organizations have multiple goals rather than a single goal.* A useful schema for viewing agencies from a multiple-goal framework is offered by Perrow,[8] who distinguishes six types of goals:

1 *Societal goals,* which relate to an organization's efforts to

[5]J. Gusfield, "Social Structure and Moral Reform: A Study of the Women's Christian Temperance Union," *American Journal of Sociology, 61* (3) (1955), 221-239; J. Gusfield, "The Problem of Generations in Organizational Structure," *Social Forces, 35* (4) (1957), 323-330.

[6]J. Mehina and C. Perrow, "The Reluctant Organizations and the Aggressive Environment," *Administrative Science Quarterly, 10* (2) (1965), 229-257.

[7]Talcott Parsons, "Suggestions for a Sociological Approach to a Theory of Organizations," *Administrative Science Quarterly, 1* (1965), 64.

[8]Charles Perrow, "Organizational Goals," *International Encyclopedia of the Social Sciences,* (New York: Macmillan and Free Press, 1968), Vol. II, pp. 305-310.

mobilize legitimation for its existence from the larger society. [Example: A clinic for drug-addicted youth that wishes to obtain legitimation from the larger society (a legitimation that may ensure financial support) may emphasize its possible contribution to the solution of the general drug problem.]

2 *Output goals*, which relate to the public constituency or clientele of the organization, that is, to the groups that directly receive the organization's outputs or benefits. (Example: Help provided by the aforementioned clinic to drug-addicted youth.)

3 *Investor goals*, which relate to the return that the investors, such as contributors, board members, or volunteers, receive for their investments of time or money in the organization. (Example: Individuals may receive favorable newspaper mention, for instance, for assisting the clinic in its work.)

4 *System goals*, which relate to the organization's efforts to maintain its own equilibrium and stability. (Example: Activities designed to ensure a solid resource base for the organization—money and professional manpower, for instance.)

5 *Product goals*, which relate to the specific "product" of the organization. (Example: In the case of a welfare department, the clients' checks. In human service organizations, many output goals are the same as product goals.)

6 *Derived goals*, which relate to functions that have only an indirect relation to the organization's main goals. (Example: In the case of the clinic, its involvement in radical political activities that many of the clients support.)

In designating a goal to change, then, a practitioner must specify which of multiple goals is being singled out for attention. An organization may be differentially subject to influence, based on which subgoal (or subgoals) is delineated as the target of intervention.

Second, *organizations' goals are not static; they shift over time.* In sociologists' terms, what takes place is either "goal displacement" (substituting one goal for another) or "goal succession" (adding new goals when old ones have been realized or cannot be attained).

Zald and Denton's examination of the YMCA[9] illustrates how an organization shifts its goals in order to adjust to a new social

[9] M. Zald and P. Denton, "From Evangelism to General Service: The Transformation of the YMCA," *Administrative Science Quarterly, 8* (2) (1963), 216-234.

environment and thereby protects its survival. The original goals of the "Y" included improving the social conditions of lower class people through religious indoctrination and educational activities. Over time, these goals broadened to include more general all-purpose service activities aimed at middle as well as lower class people.

A useful illustration of a shift in an organization's goal emphasis is provided by Perrow[10] in his study of voluntary general hospitals. He shows how changes in organizational needs modify the composition of internal goals. When the hospitals needed financial resources, the trustees were the dominant group that shaped major goals. The situation changed, however, after the organization's financial situation became secure and the need for professional prestige emerged. Domination in the organization was then transferred to the medical staff. With the development and expansion of hospitals, however, the need for coordinating complex functions, including interdependent and specialized health services, paved the way for domination by the administrative staff. Focal organizational goals may be viewed, therefore, as phases that dominante and fade according to organizational needs. Equally significant, different organizational factions may attain varying level of influence as goals shift over time.

It may be useful to view an organization's goals from an historical perspective, in order to assess dysfunctional goals that have been inadvertently adopted, as well as to make use of natural trends and tendencies in transformation of goals.

OPERATIONALIZING THE GUIDELINE

This guideline has four components: (1) changing an organization's goals; (2) altering the structure of influence; and either (3) increasing the power of groups already functioning in the organization or (4) introducing new groups into the organization. We have discussed goals in the previous section. Now we shall examine the action components.

Altering the Structure of Influence

There may be many centers of power or influence in an organization: an agency's board, the executive, the staff, membership

[10] C. Perrow, "Organizational Prestige, Some Functions and Dysfunctions," *American Journal of Sociology, 66* (4) (1961), 335-341.

or clientele, or community elites. Furthermore, different groups may be influential for achieving different goals. Thus, to change a particular goal, one might need to make a shift within a particular group (for example, certain program goals may be changed by shifts within the staff; procedural goals by shifts within the administration; and policy goals by shifts within the board). On the other hand, to change another goal might necessitate a shift in influence from one group to another (for example, strengthening the hand of the staff as opposed to the board). In the case of the welfare workers union referred to at the beginning of the chapter, the chairman shifted a particular segment of the membership into a stronger position within the leadership or decision-making hierarchy:

> *The question I had to deal with was the nature of the relationship between organizational goals and power distribution within the organization. What I set to do was to increase the relative power of the black members and of the non-college degree holding members of the organization. Conversely the power of the white members of the organization would be decreased, as would that of the college degree holding members. In a general sense, the race and the class variables converged. The majority of the blacks did not hold college degrees while the majority of the whites did have BA's. At the outset, the power of the whites in the organization was disproportionately high in relation to their numbers. In this context it was specifically attempted to increase the power of the non-college degree holding blacks by increasing their ability and opportunity to move into leadership positions within the organization. This educational component was vital in this process.*
>
> *Not all members of the non-college work forces were sympathetic to a working class point of view. In fact some of the more conflictual relationships in the whole agency were between clerical staff and clients. My concern was that by altering the power within the organization (increasing the power of the non-professionals) I might set in motion a process of unwanted organizational goal changes through giving leadership to even more conservative elements. This did not happen. To ensure that it did not happen, a strong educational component was included which involved both those who would be increasing their relative power and those who would have less. We set up a "labor school" program to which we invited the entire membership. At the same time we did active recruiting*

among those members of the non-college, black staff who we knew had a progressive attitude and who had been critical of the organization for functioning as a traditional trade union.

The training program dealt with subjects such as the history of the labor movement in the United States and Europe, the rise of militant unionism during the depression, blacks and labor unions and shop "floor" strategy. Training was used as a means of increasing the effectiveness of those who viewed the union from a working class perspective. This did two things. First, it created a feeling of confidence that we really meant business in implementing the stated working class goals of the union. Second, it provided folks with more expertise in operating as organizers at their place of work.

A real risk of this guideline (in organizations like mine) is that the perceived loss of influence by those whose relative power is declining can result in their taking divisive actions which cause the splintering or disintegration of the organization. In this instance, if that had occurred, it might well have taken on racial overtones as well as class conflict (this happened only on an individual basis and involved only two people). It is for this reason that a great deal of priority was placed on the educational component, involving both those who were losing power and those who were gaining power. That is to say, the decision to proceed with the educational program was made democratically and everyone was invited to participate through a general mailing to the entire membership.

We are now in a much better position to continue moving in this direction. We have already established definite linkages with welfare reform and welfare rights groups. Levels of antagonism between clerical staff and clients are being reduced. With time the effect of the new leadership should produce some very important payoffs in better services for clients as well as in the development of a more relevant and powerful union.

The type of organizational structure involved affects the choice of approaches to the influence system. For example, in a "rationalistic" organization, one that has the classic top-to-down authority structure typical of formal bureaucracies, it may be essential to influence the director, board, or some other level higher than the one at which a change is sought. On the other hand, in a "human relations" type of organization, which has a diffuse or decentralized authority structure with decisions made among the workers themselves, it may be necessary to achieve a staff rather than an executive decision. In some professional organizations personnel cherish their autonomy and are not likely to carry out conscientiously directives handed to them from above.

Influence in an organization may be a subtle and complex phenomenon. The idea behind this guideline is that influence should be sufficient to affect a goal in a particular direction. A shift in influence may in one instance require a formal modification of the authority structure of the organization, perhaps through a change in the bylaws. In another case a staff group may be brought together informally and, by speaking with a unified voice, may force the agency director to steer a different course. The point is that power and influence may be formal or informal, *de jure* or *de facto*, depending on the situation and the objective.

This guideline has a branching aspect — a kind of fork in the road — with a choice of two courses of action. A shift of influence may be executed either through *internal adjustments alone* or through the introduction of *new elements from outside the organization.* While both logic and experience suggest that both may be used simultaneously, for purposes of an orderly presentation we will treat them as separate alternatives.

Increasing the Power of Groups within the Organization

Often it is possible for the practitioner to find factions of the organization who are in sympathy with his aims. The task then is to strengthen the status, resources, or formal decision-making roles of these groups. In the example of the welfare workers' union, members with a working class orientation were singled out as a compatible intraorganizational faction. Through a training program these people were provided access to leadership roles in the organization. Of course, as the practitioner stated, there is always the danger of a reaction by the people whose influence is proportionately reduced. As in any "political" strategy, this countervailing potential has to be anticipated and taken into account in the primary and contingency strategy measures being used. In the example, the chairman neutralized the potential reaction by having the training program adopted openly by the organization as a whole and by publicly inviting the participation of all people (while privately actively recruiting among the progressive faction).

Other strategies for increasing the power of sympathetic groups within an agency are illustrated by the experiences of two practitioners, one working in a family service agency and the other in a regional planning council:

1 Family Service Agency

My specific goal in using the guideline was to use the mental retardation program as a wedge in the agency and through it to move to a position of advocacy. My particular methodology was a slow process, but it is on the way to working now.

Altering the structure of influence—an element in this guideline—could be accomplished by introducing new people and new ideas to the board. I decided to do this through my program committee: the advisory committee on mental retardation. This was a new group in the agency which embraced the advocacy position, and had access to the board through the committee chairman, a board member. It was a board-appointed committee and at the board level, but board committees were often only pro forma. To move toward accomplishing my objective took some real planning. Initially, I had to be sure that the mental retardation committee accepted the advocacy position, and did this by submitting to them a "proposed" set of committee objectives which included advocacy. They not only accepted it, but strengthened it.

A device I used was to make sure that our mental retardation committee chairman always has something to report at the board meetings. This served to create an awareness about our group on the part of the board, so that when issues arose, the board would listen. As yet we have not had a chance to test the "issue" idea, but we did get listened to with much interest. I have no doubt but that the question of advocacy can and will be raised through this committee given time and the right conditions.

2 Regional Planning Council

The Federal Office of Management and Budget requires that state and regional planning agencies review federal grant applications for a number of programs, including housing. The Regional Planning Council performed these reviews in a very perfunctory fashion. A long-time and fairly traditional planner had handled this responsibility for the Council and had been assisted by a technical advisory committee appointed by the board, largely composed of county planners and other city and state officials who were content to keep the Council in a relatively passive role. I and a couple of other Council staff members also were official participants of the ad hoc committee.

My objective in terms of this guideline was to change the Council's implicit organizational goal of a perfunctory, passive review of housing applications to a more aggressive policy which has the goal of actively influencing the housing situation. In the past, for example, grant applications were reviewed only in comparison with existing regional plans. (If a proposed highway was in conflict with the regional highway plan it would be rejected.) I wanted to expand housing reviews to take into account a number of humanistic criteria, which although not yet part of a formalized regional plan, were important factors to consider in the development of housing programs. Such criteria include the community's need for the income-level of housing proposed, equal housing opportunities to be offered, etc. In order to attain this goal change, I felt that I would have to revise the balance of decision-making process within the Council, shifting the weight of influence from those who favored an inert role to those who favored an assertive role. I felt that this goal change would not be accepted by the advisory committee, given the policies followed and the membership of the committee.

My strategy therefore was to avoid bringing up housing reviews before the committee. I was able to do this as a result of certain delays produced by negotiating problems in the Council's dealings with HUD. I kept telling the committee members that we would consider the housing reviews in a separate appendix of the general review manual which the committee was preparing. Finally the committee disbanded before any matters relating to housing were decided.

In the meantime, I had been conferring with some Council staff members, including the deputy director, who I believed would favor a more out-front housing policy. Based on my discussions with the staff program heads of such areas as transportation, environmental health, education, and recreation, the deputy director decided that my proposal for a more-encompassing housing review policy to be conducted by selected staff would be accepted by the agency.

Thus I believe that by shifting the balance of influence away from the board advisory committee and to an informal set of persons composed of certain agency program heads and the deputy director, I was able to change the organizational goals of the Council with regard to housing in the region.

An interesting twist in interpretation was used in the second example. In this case, the power of one group was reduced or phased out prior to the shift of influence to an alternate group. This pattern may reduce some of the resistance and opposition that is likely to occur when the shift is simultaneous.

Introducing New Groups into the Organization

Sometimes a practitioner may find that no groups in the organization favor the goals he is pursuing or that the supporting groups are weak. One attractive course of action is to engage in educational work within the organization in order to build one or more clusters of support or strength. Another is to introduce new groups into the organization with compatible values and objectives. These new groups might be board members, staff, or clients. It may be especially useful to draw on the "outside" strategy when particular outside influences are implicated in the desired goal change, or when the target agency has strong interdependent relationships with external units. Within the general format of a political strategy, this external approach is probably more threatening, volatile, and risky (essentially, more "political") than the internal one. Perhaps for this reason few project practitioners used this option. One who did, a worker in a neighborhood service center, met with some success:

While the Neighborhood Service Center was supposed to be servicing the needs of the poor in our geographic area, the preschool program was definitely reaching primarily middle class families. Mothers were using our center to dump kids for a morning or an afternoon while they went shopping or played bridge. I felt that we ought to drop this activity so that the resources could be shifted to assist the target population of poor residents. Part of the problem in changing the situation was that some of the middle class black and white board members were intent on preserving this program, since it was one of the few integrated ones the center was running. I decided to use the guideline to try and institute some changes in the present mode of operations.

I met with my supervisor to discuss my idea and also to seek support and approval. After this meeting, I proceeded to arrange a meeting with the Director of the Child Care Federation of the county. We discussed what I wanted to do, the information I wanted from her, and the role I wanted her to play. I got what information I needed and proceeded to contact directors of day care centers to get additional information. After collecting, analyzing, and writing this up, I gave it to my supervisor for approval and suggestions.

At this point I was asked to arrange for the Child Care Federation Director to attend the program committee with us. At the meeting all of us presented information, and the Federation Director stressed the needs of the poor, but no final decision was made....Later the matter was referred to the entire board with a suggestion from the program committee that the program be discontinued as it is and other alternatives be sought. (The program was subsequently discontinued.)

So far we have given four examples of how our project practitioners implemented this guideline. In the chart on the following page, these narratives are summarized under the headings of the guideline's four components.

PATTERNS OF IMPLEMENTATION

As we have seen in implementing this guideline, a practitioner has a choice of two means, either shifting the influence of groups within the agency or introducing new groups into the agency. In addition, the context of this action may be either his own agency or an external agency. Thus there are four possible patterns of implementation, which may be seen most easily in a simple four-cell table:

MEANS	CONTEXT	
	Own Agency	External Target Agency
Shifting influence of groups within the agency	a	c
Introducing new groups into the agency	b	d

As we have already noted, making internal changes is more manageable and tends to be less political than introducing new ele-

Setting	Changing an Organization's Goals	Altering Structure of Influence within the Organization	Increasing Powers of Groups within the Organization that Hold Goals Compatible with the Practitioner
Welfare Workers Union	From traditional trade union goals to working class orientation goals	Shifting progressive black members into the leadership, decision-making structure	Giving progressive black members training, increasing their expertise, and bringing them into leadership roles
Regional Planning Council	From passive housing review policy to active housing review policy	Phasing out the board appointed review committee and setting up an informal staff review group	Assigning responsibility for housing review decisions to the new informal staff group
Family Service Agency	From traditional in-house service policy to out-reach	Increasing the influence of a board-appointed committee	Making the board-appointed committee more active in its pro-advocacy input into the board
			Introducing New Groups into the Organization that Hold Goald Compatible with the Practitioners.
Neighborhood Service Center	Eliminate day-care program serving a middle class clientele	Introducing new authoritative information into program committee deliberations	Having director of Child Care Federation take part in program committee deliberations

Figure 3.1 Elements of the Goal Change Guideline Operationalized

ments into an organization. And it is easier and safer to work within one's own agency than to try to change an external organization. As one moves through the cells from *a* to *b* to *c* to *d* the task becomes less controllable and riskier, and accessibility becomes more difficult. Thus, in our field tests, most implementation examples fell into *cell a*, a small number in *cell b*, and none in cells *c* and *d*.[11]

In the cell *a* pattern (own agency, "inside" strategy), the locus of influence being affected may be the board or executive group, the executive staff, the operating or program staff, the organization members, or the agency clients. For a practitioner, the board may be the most difficult locus and the staff perhaps the easiest in terms of accessibility and manipulability. As we indicated earlier, shifts may take place within one group, or from one group to another. In the example of the family service agency, the shift of influence took place within the board. In the case of the regional planning council, the staff gained influence at the expense of the board.

The cell *b* pattern (own agency, "outside" strategy) was followed by the practitioner in our example of the neighborhood service center. He chose to bring a single individual from the outside (an "expert") into the situation in order to influence the board in the desired direction. While relying on an individual rather than a group was effective here, in another case in the field test the selected individual was not able to follow through, and the entire effort collapsed. Working through a group may be more difficult and time-consuming in some ways, but it also may be a safer way to proceed. Outside elements may also be injected at the staff or membership-client levels of an organization depending on the type of decision one is attempting to effect and on who has the power to make that decision.

In another case a school-community agent working in an elementary school used several external trainers (a group of experts) to influence teachers to accept certain curriculum wishes of low-income parents.

QUANTITATIVE FINDINGS FROM PRACTITIONER LOGS

In the field study practitioners had a somewhat lower success rate with this guideline than with the others. Of the 19 who implemented the guideline, 13 were judged to have completely or almost

[11]The implementation of an outside strategy as in cells *c* and *d* may require a longer time frame than we have employed in this study.

completely attained their intended outcome. Changing organization goals, as may be expected, seemed to present greater obstacles and challenges than other practice tasks.

The "inside strategy" was used by most practitioners in the field test. Shifts in influence were made primarily within the agency structure rather than through the introduction of new groups from the outside. For this reason not much contact with key community groups was reported (Table 3-1). Some 54 percent of the practitioners stated that no community groups were important and another 31 percent found between one and five groups important. Ten groups were the most reported.

Public agencies and voluntary associations were noted as being most important (checked by 39 percent of the practitioners each) and private agencies somewhat less (checked by about 23 percent of the practitioners). Voluntary associations were frequently found to be important sources of information and guidance. This was a key trend among reasons for community group contacts.

A larger number of individuals were contacted than were community groups. The range was 1 to 25, with the concentration between six and 15 (Table 3-2). In retrospect, practitioners increased the number of individuals seen as important (as contrasted with the community groups section where the number of important groups was subsequently reduced).

Agency supervisors (62%) and peers (54%) were considered important by the largest percentage of successful practitioners. In addition, board committee members ($\overline{6.2}$), agency subordinates ($\overline{9.8}$), community people ($\overline{4.0}$), and clients ($\overline{4.7}$) were contacted in large numbers by those who utilized these categories.

Immediate participation was sought from agency supervisors (12%), peers (15%), and subordinates (19%), while future participation was sought from agency supervisors (12%) and clients (12%). In addition, agency supervisors were frequently contacted to obtain legitimation (15%), and peers were asked to exercise personal influence (12%).

Thus, in implementing this guideline, you are not likely to involve many outside community groups (unless, perhaps, when employing the "outside" strategy). When you make such contacts they are more likely to be with public or private agencies. Voluntary associations, however, may play a crucial part, and such group contacts when made should be carried through carefully. You are likely to take advantage of such voluntary groups mainly for information and guidance.

Individuals are apt to be contacted by you in greater numbers. Many contacts will fall within the agency hierarchical structure in im-

Table 3-1
Key Community Groups Contacted[a,b]

Type of Group Contacted	Percent of Practitioners Who Considered This Group Important	Major Reasons for Contact
Public agency	39	Variation, no strong tendencies
Private agency	23	Variation, no strong tendencies
Voluntary associations	39	Information and guidance

[a]Refer to the logs in the Appendix B for full range of variables from among which those cited here are reported.

[b]Number of groups considered important: Range was 0-10; 54% considered no groups, 31% indicated from 1 to 5 as important.

plementing the guideline. Most of such people, as well as clients, are to be contacted for purposes of participation, immediate or future. Also, executives, board members, and supervisors may be contacted for legitimation or approval, while peers within the agency may be asked to exert personal influence.

Practitioners viewed facilitating factors as having greater weight in implementing the guideline than limiting factors. All of the

Table 3-2
Key Individuals Contacted[a]

Types Most Frequently Considered Important	Major Reasons for Contact
Agency supervisors	Future participation Immediate participation Legitimation
Agency peers	Exercise of personal influence Immediate participation
Board committee members	No trends
Agency subordinates	Immediate participation
Community people	No trends
Clients	Future participation

[a]Number of individuals considered important: Range was 1 to over 30.

factors (personal, agency, client, and community) were seen as somewhat facilitating, with personal and client highest, followed by agency, and then community. As usual, personal factors were prominent, but in this instance they were rivaled by client factors rather than standing alone. (However, in retrospect, personal factors increased and client factors decreased in saliency.) When a goal of considerable difficulty (such as changing an organization's goals, is confronted, personal factors are not as likely to be seen as sufficient. Allies and additional supporting elements are viewed as necessary to a greater extent.

As with other guidelines, you should capitalize on the facilitating factors in the situation.

In the personal area it would be well to choose a goal change that falls within your position or role in the agency. This may provide a certain level of legitimation for your activities and permit a concentration of effort. It may be helpful if the action grows out of your prior experiences, so that this too can be applied toward optimizing the outcome. Relevant background knowledge also is of special assistance. Such background knowledge should be sought out, or the area selected should be one in which you already have background knowledge. It also helps to pick a program to which you have some commitment. You should take care to maintain good working relationships with staff members, administrators, and board members. Patience is not a particular virtue in implementing this guideline. Commitment rather than patience, practitioners state, is the important consideration when aiming at short-term, proximate goal changes. As in many situations, a good reputation helps.

With regard to clients, the next most important facilitating factor, interest and receptivity, are important. Choose a goal that is of interest to the client group or to which they are receptive. As an alternative, make it your business to work on building such interest and receptivity.

In the community, disinterest or dissatisfaction are useful facilitating factors. Such dissatisfaction may provide background pressure that stimulates change, and enables client involvement to have an impact. You may select a goal in an area in which such dissatisfaction or disinterest already exist or attempt to develop a sense of dissatisfaction in the community as part of the implementation strategy.

In the agency sector it is facilitating if the intervention is consistent with your already assigned tasks. Again, legitimation and concentration of energy may be the operating variables here. It is useful to obtain the support of staff and perhaps to a lesser degree that of supervisors. During implementation it may appear helpful to have administration support also. However, administrators may block goal

Table 3-3
Facilitating and Limiting Factors. Scores from Intensity Scale (0=None, 4=Great Deal)

	Facilitating Factors (General Intensity $\overline{2.8}$)		Limiting Factors (General Intensity $\overline{1.6}$)
	Personal ($\overline{3.2}$)[a]		Personal ($\overline{1.6}$)
1	Position or role in the agency	1	Lack of time
2	Prior experience	2	Fatigue
3	Knowledge of ideology or theory	3	Overinvolvement
4	Commitment to program		
5	Commitment to guideline		
6	Good relationships with administrators, supervisors, staff		
7	Good reputation		
	Client ($\overline{2.9}$)		Client ($\overline{1.2}$)
1	Participation in organization or program	1	Competition from other activities
2	Interest in program		
3	Receptivity		
	Agency ($\overline{2.6}$)		Agency ($\overline{2.1}$)
1	Assignments and tasks consistent with efforts	1	Unclear or shifting goals, programs, assignments
2	Staff support	2	Hindering structure
3	Supervisor support	3	Lack of resources
4	Staff involvement		
	Community ($\overline{2.4}$)		Community ($\overline{1.4}$)
1	Disinterest or dissatisfaction	1	Competition from other activities

[a]Figures represent mean scores.

changes in the end for various reasons having to do with use of resources or the politics of the situation, for example. In retrospect, practitioners found the support of administrators to be less helpful than they had considered this to be during implementation.

The greatest limitations may be anticipated in the agency and personal sectors. The community is likely to be less limiting and clients the least. Agency structural factors may be a special problem, particularly unclear or shifting goals. Perhaps it is possible to turn the fluidity of such a situation to an advantage by approaching it as an occasion that provides openings for the introduction of new goals. Lack of resources is another inhibiting factor. It may be useful to seek out possible resource inputs from outside sources (such as other agencies with similar objectives). Availability of such external resources is likely to remove important resistances to adopting some types of new goals.

On the personal side, pressures of time, involvement, and fatigue may inhibit movement. The principle of concentration of energy applies here. It is important for community practitioners to use their time efficiently, to set priorities, and to eliminate less productive involvements.

Clients are not likely to be a problem, competition of other activities for their time and interest constituting perhaps the greatest difficulty. This suggests selecting a goal that is salient to clients or working to stir up such interest. At the same time other educational work with clients may be needed in providing either background knowledge about the organization or program, or skills necessary to the carrying out of certain client roles. The same types of difficulties may be anticipated from the wider community, and similar approaches should be considered at the community level. Lack of community funds may turn out not to be as large a problem as it appears during implementation and should not be a deterrent to moving ahead.

Let us now look at more narrative comments of practitioners.

PRACTITIONERS' VIEW OF PROBLEMS AND PROSPECTS

Changing goals of organizations is obviously an important part of community practice. At the same time, this is extremely difficult to accomplish. Practitioners in the field study ran into many obstacles and resistances in implementing this guideline, and the success rate was lower than for the others that were tested. (Nevertheless the guideline was rated 3.7, on the 5-point usefulness continuum, and 36.8 percent of the practitioners gave it the highest rating of 5 for usefulness.)

What our practitioners seemed to be saying was that the strategy is potentially very effective, but that it also may be political, controversial, and hazardous. A succinct summary of the views of many is contained in these comments by three practitioners:

1 *I think that this is important because it offers possibilities whenever a practitioner is blocked in the system. He has the*

option of changing from the inside or attempting to do what I did in bringing someone in who may have an impact.

2 *This guideline seems to allow for considerable potential change, while also necessitating some risk for the practitioner in the area of power politics and group conflict.*

3 *Some changes carry the concept of "winners" and "losers" within them. It requires some study as to how to achieve a balance so that more is not lost than is gained. Decreasing the influence of certain groups may be a source of future conflict.*

Some practitioners obviously found this realm personally threatening or incompatible with their professional philosophy.

> *The political aspects of it made me feel uncomfortable because I am much more accustomed to using persuasion.*

In making suggestions to the project staff concerning how this chapter should be presented to readers, one practitioner echoed others in advising: "Put more emphasis on the difficulties and constraints in attempting to change organizational goals."

Practitioners spoke also of various benefits they saw in using this guideline:

> *I consistently find myself in practice situations that warrant goal change. I think that when a practitioner is in an agency setting he must attempt to change the goals if he finds them counterproductive.*

Practitioners indicated that demonstrated capability in performing this function can serve as a sign of competence, both to oneself and to others.

> *I feel that this guideline can definitely help practitioners new and old to the job establish themselves and feel more comfortable if they are truly able to change an organization's goals to be more in keeping with their own. It is an excellent measure of a practitioner's effectiveness if he is able to effect the organization's goals.*

One value of the guideline is that it offers a *diagnostic tool* for assessing what is actually happening in organizational settings.

> *It lays out some basic truths about institutions and gives one a handle on thinking about the system.*

Even if the guideline is employed unsuccessfully on the first try, the experience and diagnostic skills gained can carry over and be the basis for a more successful second implementation.

> *I have no reservations in using this guideline again. I think I will be able to diagnose the situation much better and not use it as a threat to the power group as I think it became this time.*

The three most common types of problems pointed out by practitioners as a result of their experience revolved around time considerations, the selection of obtainable objectives, and the practitioner's position in the hierarchy of the organization.

1 Time

The problem cited most often was the great amount of time needed to bring about even a small change in an organization's goals. One practitioner noted that the next time he uses the guideline, he will give himself "a much longer period of time to carry it out, realizing the difficulty of dealing with the goals of an organization." And over this long period of time, a great deal of the community worker's time must be committed to the effort. One's schedule has to be adjusted and cleared for the task:

> *It is clearly possible to change organizational goals as this guideline indicates. Practitioners, however, are well aware that doing so may add to their work unless some other assignments are eliminated — or subordinated. It adds new volume to an already heavy workload.*

Even after the changes are effected, the follow-up activities may be demanding. One practitioner warns:

> *The group that loses influence is likely to become incensed. This means that there will be a lot of "mopping up" to do afterward, a lot of effort put in toward helping the two groups learn to respect each other and work together on the new basis.*

2 Obtainable Objectives

Practitioners cautioned that one must be practical in choosing an objective. It is not necessary (and often not desirable) to set out to change the entire organization's goals. It is possible to partialize either the organization (changing only one department) or the goals (attacking only one of an organization's many goals, or part of a particular goal). From their experience, practitioners recommended both approaches:

> *I would advise that staff using this guideline take on a portion at a time. In other words, do not try to take on the whole organization at once or do it alone. Other people may have ideas as good. Form coalitions when possible.*
>
> *Again, I would caution workers to change goals that they have easy access to. In other words, take the mountain a piece at a time. In this instance I was successful and that gives me a positive feeling about using it again. It would have been tricky if we were trying to change larger organizational goals.*

Feasibility also involves assessing the power of the group you are attempting to influence. In one instance, an agency director was concerned about a conservative executive committee that dominated the board. He wished to change the organization's goals in the direction of more service-oriented programs by enhancing the position of certain members of the board who were not part of the executive clique. He drew these members together in a small group that he hoped would be a countervailing force, but he had not fully recognized the ability of the executive elite to crush a weak opposition. The practitioner summed up his experience as follows:

> *I think this guideline can be most useful when there is a willingness on the part of the power group to respect the position and contributions of the newly developed group. It was not helpful with a group that had extreme power and knew how to manipulate behind the scenes and to discredit others. I do not think that this guideline can be effective when the group in power can use the technique of discrediting and belittling its opposition.*

3 Position in the Hierarchy

Many of the practitioners felt impotent to influence their organization on the level of goal formulation. This was particularly true of younger or less experienced workers (although we saw in the previous illustration that even an agency director is not immune to frustration on this account).

The practitioners suggested two approaches to overcoming this obstacle. First, it may be possible to work through some other individual who has greater authority. If he collaborates with such an individual, the practitioner can take a back seat, allowing a qualified substitute to function in his place. In a certain sense such a strategy involves persuading and training a stronger ally to carry out the action principle of the guideline.

The other suggestion involves selecting an existing and accessible locus of power within the agency, rather than attempting to institute an entirely new center of influence. A practitioner explained his successful implementation:

> *In my situation, I made use of latent power of a group already formed (and it was a very small goal).*

A review of the cases of implementation by practitioners who did not have high administrative posts suggests two sources of strength for lower level workers. One is the control and use of information as an instrument of power; the other is mobilization of the staff from a latent to an active force in the organization. From its frequency of occurrence, it would appear that control of information is a type of power available to most practitioners. It appears in such varied circumstances as the gathering and provision of data on child care services, the release of budget information to a staff cohort, the presentation of the results of a student survey to a board of education, and the development of an information system for the juvenile courts. In other words, connecting up new information with newly formed power blocs seems to be a useful way to accumulate a "critical mass" of influence.

In several instances the staff was able to influence goals after the practitioner had helped them to consolidate around a particular objective. As one practitioner analyzed his situation:

> *Our staff had compatible goals, but we had not used our power as a group before. It became a matter of getting them to act as a unit, which gave us more power than if we had taken action as individual members.*

In this instance, the practitioner was able to build upon previous relationships and staff consensus, and was assisted by a critical issue (the arbitrary shifting of office space by a superordinate) to develop a sense of solidarity among the group. Unionization epitomizes this idea, but the concept can also be applied in a less formal way, and with regard to *ad hoc* situations. Very few staff groups, apparently, maximize the impact they could have were they to operate in a collective fashion.

In addition to these three major areas, a few other problematic factors were identified. One practitioner noted that sometimes there are no compatible groups within the organization with which to align oneself. It may be necessary to abandon this guideline in such a situation, or perhaps to shift to the outside strategy. Even when new groups are introduced into an organization, they may gain no real influence on the organization's goals. This again points up the need for careful diagnostic thinking in designing a plan of implementation.

A middle-level supervisor in a mental health clinic attempted to use the staff as a wedge in moving the director toward serving neglected groups. She encountered difficulties in convincing the staff that she was an ally with a mutual interest in improving the quality of services. It took time for trust to be established across hierarchy levels. Another practitioner in a juvenile court setting found numerous enclaves of people from different disciplines. She underestimated the effort required to get people to cross professional boundaries and form a new common interest staff group.

GETTING STARTED

1 Think of some situation or problem in your practice situation that could be improved through a change in organizational goals. The goal should be modest in scope, not involving the entire organization, but perhaps a specific program, activity, or department. This permits modification of the goal to take place within a three-month period. (The organization may be your own or an external target agency.)

2 What type of goal is involved among multiple organizational goals? Has this goal been in flux historically? Can the direction of change be capitalized on?

3 What locus of organizational operation is instrumental in maintaining or changing this goal: board, the executive staff, operating staff, members, clients, etc?

4 Are there individuals or groups in the agency who are in tune with your desired goals? Are they situated close to the primary locus of influence or at another locus?

5 How can the power or influence of these groups be strengthened? Is a shift from one locus to another necessary? How can the power or influence of the people in the current critical locus be reduced, either prior to or simultaneously with a shift of influence to the new group?

6 If there are no such internal groups, are there external groups of this type? Can they be moved into relevant positions of influence within the organization?

7 How can the reaction of current power holders be neutralized or minimized during the transition process?

8 How can the influence of the new group be stabilized or institutionalized?
9 When the transference of influences has been achieved, have the desired changes in goal orientation been realized?

INITIAL LOG FORM

As a further step toward getting started, we suggest that you put down your tentative thoughts on the implementation of the guideline. The Initial Log Form we developed for the field test was helpful to practitioners in that connection. The Initial Log is a tool for organizing your thinking in a systematic way. It is geared especially to helping you think about your goal, ways of operationalizing the guideline, the key individual and community groups to involve, and the facilitating and limiting factors in the situation (personal, agency, client, community).

Following the Log Form you will find illustrations of key sections that were completed by project practitioners.

INITIAL LOG

A Preliminary Guide for Action

1 Date of Preparation of Guide for Action ______________.

2 In relation to using the guideline, what is your objective (i.e., the organization goal you wish to change - from, or to). Keep a short-term time perspective (between 5 and 12 weeks); the *proximate* goal should be indicated.

3 Describe the circumstances (conditions, events, assignments, requests, etc.) that led you to use this guideline to achieve the goal above.

4 Look back at the intervention guideline. How would you begin to define or concretize *each* element of the guideline in your immediate practice situation (i.e., how might you operationalize these components)? Keep in mind the proximate goal stated in part 2.

How do you intend to alter the structure of influence?

Will this be brought about by increasing the power of those groups *within* the organization holding compatible goals with the practitioners. Specify.

Or will it be brought about by introducing new groups into the organization that hold compatible goals with the practitioner's. Specify.

5 List the *major* steps you anticipate going through in order to utilize this guideline. Describe specific behaviors in the order in which you expect they will occur.

6 What *key* community groups will you probably involve (if any)?

Group	Reason for Contact

7 What *key* individuals will you probably involve (if any)?

Individual(s)	Title and/ or Affiliation	Reason for Contact

8 Facilitating and limiting factors in guideline implementation:

As an aid to implementation you should consider factors that will affect your progress. We have provided checklists of common-*facilitating factors*, those that will assist you to carry out the guideline, and typical *limiting factors*, those that may inhibit your success. In the checklists we have included conditions that were frequently indicated by practitioners in the field study. Others may be important in your own situation, and space is provided for you to note these.

Following the itemized checklists, you are asked to estimate the relative importance of various facilitating and limiting factors.

Personal Factors

Facilitating

- ☐ Good personal relationships with board/board members
- ☐ Good personal relationship with administrator
- ☐ Good personal relationship with supervisor
- ☐ Good personal relationships with staff
- ☐ Good personal relationships with clients
- ☐ Good personal relationships with community people
- ☐ Good personal relationships with nonstaff professional peers and friends
- ☐ Positive effects of commitment to agency
- ☐ Positive effects of commitment to program
- ☐ Positive effects of commitment to guideline
- ☐ Other: ______________________________

  ____

Limiting

- ☐ Poor relationships with board/board members
- ☐ Poor relationships with staff
- ☐ Negative effects of lack of commitment to agency
- ☐ Personal knowledge of community
- ☐ Personal knowledge of clients
- ☐ Personal loss (demotion, job title, etc.)
- ☐ Negative effects of not enjoying the job
- ☐ Fatigue
- ☐ Other: ______________________________

  ____

Agency Factors

Facilitating

- ☐ External authority requirements of organization support effort
- ☐ Affiliated organizational support or involvement
- ☐ Board support or involvement
- ☐ Administration support or involvement
- ☐ Administration disinterest
- ☐ Supervisor disinterest
- ☐ Staff involvement
- ☐ Practitioner assignments are consistent with effort
- ☐ Physical facilities aid the effort
- ☐ Other: ____________________

____

Limiting

- ☐ External authority requirements hamper efforts
- ☐ Lack of power and/or authority of organization
- ☐ Hindering structure of organization
- ☐ Negative agency attitudes toward the clients or community
- ☐ Lack of knowledge of clients or community
- ☐ Lack of staff or training
- ☐ Lack of support of board
- ☐ Lack of support of administration
- ☐ Lack of support of supervisor
- ☐ Other: ____________________

____

Client Factors

Facilitating

- ☐ Client support of other clients
- ☐ Client support of practitioner
- ☐ Other: ______________________________

____

Limiting

- ☐ Dissensus among clients
- ☐ Other: ______________________________

____

Community Factors

Facilitating

- ☐ Community participation in your organization or program (through legal or administrative ruling)
- ☐ Community support of your organization generally
- ☐ Community interest in your program specifically
- ☐ Support of (influential) community groups for your organization or program
- ☐ Influential or other community groups involved with organization or program
- ☐ Community disinterest in, or dissatisfaction with, organization or program (leading to a desire for change)
- ☐ Changes in community tend to support organization or program
- ☐ External influences making the community support your organization or program
- ☐ Community support of clients
- ☐ Other: ______________________________

____

Limiting

- ☐ Pressure from community residents
- ☐ External influences make community unsupportive of organization or program
- ☐ Community residents not interested in program specifically
- ☐ Differences in life styles between staff (including practitioner) and community residents
- ☐ Other: ______________________________

____

9 Facilitating factors—relative importance

In general, to what degree do you think *personal factors related to yourself* may be facilitating in implementing this guideline? (These factors might include good relationships with staff, good relationships with community people, personal knowledge of community, and positive effects of skill.)

Rate the degree of facilitation:

None ______ ______ ______ ______ ______ Great Deal
0 1 2 3 4

In general, to what degree do you think *agency* factors may be facilitating in implementing this guideline? (These factors might include administration support, supervisor support, staff support, and physical facilities aid effort.)

Rate the degree of facilitation:

None ______ ______ ______ ______ ______ Great Deal
0 1 2 3 4

In general, to what degree do you think *client* factors may be facilitating in implementing this guideline? (These factors might include client participation in organization or program, client receptivity to organization or program, and client support of practitioner.)

Rate the degree of facilitation:

None ______ ______ ______ ______ ______ Great Deal
0 1 2 3 4

In general, to what degree do you think *community* factors may be facilitating in implementing this guideline? (These factors might include community support of organization generally, influential and other community groups support organization or program, changes in community tend to support organization or program, and community support of practitioner.)

Rate the degree of facilitation:

None ______ ______ ______ ______ ______ *Great Deal*
0 1 2 3 4

10 Limiting factors—relative importance

In general, to what degree do you think *personal factors related to yourself* may be limiting in implementing this guideline? (These factors might include poor relationships with staff, poor relationships with community people, lack of personal knowledge of community, and negative effects of insufficient skills.)

Rate the degree of limitation:

None ______ ______ ______ ______ ______ Great Deal
0 1 2 3 4

In general, to what degree do you think *agency* factors may be limiting in implementing this guideline? (These factors might include unclear or shifting goals, programs or assignments; lack of funds, facilities, and other resources; lack of support or hindering action of supervisor; and lack of support or hindering action of staff.)

Rate the degree of limitation:

None ______ ______ ______ ______ ______ Great Deal
0 1 2 3 4

In general, to what degree do you think *client* factors may be limiting in implementing this guideline? (These factors might include negative response to organization generally, client interference with organization activities, and dissensus among clients.)

Rate the degree of limitation:

None ______ ______ ______ ______ ______ Great Deal
0 1 2 3 4

In general, to what degree do you think *community* factors may be limiting in implementing this guideline? (These factors might include negative response to organization generally; lack of knowledge of organization purposes, programs or activities; influential community groups or leaders that do not support organization or program; and competition by other activities with community residents' time and interests.)

Rate the degree of limitation:

None ______ ______ ______ ______ ______ Great Deal
0 1 2 3 4

ILLUSTRATIONS OF INITIAL LOGS COMPLETED BY PRACTITIONERS

I. EXAMPLE OF PRACTITIONER IN A WELFARE EMPLOYEES UNION

A. Goal Statement

Strengthen the union by developing its working class orientation and efforts through increasing the relative power of black and noncollege degree-holding members of the union. Shift organizational objectives from those of a traditional trade union to a greater working class orientation. Specifically, the proximate goal is to increase the effectiveness in performing union roles of members having a working class perspective. This will put into operation existing but dormant organizational goals.

B. Concretization (Operationalization) of Guideline Elements

Altering the structure of influence within the organization: Increase the relative (compared with white, middle class degree-holders) influence of progressive black and non-college degree members of the organization.

Increase the power of groups within the organization that have goals compatible with theirs: Through an educational program, increase the knowledge and competency of blacks and clericals; at the same time facilitate their movement into leadership positions.

II. EXAMPLE OF PRACTITIONER IN FAMILY SERVICE AGENCY

A. Goal Statement

Shift goals from serving clients one to one within the agency to serving categories of clients through outreach advocacy approaches. Specifically, the proximate goal is to have the board adopt a policy of advocacy for the mentally retarded population of the city.

B. Concretization (Operationalization) of Guideline Elements

Altering the power of influence within the organization:

Increase the influence of the Advisory Committee on Mental Retardation.

Increase the power of groups within the organization that have goals compatible with theirs: Helping the Advisory Committee on Mental Retardation to be active and competent in introducing pro-advocacy proposals into the board. The committee will be strengthened by making it more vocal, more unified, and more focused as a unit within the organization.

4

FOSTERING PARTICIPATION

For many human service and community workers the subject of participation is central to their practice. Neighborhood and community development workers, including those in the early settlement house movement, have viewed grass-roots participation as essential to their efforts.[1] Planners in institutions such as Community Welfare Councils and United Funds have long embraced "voluntarism," which in practice has meant the involvement of a cross-section of community "leaders" in policy formulation and program implementation. Social activists have viewed the mobilization of masses of people as an ideological imperative as well as a strategic necessity.

In the field of community organization, participation has been viewed in various, but not always compatible, ways. In one view, participation is *a goal in its own right.* That is, in an impersonal urban environment where associational ties have been weakened and individual citizens feel impotent, the basic objective of community practice is the restoration of meaningful human involvement through participation.[2] Phrases such as "local initiative" and "maximum feasible participation" capture this meaning. Substantive results, such as specific health and welfare programs, are not as important in this perspective as the more fundamental objective of providing channels for ties

[1]For a historical overview of the subject see Sidney Dillick, *Community Organization for Neighborhood Department—Past and Present* (New York: Women's Press and Morrow, 1953).

[2]For a prototypical representation of this position, see William W. and Loureide J. Biddle, *The Community Development Process: The Rediscovery of Local Initiative* (New York: Holt, Rinehart and Winston, 1965).

among people or increasing their decision-making capacity. Participation then is an overriding objective.

In contrast, other people view participation as a means for achieving more concrete programmatic ends—but also as a *constant, unvarying means.*[3] The arguments for this view are both philosophical and practical. In the first place, it is argued, democratic values require self-determination and the broadest possible involvement of the effected community in the development and enactment of policies and programs. Hence, maximizing participation represents a fundamental philosophical creed. In the second place, only those programs which are determined by citizens will be vigorously carried out; that is, when people take part in decisions affecting their lives they will support the resulting public policies and programs. Thus, on a practical basis, participation is correlated with effective policy and program implementation.

A third view of participation is even more practical. In this view, participation is a *conditional means*, to be employed selectively for certain goals and under given circumstances.[4] Not all valued social objectives, in this conception, will be achieved or maximized through broad participation. Some research studies, for example, suggest that raising the level of community involvement has had a negative impact on certain programs, such as school desegregation, school bond drives, and fluoridation. In this third orientation the practitioner would weigh the costs and benefits of participation in specific consequences to human welfare.

Regardless of which perspective one adopts, however, there follows the more pragmatic, "nuts and bolts" question of the best ways to get people to join up, attend a meeting, work on a committee, or help raise money for an organization. A school-community worker in an elementary school faced this kind of practical problem:

[3]Murray G. Ross, in his widely read book on community organization, advocates this view. He states: "Community organization as it has been described here requires the participation of the people of a community. For what is to be united in common action is people. And what is to be changed is to be changed by people...." Murray G. Ross,- *Community Organization: Theory, Principles and Practice* (New York: Harper and Row, 1967), pp. 168-169. This view may also be inferred from Foskett's writing. John M. Foskett, "The Influence of Social Participation on Community Programs and Activities," in Marvin B. Sussman, ed., *Community Structure and Analysis* (New York: Thomas Y. Cromwell, 1959), pp. 311-330.

[4]This more analytical orientation is suggested by William Gamson, "Community Issues and Their Outcome: How to Lose a Fluoridation Referendum," in *Applied Sociology: Principles and Problems*, A. Gouldner and S.M. Miller, eds., (Glencoe, Ill.: The Free Press, 1965).

The mothers program began in October and ultimately involved nine mothers — seven of whom did tutoring in the school with youngsters needing extra help and two helping to maintain and operate the materials center. In April, the helping teacher who was in charge of the program came to me seeking assistance because two mothers had recently dropped out of the program and because she had only an average of three mothers attending their meetings.

We will focus our attention on this type of concrete practice task and set aside the philosophical ramifications of participation.

RESEARCH ON PARTICIPATION

Findings of recent research on the subject of participation can be summarized as follows: The amount of participation in voluntary associations varies directly with both the number of benefits (rewards, satisfactions) offered by an organization and the degree to which the benefits are contingent on participation.[5]

Several studies suggest various refinements and elaborations of this proposition. Four points are particularly useful for our purposes:

1 There appear to be four important sources of benefits that community-oriented voluntary associations can exchange for members' contributions: (a) achievement of specific goals; (b) rewarding goal-achievement procedures; (c) rewarding structural devices, such as formal offices; and (d) informal cliques.[6]

2 Low income persons show more interest in participating in activities that have direct and immediate benefits than in

[5]Charles Lee Mulford and Gerald E. Klonglan, "The Significance of Attitudes for Formal Voluntary Organizations: A Synthesis of Existing Research and Theory," paper presented at a meeting of the American Sociological Association, Washington, D.C. (September 1970). Anthony Orum, "Structural Sources of Negro Student Protest: Campus and Community," paper presented at a meeting of the American Sociological Association, San Francisco, California (September 1969). Leonard Schneiderman, "Value Orientation Preferences of Chronic Relief Recipients," *Social Work, 9* (3) (July 1964), 13-18. Alvin Seals and Jiri Kolaja, "A Study of Negro Voluntary Organizations in Lexington, Kentucky," *Phylon, 25* (1) (Spring 1964), 27-31. Keith W. Warner and William Hefferman, "The Benefit-Participation Contingency in Voluntary Farm Organizations," *Rural Sociology, 32* (2) (June 1967), 133-153. Harold Weissman, "An Exploratory Study of a Neighborhood Council," dissertation, Columbia University, 1966.

[6]Harold Weissman, "An Exploratory Study of a Neighborhood Council," dissertation, Columbia University, 1966.

long-term activities with long-range payoffs.[7] Various studies of time orientation have shown that lower-class individuals have a greater present-time orientation, as compared with a future-time orientation, than middle-class people. (Some researchers have hypothesized that this difference is caused by pressures on the low-income person to be preoccupied with immediate, recurrent daily problems of survival.) Schneiderman,[8] for example, compared a sample of welfare recipients with a sample of middle-class school teachers and social workers and found that welfare recipients were significantly more likely to emphasize "present time" over "future time," and "being" over "doing" on a value-orientation scale based on an instrument developed by Kluckhohn and Strodtbeck.

3 Low-income persons seem to prefer activities that provide opportunities for spontaneous, expressive behavior.[9]

4 When benefits are explicitly tied to participation in a direct way, they have the greatest effect on participation. Warner and Hefferman,[10] for example, in a study of farmers' organizations, found that the greater the number of benefits that were contingent upon participation, the higher the attendance at association meetings.

ACTION GUIDELINE

PRACTITIONERS WISHING TO FOSTER PARTICIPATION IN ORGANIZATIONS, VOLUNTARY ASSOCIATIONS, OR TASK GROUPS SHOULD PROVIDE (OR INCREASE) APPROPRIATE BENEFITS.

---

[7] Leonard Schneiderman, "The Culture of Poverty: A Study of the Value Orientation Preferences of the Chronically Impoverished," dissertation abstract, University of Minnesota (1963). Leonard Schneiderman, "Value Orientation Preferences of Chronic Relief Recipients," *Social Work, 9* (3) (July 1964), 13-18.

[8] Schneiderman, *op. cit.*

[9] Anthony M. Orum, "Structural Sources of Negro Student Protest: Campus and Community," paper presented at a meeting of the American Sociological Association, San Francisco, California (September 1969). Schneiderman, *op. cit.* Alvin Seals and Jiri Kolaja, "A Study of Negro Voluntary Organizations in Lexington, Kentucky." *Phylon, 25* (1) (Spring 1964), 27-31.

[10] Keith W. Warner and William Hefferman, "The Benefit-Participation Contingency in Voluntary Farm Organizations," *Rural Sociology, 32* (2) (June 1967), 133-153.

The term participation in the guideline should be interpreted in a broad sense. It is meant to include not only the recruitment of new members but also changes in the pattern of existing member's participation. For example, an individual who had only attended general membership meetings might begin to participate in committee activities. We have not included the contingency notion in the guideline itself. It may not always be necessary or feasible, and some practitioners may find ethical dilemmas in making rewards explicitly contingent on participation.

ILLUSTRATING AND OPERATIONALIZING THE GUIDELINE

Of course, this guideline may be viewed as stating an obvious and well-known approach to fostering participation—that is, the provision of benefits to people to reward past participation and thus to motivate continued participation. Many practitioners intuitively use rewards linked to participation in this way. For example, Spergel in a widely used community organization text book states: "A service program tied in with community action assumes that there are persons who want to receive personal gratification as well as give energy and time to other people's problems. People expect a *quid pro quo*, one way or the other, for efforts expended."[11] What we are trying to do here is to make this common assumption and approach more explicit and more systematic, so that it may have a more effective impact on participation rates in community groups. We shall first describe the types of benefits related to participation, and then demonstrate the use of each of these benefits through direct illustrations from practice.

Essentially one may describe rewards in terms of *instrumental-* and *expressive* components. Instrumental benefits provide material, tangible, task-oriented returns (such as getting favorable legislation passed or a traffic light installed). Expressive benefits are intangible and psychological in character, such as increased friendships, personal satisfaction, and pride. (For some this may be reminiscient of task and socioemotional aspects of group process.) Further distinctions may be made within the two categories:

1 *Instrumental benefits* may be:

a *Material:* Obtaining an increased welfare allotment, securing needed information, or authorization, etc.

[11]Irving A. Spergel, *Community Problem Solving: The Delinquency Example.* (Chicago and London: The University of Chicago Press), 1969, p. 136.

b *Interim-anticipatory:* Setting up an action structure or obtaining a verbal commitment that is a partial achievement leading up to the longer-term material gain. (Indeed, these may also occur in steps together.)

2 *Expressive benefits* may be:

a *Social-interpersonal:* Making new friends, having an enjoyable social experience, etc.

b *Symbolic:* Receiving an award that represents public approval or recognition of an individual's participatory activities, being mentioned in a newspaper article, etc.

In practice these approaches may quite often be used in combination; sometimes one is given special emphasis and supplemented by other people.

In the section that follows, practitioners describe how they used these four different forms of benefits with different client groups.

1 Instrumental: Material

Our Community Mental Health program in the housing project was floundering. I decided to use the participation guideline out of a real need for it. I had been working with a small cluster of residents in the project to develop a self-help group. At one point, in the work with that group, our efforts began to falter, and we were threatened with losing the group, as a unit, although our consultations with individual families were going well. I decided to carry out this guideline with the goal of increasing participation in group meetings in that area of the project.

Following the elements of the guideline in this case really saved the group. We decided to increase benefits by making sure that specific personal problems were resolved for each family — for example, getting roach spray free from the Manager (he usually charged residents) for two women; getting a toilet repaired; following through with the school in getting special attention for specific children; and transporting families to the dentist. At the same time we saw the families individually and informally, and decreased the number of group meetings (where they had been weekly, we tried bi-weekly; then "on call"). In a certain sense, elimination of unnecessary meetings was a reward also. On a group level, when tenants ran into a disagreement with the management concerning arrangements for paying rent, we facilitated a linkage with Legal Aid.

When we felt that the time was right to call the group together we did this, and then personally visited those who did not attend, suggesting that we could not continue to work with them individually, if they did not attend the group sessions! It absolutely worked—and the group was able to begin operating again. Thus by providing concrete benefits and at the same time making them contingent upon participation in the group, the group began to function again.

2 Instrumental: Interim-Anticipatory

I used this guideline to help me in organizing the Black Student Union at the Junior High School. Although attempts had been made by the administrators of the school to organize the black students, lack of organizational skills had prevented the organization from functioning. After a meeting with the administrators, it was suggested that our Community Center give necessary assistance to organize such a group.

The assistant principal called a meeting of selected people to discuss organizational strategy. This step created some personality conflicts among students who were selected. Nonetheless, in that meeting I had the students identify the areas they felt the organization should concern itself with and had them divide into different committees. I assigned my staff to work as advisors to each committee, with me taking the Goals and Structure Committee. The Goals and Structure Committee, composed of about ten students, met for five days to discuss the goals and objectives of the organization. Allowing the students to develop their ideas, and at the same time influencing them to deal with concrete problems confronting black students, the committee developed a structure that would be composed of a Steering Committee with representation from each grade level. I recommend that as opposed to the traditional competitive election method, those students in each grade that were interested, volunteer and place their names in a box. The three names selected from the box would be the persons on the Steering Committee. Other students would become members of the different committees. Thus this method enabled students to be structured so that their participation would provide some immediate resolution to their problems. The Steering Committee began to function immediately, and staff again were assigned to provide technical assistance. The first step was for the organization to proceed with plans for Black History Week. This effort enabled the organization to immediately develop a program, carry it out, and allow for a large number of black students to participate — thus providing the students with activities that gave concrete evidence of making progress toward their goals, while gaining organizational experience.

After the black history program, the organization was functioning well enough, and had the necessary support and direction, that I could withdraw my staff. Periodically, the students would call upon us for assistance, but we had basically accomplished our task.

3 Expressive: Social-Interpersonal

Our union needed to increase the participation of the clerical members in our programs. A clerical caucus exists, but it is small, not highly active, and has not engaged in any activity that has resulted in the resolution of pressing problems or in satisfaction for members. Given the realities of our situation, it is not likely that there will be any immediate resolution of these pressing problems, but through sustained participation of clerical employees, along with other groups, over a longer period such resolution is anticipated. Nevertheless, to sustain the necessary participation it is important that there be some short-term gratifications. The clerical caucus was encouraged to sponsor a social event which could raise money to finance legal support of our members and, equally as important, would bring more clericals together socially.

At a clerical caucus meeting in April, the decision was made to plan a cabaret night. Division of responsibilities for carrying out the decision was made. A day in late May was chosen for the event. During the remainder of April, the clerical caucus met regularly to plan the details of the party, chose the band, selected the site, and distributed tickets to various union members to sell. People were obviously having fun and relating to each other differently from on the job or even in previous union business. My role was limited to securing from the union executive board the necessary advances in funds for deposits on the band and the hall and for the purchase and printing of the tickets.

The cabaret was a huge social success (although very little profit was realized). There was a competing cabaret which was sponsored by another employee organization that was held several days later. It cut down on the attendance at our social. However, reports from persons who attended the competing cabaret indicated it was a drag compared with the clerical caucus cabaret. This led to an increased sense of camaradarie among those who had worked together on our event. Members of the caucus have a closer social bond among them now.

At a meeting in June there was a general feeling of job well done. Most of the meeting was spent recapitulating the events around the cabaret, and as we were about to adjourn, the decision was made to hold another meeting the following week and to begin to deal programmatically with the needs of the clerical employees, including how to recruit more into the union.

4 Expressive: Symbolic

As a school-community agent I was interested in increasing community participation in the school and at the same time improving services to children through use of volunteers. Special classes were decided upon according to the interests of the volunteers and students alike. They included arts and crafts, cooking, crochet, dramatics, modern dance, and sewing.

I decided to use this guideline in relation to the project in order to give continuity to the program. The "expressive" approach I took was to provide recognition for the work done by volunteers. This included: working toward a final presentation of activity "products" at the end of the program; giving out of service awards; and pictures and publicity for the program. I kept the time period short so that the end point would not seem too distant. I attended also to providing sufficient supplies; including the volunteers themselves in planning; holding frequent staff meetings to offer encouragement; and individual letters and phone contacts with volunteers. Much interest was developed in the volunteer program and it ran quite smoothly.

The continued staff meetings with the volunteers — and having the final event with publicity and service awards to look forward to — sustained interest in the program. The school administrator also took pictures and brought supplies around during the six-week session. Weekly plans were required from the volunteers so that I would know what specific activities were scheduled and what could be done for the final presentation.

I requested that a regular PTO meeting be given over to the final presentation, in order to reach a large number of community people. There was a great deal of publicity for the event in the neighborhood, as well as a picture and story in the State Chronicle. Volunteers and parents helped to publicize the program by word of mouth. I was delighted to see 200 persons in attendance at the meeting. (This served a double purpose, because the School-Community Council elections were held that night and this certainly helped to get the vote out.)

Because of the success of the program, the volunteers wanted to repeat it for another six-week session, and students also looked forward to it.

In contrast, the second session was not as successful. Because of a conflict between the principal and myself, I lost some of my drive—there were fewer staff meetings, no pictures, and the final presentation, being repetitious, was rather anti-climatic compared with the first. I feel that because the quantity and quality of "expressive experiences" were less, participation and enthusiasm in the second session declined.

It is not necessary to dwell on the operationalization of this guideline, since the "benefit" notion is clear and is widely employed in the field. For a quick summary, the four illustrations from practice are laid out in chart form (Figure 4-1) according to the three components of the guideline: increase participation, voluntary associations and task groups, and benefits.

PERSPECTIVES FROM BEHAVIOR MODIFICATION

It is not surprising that a practitioner declared: "The guideline represents an application of 'behavior modification' theory to community practice—and this certainly seems appropriate." The benefits-reward (or reinforcement) principle is basic to behavior modification, and it would be a disservice to ignore the substantial research in this field as we apply some behaviorist concepts to community practice, an area in which they have not found systematic or direct expression. We

Setting	Increased Participation	Voluntary Association or Task Groups	Benefits
Community Mental Health Housing Project	Tenants attend meetings more regularly	Self-help Tenants Group	*Instrumental Material:* free roach spray: have management make apartment repairs such as fix toilets; getting the local school to give special attention to children of the family; transportation to the dentist; legal aid service procurred
Junior High School Community Center	Increase number of black students serving on committees	Black Student Association	*Instrumental Interim-anticipatory:* successfully conducting a black history program
Trade Union	Maintain membership and attendance at meetings of clerical workers	Social Work Union	*Expressive Social-interpersonal:* carrying out a successful cabaret night social event
School-Community Agent Program	Prevent loss off of participation of volunteers in providing after-school activities	Volunteer Service Program	*Expressive Symbolic:* a public PTO meeting featuring publicity, service awards, pictures, and display of products of volunteer services.

Figure 4.1. Elements of the Participation Guideline Operationalized

have selected a few behaviorist terms and concepts that have a reasonable degree of relevance to community and organizational level intervention.

Behavior Specification

It is essential that the practitioner specify the exact nature of the behavior to be changed. In the case of participation, we may attempt to increase the following:

1 *Rate:* The frequency with which an individual attends meetings.

2 *Form:* The type or quality of participation—for example, attendance, committee chairmanship, financial or other material contributions, and speaking up more at meetings.

3 *Duration:* The extent of participation—that is, retention or maintenance of participation over time.

4 *Variability:* The stability or regularity of participation.

The assumption is that different types of benefits may be effective in encouraging various aspects of participation behavior.

Positive Reinforcement

Essentially this refers to the provision of benefits contingent upon the performance of some desired behavior. Thomas points out that the social worker has certain direct interpersonal reinforcers available in his relationship with clients.[12] These include approval, attention, and affection. In a group or community context, these rewards may be offered to a specific individual through other individuals. In classroom situations the following positive reinforcements have been suggested: information regarding performance ("your answer is correct!"), material rewards (good grades, candy), social rewards (praise, affectionate embrace), and opportunity to engage in preferred behaviors (extra recess, personal selection of preferred study subjects).[13] In human service work the agency's resources offer many

[12]Edwin Thomas and Esther Goodman, eds., *Socio-Behavioral Theory and Interpersonal Helping in Social Work,* (Ann Arbor: Campus Publishers, 1965).

[13]Mary B. Harris, *Classroom Uses of Behavior Modification,* (Columbus, Ohio: Charles E. Merrill, 1972).

reinforcement possibilities, as do those external community resources with which the agency has operating linkages.

Contracting

There has been increasing use of this concept in various settings such as schools and community mental health programs. In our immediate area of interest it might be possible for a practitioner to come to an agreement about a level of participation, which if followed for a designated time might result in a pleasing outcome. For example, contracting was used in the issuance of a certificate to leaders who completed the six-week volunteer service session in the school-community example cited earlier.

Shaping

This involves establishing a series of sequential goals leading up to a longer range goal. The technical behavioral language refers to "successive approximations." In community practice one is more likely to speak of *interim goals* or incrementalism. As a hypothetical example, a community worker wants a woman to take on an appointive office; she starts by asking her to attend a committee, then later asks her to chair a committee, and finally to hold an office. (Here again we see that behavior modification techniques are not unknown in community intervention, although they may be called by different names.)

Group Contingencies

Benefits may be offered to groups as well as to individuals. The United Fund offers a great number of social and symbolic rewards to volunteers who go over the goal, often using graphs and charts to dramatize the group objective. A committee or organization might set certain goals or standards for participation and foster group achievement satisfactions for successful attainment.

Extinction

The extinction principle probably has a limited use in community practice generally. Here we are dealing not with rewarding a desired behavior, but with attempting to decrease undesirable behavior. This is riskier and more difficult, because it often evokes the use of punishing or aversive stimuli, usually by removing the reinforcing aspect of the interfering behavior.

For example, a member of the group persists in making very impractical suggestions, largely as a way of calling attention to himself. This throws the group off track and also causes the chairman to lose for the moment his control and effectiveness. The practitioner might suggest to the chairman that by responding in this overt way he is reinforcing this undesirable participation by giving special attention to it. Perhaps an alternative would be to ignore or to handle in a brief, routine manner these inappropriate comments and to proceed with the business at hand. The inappropriate participation thus might be extinguished when the psychologically desired rewards were no longer attached to it. At the same time, the chairman or the practitioner could respond with support and enthusiasm when the member makes appropriate and "practical" suggestions.[14]

PATTERNS OF IMPLEMENTATION

In our review of the experience with this guideline, we found that one general pattern of implementation was followed in all the cases in the field test. This pattern consisted of five steps: (1) goal determination, (2) selection of benefits to be used, (3) initial contact with potential participants, (4) follow-up contact with potential participants, and (5) delivery of benefits or operation of the event.

1 Goal Determination

The first step was to select the participation objective. The guideline was used to form new groups or to maintain or to increase participation in existing groups. Illustrations of these three objectives are given in goal statements of practitioners:

> *My goal is to get those WRO (Welfare Rights Organization) groups in the metropolitan area which are not working to have the Early Preventive Screening, Diagnosis, and Treatment*

[14]Aversive tactics are used by certain social activists (i.e., Alinsky) or agency personnel (i.e., supervisors) to eliminate or shift particular behavior patterns or modes of participation.

program implemented in their communities to participate actively in the efforts to secure this program for their communities.

My goal is to maintain the current level of mothers now participating weekly in the mothers tutoring program in the school and to increase the number who attend the group meetings of the mothers.

My goal is to increase the number of participants in the Mental Health Association's annual chapter leadership workshop.

The relatively high level of success in the use of this guideline was distributed rather evenly across the three goals.

2 Selection of Benefits

The selection of the means of increasing participation may be seen as a two-stage process of identifying the benefits available or subject to the control of the practitioner and matching the benefits to the target population. One practitioner explicitly made this distinction when outlining her course of action:

(a) Figure out what might be the most effective reinforcers for this group.

(b) Figure out the most feasible reinforcers in terms of administration.

The order in which she lists the two stages is illuminating, since it suggests that practitioners may start by defining the benefits needed to increase participation and then attempt to obtain them, or first determine the types of benefits available and feasible in their situation. There is some support for giving early attention to the feasibility factor in the case of a practitioner who settled upon a benefit before verifying that it was, in fact, available: "During the week following this staff meeting I found that it would be impossible for the agency to pay for a luncheon for any portion of the staff." From the high success rate and the range of benefits provided, however, it would seem that the practitioners had access to sufficient benefits. (Problems and obstacles will be recounted later.)

The main concern, thus, would seem to be matching the benefits to the target system. Whether because they had trouble predicting the needs and desires of the target population or because they simply wanted to insure the success of the intervention, the most practitioners (13 out of 18) who implemented this guideline provided multiple benefits. All but one of the 13 opted for a combination of instrumental and expressive benefits. The modal category within this combination (eight cases) combined material and social interaction benefits. The lone exception was a union president who used material (refreshments) and interim-anticipatory (legal consultation) benefits. In the absence of strong evidence concerning what benefits apply to which clients and constituents, the use of *multiple rewards* seems a wise course. It appears that practitioners were as likely to use the instrumental-expressive combination with nonpoor as with poor target populations. The same was true of the use of single and dual-instrumental benefits.

3 Initial Contact with Potential Participants

As might be expected, the method used for the initial contact varied with the nature of the target system, although the differences were not marked. The major difference in approach lay in the degree to which the potential membership could be easily identified and located, and in the degree to which the practitioner was in day-to-day contact with that membership. Ten of the field interventions took place within the practitioner's agency (four with staff or board as the target and six with consumers). Four interventions were directed toward external organizations and four toward the community at large. The types of initial contacts varied, ranging from direct personal conversations and telephone discussions to flyers, mailings, and notices in the newspapers.

4 Follow-up Contact with Potential Participants

An interesting trend concerning the follow-up or recontact stage was a tendency for practitioners to use a different medium for the recontact than was used for the initial contact. When each individual of the potential membership could be identified, the contact and recontact were usually made by a formal letter or memo alternating with an informal conversation, either face-to-face or by telephone. When potential members could not be identified individually, practitioners tended to use a different means of communication for the recontact stage than they had used for the contact stage. Although it might be argued that the alternative means of publicity simply reaches a somewhat different population, the value of newspapers, radio, or television in legitimizing or reinforcing handbills and posters should not be ignored. We are not able to state that a varied follow-up is effective or successful; we only note that it is a common or typical practice.

5 Delivery of Benefits or Operation of the Event

The actual delivery of the promised benefits was particularly important when the event was one in a series that was expected to continue; this situation applied to most of the practitioners. It appears from four cases that involved somewhat extensive benefits that the practitioner had to expend considerable effort to assure the delivery of the benefits, although most of the effort took place prior to the event.

In several cases practitioners developed contingency plans, so that if one benefit turned out not to be available, another could be substituted. If the benefits were social-interpersonal, a good deal of energy had to be expended during the event itself; other types of benefits, particularly material, required much effort prior to the event. In general, the less certainty about the benefit—meaning the less control the practitioner had over the delivery of the reward—the more effort the worker had to expend on benefit provision. Practitioners just had to work harder, using multiple and contingency approaches, when their capability for "delivering the goods" was limited.

QUANTITATIVE FINDINGS FROM PRACTITIONER LOGS

The portrait of successful implementation presented below is based on 16 cases (out of 18 implementation attempts) in which use of the guideline resulted in complete or almost complete attainment of the intended goal, as judged by the panel of evaluators. As usual, the information will be given in four categories: key community groups contacted during implementation, key individuals contacted, facilitating factors in implementation, and limiting factors in implementation.

In carrying out this guideline, practitioners tended to indicate a relatively small number of community groups to be important (See Table 4-1). The mode was one to five groups (in 50 percent of the cases), while another 19 percent of the practitioners indicated no such groups.

The percentage of practitioners reporting each type of contact as important was: public agencies, 50; private agencies, 44; and voluntary associations, 69.

The practitioners' reasons for contacting community groups varied considerably. The reasons for dealing with public agencies were to gain legitimation or approval as well as participation. With regard

Table 4-1
Key Community Groups Contacted[a,b]

Type of Group Contacted	Percent of Practitioners Who Considered This Group Important	Major Reasons for Contact
Public agency	50	Legitimation or approval Immediate participation
Private agency	44	Immediate participation
Voluntary association	69	Immediate participation

[a]For Tables 4-1 and 4-2, refer to the logs in Appendix B for full range of variables from those cited here are reported.

[b]Number of groups considered important: range was 0 to over 30. Mode (50%) was 1 to 5 groups; 19% indicated no groups as important.

to the other two types of groups, the main reason was to gain immediate participation. Community groups were rarely approached for financial support or for public relations purposes. There is evident logic to using governmental agencies as a source of legitimation and private agencies and voluntary associations as a source of recruitment.

While practitioners found few community groups important, they indicated larger numbers of individuals (Table 4-2). The dispersion was from six to over 30, with 50 percent reporting over 30 important individuals.

Practitioners considered a variety of individuals important, with no outstanding trends. Board members ($\overline{12.3}$), community people ($\overline{81}$),

Table 4-2
Key Individuals Contacted[a]

Types Most Frequently Considered Important	Major Reasons for Contact
Board members	No trends
Community people	Immediate participation
Clients	Immediate participation

[a]Number of individuals considered important: range was 6 to over 30; 50 considered over 30 important.

were contacted in large numbers by those who considered these categories important.

Community people and clients were contacted most frequently to obtain immediate participation.

In following this guideline you may find a relatively small number of community groups (somewhere between one and five) to be important but a larger number of individuals to be important contacts. Quite often you may be attempting to increase participation by clients or staff members in your own agency. Public agencies are likely to be contacted to obtain legitimation, and private agencies and voluntary associations to recruit participants. Client and community people will probably be recruited for immediate participation.

Practitioners reported that facilitating factors had much greater influence on the outcome of this guideline than limiting factors. (Table 4-3). This is not surprising, since participation is not usually a controversial subject, particularly when it is related to meeting service and program objectives of human service agencies. Organized opposition and policy obstacles are not likely to exist. Thus, if the practitioner is able to mobilize favorable factors and provide powerful enough incentives, he is likely to achieve the goal of enhanced participation.

All facilitating factors (personal, agency, client, and community) were rated high in influencing the outcome, but personal factors were viewed as most important, particularly in retrospect. These findings underline "use of self" as a significant element in executing this intervention. The personal resources of the practitioner seem to be highlighted in terms of selecting appropriate benefits, announcing them, motivating people, and delivering both interpersonal and material rewards.

It is important to capitalize on the facilitating factors in the situation. It would be advisable to choose a goal and a strategy that are consistent with (or which can be enhanced by) your position or role in the agency and your past experience. Since sense of commitment is also given emphasis, choose a goal and program for which you have conviction and enthusiasm. Attempt to develop good relationships with individuals in the agency network.

With regard to your agency situation, seek a goal that is consistent with or that may expedite your other assignments, and attempt to gain whatever support you can from fellow staff members and agency administrators. Try to locate suitable physical facilities, or plan a program that fits well with the available facilities.

Choose a program that will be of specific interest to clients, or work hard at developing their interest. Likewise, it helps if you choose a group of clients to deal with who are receptive to your agency and the program, or attempt to build this kind of receptivity as you go

Table 4-3
Facilitating and Limiting Factors[a]

Facilitating Factors (general intensity $\overline{2.9}$)		Limiting Factors (general intensity $\overline{1.6}$)	
	Personal ($\overline{3.4}$)[b]		Personal ($\overline{1.3}$)
1	Good relationships within agency, particularly supervisors and staff	1	Overinvolvement
		2	Fatigue
2	Commitment to program	3	Lack of time
3	Position or role		
4	Prior experience		
5	Knowledge of programs		
6	Commitment to agency		
7	Commitment to guideline		
8	Good reputation		
	Client ($\overline{2.7}$)		Client ($\overline{1.6}$)
1	Interest in program	1	Competition from other activities
2	Receptivity	2	Lack of knowledge of the organization
3	Support of other clients	3	Lack of other knowledge and skills
	Agency ($\overline{2.7}$)		Agency ($\overline{2.0}$)
1	Assignments and tasks consistent with effort	1	Lack of funds and resources
		2	Lack of staff
2	Staff support	3	Unclear or shifting goals, programs and/or assignments
3	Administrative support		
4	Staff involvement		
	Community ($\overline{2.6}$)		Community ($\overline{1.5}$)
1	Interest in program	1	Competition from other activities
2	Community group involvement	2	Lack of knowledge of organization
3	Participation	3	Lack of other knowledge and skills
4	Support		
5	Receptivity		

[a]Scores from intensity scale (0 = None, 4 = Great Deal).

[b]Figure represents mean scores.

along. The same goes for the outside community.

It is also necessary, though less important, to be alert to certain negative factors. Try to clarify your personal goals and assignments in the agency so that you are free to concentrate on this task without an inordinate amount of pressure from other demands or without neglecting other necessary tasks assigned to you. Lack of staff and resources may impede you. Selection of a feasible objective is an important strategic consideration in this connection. Realize also that clients and community people will have other activities that compete for their time and interests. This means that the benefits you offer must be strong enough to gain their attention and capture their motivation. Clients and residents may also lack knowledge of the organization or may not possess certain skills pertinent to the participation objective. Therefore, you may need to give attention to making up these deficits as you go along. Direct quotes and advice from practitioners follow.

PRACTITIONERS' VIEWS OF PROBLEMS AND PROSPECTS

Practitioners in the field study found this to be the easiest and most successful guideline with which they worked. In rating this guideline on a scale ranging from *1* (not useful) to *5* (useful), 55.6 percent of the practitioners checked off category 5, and the average response was 4.6. One worker notes, "The high rate of retention of client involvement I experienced suggests this guideline has a lot of power."

A number of reasons were offered for the utility of the approach. Several people commented that it was helpful in analyzing and planning their work:

> *Most of us intuitively provide benefits for our clients and the groups with which we work. This guideline and the chapter accompanying it, help us to analyze a situation much more carefully, to see elements we might not have, and to act in a more planful manner.*
>
> *The guideline illustrates the range of reinforcements potentially available and provides rationales for selecting rewards according to type of program and clientele.*

Others noted its wide range of application:

> *New workers to an agency after appropriate orientation can use the guideline to get some things started. Workers who have been in the field should find the guideline helpful in the event they have become bogged down with the routine. All could find it useful in various kinds of experimentation in bringing different groups of varied backgrounds together.*

> *Particularly when working with low-income groups, practitioners must be able to provide some rewards to keep these persons as functioning members.*

At the same time, practitioners encountered some difficulties and made a variety of suggestions on implementation of the guideline.

First, they pointed out that the benefits selected must have real meaning or significance for the target group. One practitioner stated: "You must be sure that the benefits are really viewed as worthy by the group members. Without this the whole thing would have failed." Another practitioner noted that the benefits must be *perceived* as important by participants, regardless of the objective reality of the matter. He also indicated that the benefits could be potential as well as actual: "I increased the members' awareness of services which potentially could be provided — even if these were in fact not provided." The practitioners' experience also lends support to a point made earlier in this chapter, that if benefits can be shown to be clearly tied to or contingent on participation, the impact of the guideline can be increased.

Several practitioners highlighted the need for interim, short-range benefits as a way of maintaining motivation over longer periods of time. As one put it: "Often I feel a long range goal is achievable, but the community group may not be able to have that goal in sight—or even agree with it at that stage of the game." Another stressed the significance of this concept in working with low-income citizens:

> *Most often, because of existing power relationships in the society, low income persons do not have the clout to make gains quickly or to resolve pressing problems besetting them. This means that their participation must be sustained while they go through the struggle to resolve these problems. The structuring of participation so as to provide expressive experiences and immediate social gratification permits this. Those of us who are highly issue-oriented tend to forget or neglect that. We dare not!*

Several practitioners warned that these interventions cannot be carried out in a mechanistic, ritualistic manner. The art of practice has to shape the "science" of any intervention strategy. This involves the practitioner's attitudes, interpersonal skills, sense of timing, and so on. As two of them advised us:

> *There is a need to develop trust and a decent relationship with client groups. This takes time and demonstrated proof that you can deliver.*

There is the consideration of the personal qualities of members as well as the level of enthusiasm conveyed by the practitioners.

In addition to the comments made above, which were somewhat general, more specific observations were offered by individual practitioners. We have grouped some of their comments under a few statements of advice that can be inferred from them.

Give Yourself Enough Time

Actually, I found little difficulty in using this guideline. The only problem was self-imposed: a limited amount of time in which to develop the "benefits" to be offered workshop participants.

One difficulty was my lack of information about the community I am working in. I was forced to form a group before I had adequate community information.

I would caution, to be very clear on the use of the guideline, do not over or under burden staff or the clientele you are trying to reach by trying to solve the problem in one day.

Expect to Encounter Some Organizational Obstacles

The usual organizational system interferences intruded; too many complicated chains of communication hindered application of a simple idea.

Choosing and Delivering Benefits Can Present Problems

Since what would function as instrumental and/or expressive rewards varies by individual and by situation, simply determining what the rewards might be was problematic. Also, it was not within my power to make available or to assure all of the rewards which might have reinforced participation.

Guaranteeing the rewards was the most difficult aspect of this approach.

Sometimes people can let the benefits go to their heads. The chairman of the S.C. Relations Committee received the "benefit" of signing the temporary food service licence. She is very excitable. Twice she got mad over something and swore she was going to have her name taken off! She even tried to get ahold of the man at the Health Department to do so.

Offer Some Real and Tangible Benefits

I think that a practitioner who gets into the bag of promising only expressive benefits without any instrumental rewards is fighting an uphill struggle. And instrumental benefits are not only for "lower class people."

Use Lots of Follow-up–Including Personal Contact

The phone conversations were interesting. They proved to be key to the success of this guideline. For through these personal contacts, we were not only able to elaborate on the content shared in our letter to them, but we were able to respond to the personal needs and concerns of those to whom we spoke.

Don't Put All Your Eggs in One Basket

A caution for new practitioners: I have learned from experience that no approach, used in isolation, is successful. I use this approach regularly in practice. I know that I can hold the most successful event, with all possible rewards, and still not get the desired participation. That is why we follow-up this approach with others to insure the involvement we desire.

The perennial problem of the weather as an influence on participation was noted by several practitioners, as both a limiting and a facilitating condition, and thus bears mention in passing. And, as a final caution, we may note the potential danger of goal displacement, if too much attention is paid to provision of benefits and concern for participation. Two practitioners, both of whom were working with task-oriented groups, became so involved in extensive and elaborate procedures to increase participation (a fashion show and an ethnic festival) that they lost sight of the goal toward which the instrumentality of participation was directed. During much of the intervention the practitioners' (and the groups') activities appeared to bear little relationship to the original purposes of the group. Both practitioners explained that the purpose of the apparent goal displacement was to "revitalize" the groups by demonstrating to them that they could succeed with a project. Such reasoning may have some validity, but it is necessary to weigh this against the danger of "going off the track."

As we have stated, the benefit concept is both simple and commonplace. The challenge in its systematic application is to find additional and more powerful incentives for participation, within contexts in which community practice typically takes place. The truly creative task is to search out benefits that are highly meaningful or relevant for client groups and, at the same time, available through agency or community structures over which the practitioner has influence, direct or indirect. Perhaps the most important contribution of the guideline may be to turn the practitioner's attention in the direction of new and more potent benefits that can be offered to clientele or constituents.

GETTING STARTED

1 Scanning Your Practice Situation

(a) Think of some voluntary association or task group with which you are working that has a participation problem, or

(b) Consider some aspect of your practice situation that would be improved through setting up a participatory voluntary association or task group.

2 Specifying Participation Behavior

Specify the nature of participation behavior that you will be dealing with and the direction in which you would like to change it. For example, will you be dealing with:

Recruitment—retention or maintenance—increasing the rate of participation—changing the form of participation (membership, committee participation, officership, contributions, volunteer work)—stabilizing or varying the pattern of participation, etc.

3 Determining Appropriate Benefits

Try to select appropriate benefits that are both attractive to clients and available to you to deliver:

What types of benefits would be potent or efficacious in stimulating the desired participation in the particular client group? Include:	What types of benefits are available to you to use through such sources? For example:

Instrumental
  material
  interim-anticipatory
	Your personal relations with clients.

Expressive
  social-interpersonal
  symbolic
	Agency resources and good will.
	
	Agency linkages with external resources.

Consider multiple rewards. Get to know your client group. Observe them. Ask them about their likes. Ask other experienced professionals.	The client group itself.

4 Selecting Specialized Reinforcement Techniques (if Appropriate)

Consider utilizing some special reinforcement technique such as

Shaping
Contracting
Group contingency
Extinction

These should be drawn on only if they are applicable and can be readily seen as potentially efficacious in your practice situation. Don't let them get in your way.

5 Phasing In – Contacting Potential Participants

Consider a way of making benefits known and available to the relevant target group.

6 Implementation – Delivering Benefits and Operation of the Event

Carry out the guideline — don't forget follow-up contact.

7 Assessing Outcome

Assess the change in participation behavior that has been brought about by specifying empirical indicators of goal attainment. Empirical indicators may include:

Change in specific number of persons at meetings.

Change in specific percentage of general membership who attend meetings.

Specific changes in number or percentage of dropouts from the organization.

Increase in or decrease in the number of individuals who declare their intention to run for elected office.

Increase the number of individuals involved in activities considered important by the group.

INITIAL LOG FORM

As a further step toward getting started, we suggest that you put down your tentative thoughts on the implementation of the guideline. The Initial Log is a tool for organizing your thinking in a systematic way. It is geared especially to helping you think about your goal, ways of operationalizing the guideline, the key individual and community groups to involve, and the facilitating and limiting factors in the situation (personal, agency, client, community).

Following the Log Form you will find illustrations of key sections that were completed by project practitioners.

INITIAL LOG

A Preliminary Guide for Action

1 Date of Preparation of Guide for action ______________.

2 In relation to using the guideline, what is your proximate goal (i.e., type of participation and the amount of it)? Be as specific and concrete as possible. The goal should be moderate and short-range in scope (something that can be accomplished in 5 to 12 weeks).

3 Describe the circumstances (conditions, events, assignments, requests, etc.) that led you to use this guideline to achieve the goal above.

4 Look back at the intervention guideline. How would you begin to define or concretize *each* element of the guideline in your immediate practice situation (i.e., how might you operationalize these components)?

(a) What is your proximate participation goal?

Indicate *current* level of participation: ______________

Indicate *intended* level of participation: ______________

Within what time period: ______________________

(b) What benefits will you offer?

Instrumental

Material: ______________________________

Interim-anticipatory: ____________________

Expressive

Social-interpersonal: ____________________

Symbolic: ______________________________

5 How will you deliver these benefits?
(Are they available to you? Do you control their use? Can you obtain some measure of control? Have you contingency benefits available?)

6 List the *major* steps you anticipate going through in order to utilize this guideline. Describe specific behaviors in the order in which you expect they will occur.

____

____

____

____

____

____

7 What *key* community groups will you probably involve (if any)?

Group	Reason for Contact

8 What *key* individuals will you probably involve (if any)?

Individual(s)	Title and/or Affiliation	Reason for Contact

9 Facilitating and limiting factors in guideline implementation:

As an aid to implementation you should consider factors that will affect your progress. We have provided checklists of common *facilitating factors*, those that will assist you to carry out the guideline, and typical *limiting factors*, those that may inhibit your success. In the checklists we have included conditions that were frequently indicated by practitioners in the field study. Others may be important in your own situation, and space is provided for you to note these.

Following the itemized checklists, you are asked to estimate the relative importance of various facilitating and limiting factors.

Personal Factors

Facilitating

- ☐ Good personal relationships with staff.
- ☐ Good personal relationships with clients.
- ☐ Personal commitment to the agency.
- ☐ Personal commitment to the program.
- ☐ Personal commitment to the guideline.
- ☐ Personal knowledge of the community.
- ☐ Personal knowledge of the programs.
- ☐ Personal knowledge of the relevant ideology (and theory).
- ☐ Personal gain (promotion, job title, etc.).
- ☐ Prior experience.
- ☐ Self-confidence.
- ☐ Other: ______________________________

____

Limiting

- ☐ Personal knowledge of clients.
- ☐ Personal position or role.
- ☐ Personal loss (demotion, job title, etc.).
- ☐ Impatience.
- ☐ Other: ______________________________

____

Agency Factors

Facilitating

- ☐ Affiliated organizational support or involvement.
- ☐ Board support or involvement.
- ☐ Administration support or involvement.
- ☐ Supervisor support or involvement.
- ☐ Supervisor disinterest.
- ☐ Practitioner assignments are consistent with effort.
- ☐ Physical facilities aid the effort.
- ☐ Other: ______________________________

____

Limiting

- ☐ Unclear or shifting goals, programs, or assignments.
- ☐ Hindering structure of the organization.
- ☐ Negative agency attitudes toward the clients or community.
- ☐ Practitioner-organization conflict.
- ☐ Lack of staff or training.
- ☐ Lack of funds, facilities, or other resources.
- ☐ Lack of support of supervisor.
- ☐ Lack of support of staff.
- ☐ Other: ______________________________

____

Client Factors

Facilitating

- ☐ Client disinterest or dissatisfaction with the agency or program, leading to a desire for change.
- ☐ Other: ______________________________

____

Limiting

- ☐ Client disinterest or dissatisfaction with the agency or its activities.
- ☐ Client specifically disinterested in your program.
- ☐ Client lack of knowledge about the organization, its purpose, programs, or activities.
- ☐ Clients interfere with organization activities.
- ☐ Pressure from clients.
- ☐ Dissension among clients.
- ☐ Other: ______________________________

____

Community Factors

Facilitating

- ☐ Community receptivity to your organization or program.
- ☐ Support of (influential) community groups for your organization or program.
- ☐ External influences making the community support your organization or program.
- ☐ Community support of the practitioner.
- ☐ Other: ______________________________

____

Limiting

- ☐ Community residents lack necessary knowledge or skills.
- ☐ Community residents interfere with organization activities.
- ☐ Other activities compete for the time and interest of residents.
- ☐ Community lacks funds needed to support your organization or program.
- ☐ Other: ______________________________

____

10 Facilitating factors—relative importance

In general, to what degree do you think *personal factors related to yourself* may be facilitating in implementing this guideline? (These factors might include good relationships with staff, good relationships with community people, personal knowledge of community, and positive effects of skill.)

Rate the degree of facilitation:

None ______ ______ ______ ______ ______ Great Deal
0 1 2 3 4

In general, to what degree do you think *agency* factors may be facilitating in implementing this guideline? (These factors might include administration support, supervisor support, staff support, and physical facilities aid effort.)

Rate the degree of facilitation:

None ______ ______ ______ ______ ______ Great Deal
0 1 2 3 4

In general, to what degree do you think *client* factors may be facilitating in implementing this guideline? (These factors might include client participation in organization or program, client receptivity to organization or program, and client support of practitioner.)

Rate the degree of facilitation:

None ______ ______ ______ ______ ______ Great Deal
0 1 2 3 4

This should indicate your perceptions of facilitating factors in a general sense.

In general, to what degree do you think *community* factors may be facilitating in implementing this guideline? (These factors might include community support of organization generally, influential and other community groups support organization or program, changes in community tend to support organization or program, and community support of practitioner.)

Rate the degree of facilitation:

None ______ ______ ______ ______ ______ Great Deal
0 1 2 3 4

11 Limiting factors—relative importance

In general, to what degree do you think *personal factors related to yourself* may be limiting in implementing this guideline? (These factors might include poor relationships with staff, poor relationships with community people, lack of personal knowledge of community, and negative effects of insufficient skills.)

Rate the degree of limitation:

None ______ ______ ______ ______ ______ Great Deal
0 1 2 3 4

In general, to what degree do you think *agency* factors may be limiting in implementing this guideline? (These factors might include unclear or shifting goals, programs, or assignments; lack of funds, facilities and other resources; lack of support or hindering action of supervisor; and lack of support or hindering action of staff.)

Rate the degree of limitation:

None ______ ______ ______ ______ ______ Great Deal
0 1 2 3 4

In general, to what degree do you think *client* factors may be limiting in implementing this guideline? (These factors might include negative response to organization generally, clients interference with organization activities, and dissensus among clients.)

Rate the degree of limitation:

None ______ ______ ______ ______ ______ Great Deal
0 1 2 3 4

This should indicate your perception of limiting factors in a general sense.

In general, to what degree do you think *community* factors may be limiting in implementing this guideline? (These factors might include negative response to organization generally; lack of knowledge of organization purposes, programs, or activities; influential community groups or leaders that do not support organization or program; and competition by other activities with community residents' time and interests.)

Rate the degree of limitation:

None ______ ______ ______ ______ ______ Great Deal
0 1 2 3 4

ILLUSTRATIONS OF INITIAL LOGS COMPLETED BY PRACTITIONERS

I. EXAMPLE OF COMMUNITY MENTAL HEALTH PROGRAM IN PUBLIC HOUSING PROJECT (FAMILY AGENCY)

A. Goal Statement

My goal is to increase tenant participation in the group meetings we are holding on "Y" Court in the Public Housing Project from representatives from five families at biweekly meetings to 10 families.

B. Concretization (Operationalization) of Guideline Elements

Increase participation in organizations, voluntary associations, or task groups.

Increase tenant participation in the group meetings we are holding on "Y" Court in the Public Housing Project.

Should increase the number of benefits (instrumental, expressive, etc.) provided.

I will try to do this by making sure that specific personal problems of each family that attends are resolved — like getting faulty plumbing repaired, obtaining free roach spray, serving as an advocate for children having difficulty in the schools, etc.

II. EXAMPLE OF BLACK STUDENT UNION IN A JUNIOR HIGH SCHOOL (SETTLEMENT HOUSE)

A. Goal Statement

My goal is to set up a black student organization which will be responsive to the needs of black students and not be controlled by the school administration.

B. Concretization (Operationalization) of Guideline Elements

Increase participation in organizations, voluntary associations, or task groups.

Increase the number of black students serving on functional committees of the black student organization from monthly average attendance of 15 on all committees to average attendance of 25 on these committees.

Should increase the number of benefits (instrumental, expressive, etc.) provided.

I am going to try to do this by having a group of students—operating as a committee—carry out a successful Black History Week program. This should not only encourage participation in the student organization, but also increase participation in the operating committees of the organization.

5

INCREASING THE EFFECTIVENESS OF ROLE PERFORMANCE

After working for a year as a housing planner for a regional planning council in a large metropolitan area, a young social worker became concerned because his influence on the important organizations that shaped regional housing policy was minimal. He decided to take on a new role in order to increase his effectiveness:

> *I had been responsible for the housing program of the Regional Planning Council without much sense of personal accomplishment and without feeling that the agency had achieved an influential role in the region with regard to housing matters. The goal was to increase my effectiveness through being viewed as an expert in the housing field by key decision-making housing agencies such as HUD [Department of Housing and Urban Development] and the State Housing Development Authority. In this way these agencies might use my advice in planning to a greater degree. The problem was they didn't expect me to function that way nor did my supervisor.*

Human service workers often find themselves caught up in a "cross-fire" of differing expectations regarding their work roles. Their own assessment of desirable goals may vary from those of supervisors, board members, community leaders, public officials, and others. Within the agency system different constituencies may have different views of a particular practitioner's roles. For example, clients and administrators may differ on how agency services of various kinds should be delivered.

It is often necessary for practitioners to deal with these contending expectations if they are to make an impact in their work. Also, in establishing a new role, or consolidating an existing one, differing expectancies sometimes become sharpened and brought into contention. Therefore, effective performance of newly emerging roles may be enhanced by developing them in such a way as to prevent, avoid, or minimize conflict.

GUIDELINES FROM RESEARCH ON ROLE CONFLICT

Various studies detail the dimensions of role conflict experienced by practitioners in the field. Gilbert,[1] for example, points up the contrasting expectations placed on OEO Community Action Agency staff members by agency executives and neighborhood client groups. Indeed, it is suggested by Krause,[2] in a study of rehabilitation counselors that conflict is structurally built into some professional roles by specific devices such as legal limitations in defining the job, workloads, and production and time pressures that make successful performance impossible.

The existing research on role conflict seems to indicate that the most effective solutions include neither entirely personalistic reactions nor restructuring of the entire role situation. Rather, a blending or balancing of expectancies within the existing role (or range of roles) appears to offer greatest potential. This suggests the following generalization:

> **Effective solution strategies for role conflict involve compromising competing expectancies. Role clarity and consensus among relevant actors facilitate effective role performance.**[3]

A natural inference to be drawn from this research generalization is contained in the Action Guideline:

[1]Neil Gilbert, "Clients or Constituents? A Case Study of Pittsburgh's War on Poverty," dissertation, University of Pittsburgh Graduate School of Social Work, 1968.

[2]Elliott A. Krause, "Structured Strain in a Marginal Profession—Rehabilitation Counseling," *Health and Social Behavior, 6* (1) (Spring 1965), 55-62.

[3]Bond L. Bible and Coy G. McNabby, "Role Consent and Administrative Effectiveness," *Rural Sociology, 31* (1) (March 1966), 5-14. Judith Cotes, "Conflict Resolution in the Mental Hospital," *Journal of Health and Social Behavior, 7* (2) (Summer 1966), 138-142. Neil Gilbert, "Neighborhood Coordinator: Advocate or Middleman?" *Social Science Review, 2* (43) (June 1969), 136-144.

PRACTITIONERS CAN INCREASE THEIR EFFECTIVENESS BY DEFINING A RELEVANT ROLE (OR ROLE ASPECT) AND CLEARLY SPECIFYING THIS ROLE OR ROLE ASPECT AND FOSTERING MUTUAL AGREEMENT AMONG RELEVANT SUPERORDINATES CONCERNING IT.

The value of role consensus and role compromise is supported by numerous studies. Some evidence suggests that clarity and agreement with regard to role definition may have an important bearing on practice outcomes. In an exploration of this issue,[4] 30 county extension directors and their 75 county extension agents were interviewed on several dimensions of the agents' role: for example, direction and coordination, extension relations, educational leadership, and personnel management. The degree of consensus between a director and his agents regarding role expectations was assessed. In addition, state personnel rated the various directors on efficiency in program development and implementation. County directors who were rated more effective had higher consensus on mutual role expectations with their county agents than did those rated less effective.

Additional studies lend further support to this position. Demerath[5] found that lack of role consensus between various program levels impeded a birth control in India. Gross et al,[6] concluded that lack of clarity concerning new roles thwarted the adoption of innovative educational practices among teachers. Rosen[7] determined that caseworkers in a public welfare bureaucracy exhibited high conformity to behavioral expectations when there was a high degree of consensus between supervisors and the practitioners, regardless of the type of influence or compliance mechanism used to achieve a designated role performance. Lyons[8] found that greater role clarity

[4]Bible, *op. cit.*, pp. 5-14.

[5]Nicholas J. Demerath, "Can India Reduce Its Birth Rate? A Question of Modernization and Governmental Capacity," *Journal of Social Issues, XXIII* (4) (October 1961), 179-195.

[6]Neal Gross, Joseph B. Giacquinta, and Marilyn Bernstein, "Complex Organizations: The Implementation of Major Organization Innovation," paper presented at the meeting of the American Sociological Association, Boston, Massachusetts, August 1968, pp. 1-27.

[7]Aaron Rosen, "The Influence of Perceived Interpersonal Power and Consensus of Expectations on Conformity of Performance of Public Assistance Workers," dissertation, University of Michigan, School of Social Work, 1963.

[8]Thomas F. Lyons, "Role Clarity, Need for Clarity, Satisfaction, and Withdrawal," *Organizational Behavior and Human Performance, 6* (January 1971), 99-110.

was correlated with lower job tension, lower job turnover, and higher job satisfaction.

In a study of professional orientations of social workers, Billingsley[9] found that workers with balanced orientations were more effective, at least according to ratings by their supervisors. A study conducted in a mental hospital[10] attempted to determine factors associated with resolving conflicts in the direction of either patient satisfaction or organizational-staff requirements. Workers who used compromise solutions were rated by fellow staff members on the wards as most effective. Those exercising preferential selection in the patients' direction received a medium effectiveness rating; preferential selection in the staff direction received a low rating. Whether the compromise solution is most effective in some ultimate sense is difficult to assess. It appears, however, to be associated with acceptance from, and good working relationships with, supervisors and staff associates, a condition that potentially could contribute to effectiveness.

Compromising differing expectations is obviously not the only possible solution to this problem. Under conditions of role conflict, other solution strategies that are typically employed are: (1) emphasizing only one set of role expectations, (2) withdrawing from role performance, (3) changing the role definition, and (4) using aggressive and symbolic adjustment patterns.[11] Let us briefly explore the research findings on these solutions.

1 *Selecting one role for emphasis.* In a study of a shelter house for alcoholics[12] it was found that counselors were expected to play the disparate roles of manager, companion, and member of the client community (counselors were former alcoholics). The main solution strategy they used was to select one key role to emphasize.
2 *Withdrawal from expected role behavior.*
3 *Realistic action to change the role definition.*
4 *Aggressive and symbolic adjustment patterns.*

[9]Andrew Billingslev, "Bureaucratic and Professional Orientation Patterns in Social Casework," *Social Service Review, 38* (4) (December 1964), 400-407.

[10]Cotes, *op. cit.*, pp. 138-142.

[11]Gilbert, *op. cit.* Krause, *op. cit.*, pp. 55-62. Lyons, *op. cit.*, pp. 99-110. Alvin Magid, "Dimensions of Administrative Role and Conflict Resolution Among Local Officials in Northern Nigeria," *Administrative Science Quarterly, 12* (2), 321-338.

[12]Krause, *op. cit.*, pp. 55-62.

The last three mechanisms were found in the Krause[13] study of rehabilitation counselors. Withdrawal implies noninvolvement—an apathetic, withdrawn response. Realistic action to change the definition suggests a mature, problem-solving posture. However, in the Krause study the situation was structured in such a way as to restrict successful employment of the strategy. Aggressive and symbolic behavior represented an acting out of frustration and anxiety in personalistic terms. Such behavior is generally not task-productive, but it may help workers maintain emotional stability when they confront an unresolvable practice task.

These empirical findings on actual behavior mesh well with the conceptual categories of role conflict solution suggested by Thomas and Feldman.[14]

> **The guideline offered here represents one way of dealing with active role conflict. On the other hand, and perhaps in its more common usage, it suggests a way of avoiding or preventing role conflict before it arises, especially in situations of ambiguity or uncharted job responsibilities. When conflict is severe or irreconcilable one of the other solution strategies may be preferable.**

OPERATIONALIZING THE GUIDELINE

An illustration of the operationalization of this guideline is provided by the experience of the housing planner in the regional planning council referred to at the beginning of the chapter. Here is his description of the steps he took to increase his (and his agency's) impact on housing developments in the area:

> *Planning agencies within the region receiving funds from the Department of Housing and Urban Development were required to annually prepare a document entitled, by HUD, "Initial Housing Condition." The nature of this report was to be a description of the "state of housing" in each particular geographical area in which a planning agency was located. The specific perspective of the Housing Condition report was, however, not detailed by HUD. I was given the responsibility by the agency to prepare this report.*

[13]Krause, *op. cit.*, pp. 55-62.

[14]Edwin J. Thomas and Ronald A. Feldman, *Concepts of Role Theory* (Ann Arbor: Ann Arbor Publishers, 1964).

Our deputy director was concerned about "shaping up" our housing program and gaining credibility with other organizations. I decided to work out a specific housing-oriented role with him.

The question for me became, "What is my role in regard to this function and what type of task will result?" For a number of reasons, I decided early in my own mind that I wanted my role developed as a housing data-expert. (I could conceive of several other roles that I might assume in regard to the preparation of the report. I might have decided, for example, to concentrate less on data, and more on implementation strategies. Or I could have highlighted problems as experienced by low income people and expressed by them, in their own words, in obtaining adequate housing. This would have been in contrast to a completely data-oriented report.) I wanted the task to be the production of an initial housing condition evaluation that would represent an analysis and interpretation of all the available data on housing in this part of the state; basically an estimate of the housing needs of the Region for the 1970-1980 period.

When I had decided what I preferred in regard to the role, I talked with our deputy director, since he had control over the internal program of the agency. He agreed to my proposal, and we further agreed that issues of strategy and policy could follow in a later report. The questions of housing data on the one hand, and housing implementation strategy on the other, would not be mixed into the initial housing condition report.

I spent virtually full-time in the next four weeks working on the report and gaining an understanding of housing data from sources such as the U.S. Census, the agency's own population projections, and other places. A reasonably high-quality report was produced. A meeting was held with a few Council staffers who had read the report. The group included the agency's director, deputy director, regional planner, and management information director. They were unanimous in their opinion that the report was the most substantial analysis of housing needs and use of housing-data that had been prepared in dealing with our section of the state.

In addition to this meeting, I also received comments from outside persons who had received copies of the report. Among them, a data analyst from the State Housing Development Authority and a noted private marketing consultant, gave their support for the report and indicated that they were planning to use parts of it.

> *I believe that the comments of these persons within and outside of the agency had the result of gaining more respect for my technical competence in the housing field, which I consider one criterion of increasing my effectiveness. I do not believe that this would have been possible, if my role had not been defined—allowing me to concentrate on data-analysis—and if I had not gained agreement for this role and task conduct by my relevant superordinate—the Deputy Director of the Planning Council.*

In summary, this young planner recognized that he was not being as effective as he wanted to be; important decision-making organizations in the housing field were not taking him seriously. He decided they would take him more seriously if he demonstrated competence as an expert in housing data analysis. Housing agencies he was dealing with were formal governmental bureaucracies who tended to respect formally established bureaucratic roles. Having clarified his desired role for himself, he thereupon discussed it with his agency supervisor, won agreement to proceed accordingly, and went on to a rather successful achievement. Obtaining this agreement with the superordinate was crucial in this case, because it permitted the practitioner to define his virtually full-time job activities for a four-week period in a particular way.

Another way to analyze the guideline is to break it down into its component sections and to discuss each in turn:

Practitioners Can Increase Their Effectiveness

The practitioner needs to determine for himself an area in which he wishes to improve or increase the impact of his performance. Effectiveness implies a projected service or policy outcome; it does not relate to technique or role performance alone. The enacting of the role is expected to lead to a desired further outcome. In the example above, effectiveness was related to being viewed and used as a data expert by outside agencies, not alone to the completion of data-analyzing tasks.

A school social worker established a role as a consultant to teachers on individualizing pupils. She describes the *outcomes* of performing this role as follows:

> *Thus far we have met with two teachers emphasing that they individualize their approach to children. The outcomes have been encouraging. I'll give an example.*
>
> *We were dealing with a girl who: (a) had a low level of emotional expression, (b) had low self-esteem, (c) needed a*

warm affectionate environment, (d) was socially isolated in a rural home setting.

(a) With regard to helping with emotional expression, the teacher set up weekly drama sessions, on a small group basis. The small group arrangement would insure participation of the student, and would provide a less threatening group situation in which to try out her emotions.

(b) With regard to self-esteem, we decided to capitalize on the girl's fondness for and skill in games. She was encouraged to develop a game of her own. The class played it, with much enjoyment. The teacher has the class play this game once a week.

(c) With regard to warmth and acceptance, the girl is released once a week to tutor younger children in a class where there is a very outgoing expressive teacher who has been briefed on the girl's needs. Also, the younger children have responded with praise and affection to the help given them.

(d) The teacher called the local Brownies troop requesting that they contact the mother with information and an offer of service for the girl. This was seen as a way of giving her more social contact in an isolated situation.

By Defining a Relevant Role (or Role Aspect)

"Relevant" suggests a link between the area of effectiveness aimed for and a role instrumental to such enhanced productiveness. In the housing planning example, successful carrying out of a data-analyzing role was connected to being viewed as a housing research expert. The term "role aspect" is used to suggest that the dimensions of the role may be appropriately wide in scope or rather narrow and modest. In the example, broader roles might have included planner, planning expert, or general research expert. A more narrow role aspect might have included data expert in public housing, or expert in use of cost-benefit analysis in housing analysis. The school social worker confined her consultation to a given population (the teachers) and to a specific purpose (helping them individualize).

Clearly Specifying This Role or Role Aspect

"Clearly specifying" is used in juxtaposition to "defining." The latter may imply a rather broad conceptualization of the role; "clearly specifying" demands that the role be sharpened fairly definitively. It means the narrower delineation of a broader role; that is, "expert" becomes clearly specified as "expert housing data analyst."

And Fostering Mutual Agreement

Agreement may take various forms: an informal verbal assent (or "gentleman's agreement"), a memorandum of understanding, a public announcement by both or one of the parties, or an official document. Any exchange from a glance or a handshake to a formal, legal paper or procedure may suffice for mutual agreement. In the housing example, there was verbal agreement in a conference between the practitioner and his immediate supervisor.

Among Relevant Superordinates Concerning It

In formal bureaucratic organizations, superordinates will usually be immediate supervisors. In the kinds of human service agencies and indigenous voluntary associations and social change organizations in which community practitioners often operate, the definition of "relevant superordinate" may be much broader. "Relevant" connotes an individual with the authority, influence, or power to legitimate or facilitate the *particular* role or role aspect that the practitioner wishes to enact. This relevant superordinate may be the immediate supervisor, or it may be a supervisor or administrative person one or two steps up the line in a larger organization. It may need to be the top executive. Alternatively, it might be the board chairman, a board committee, or the whole board. Sometimes, in the fluid and political world of community organization, a relevant superordinate may be a community person who has great influence over decisions and operations of the agency – a wealthy contributor, an important neighborhood opinion leader, or the mayor or ward chairman. Determining the key superordinate is a crucial component in carrying out this guideline. In the housing example the immediate supervisor was the relevant person. However, other possibilities were considered and discarded: "Another potential relevant superordinate, the Housing Advisory Committee or its Chairman, did not materialize, because the executive had decided that the committee should not meet until the Council had designed an initial framework for its housing program." At a later time, this committee or its chairman might be the most relevant superordinate.

PATTERNS OF IMPLEMENTATION

Many patterns of implementation logically present themselves and were in fact manifested in the field test. It is possible to use superordinates within the agency (a supervisor) or outside it (a powerful political leader with influence on the organization). Within the organization one may work through the administrative hierarchy or the board structure. Consensus may be along a continuum from highly formal (a joint letter of agreement) to quite informal (a nod of the head).

The most useful way of viewing approaches to implementation is to describe the process leading up to and following agreement with the superordinate. From our analysis of the field experiences, four modes emerge:

1 Agreement → exercising the role.
2 Environmental legitimation or support → agreement → exercising the role.
3 Demonstrating the role → agreement → expanded exercise of the role.
4 Agreement → demonstrating the role → expanded exercise of the role.

We will illustrate and discuss each of these in turn.

1 | Agreement → Exercising the Role. |

Looking at the Regional Planning Council illustration, we saw that the practitioner proceeded as follows:

1 Determined an area in which to increase his effectiveness (being viewed as a housing expert by relevant decision-making agencies).
2 Determined and specified an appropriate role (data-analysis expert).
3 Chose a pertinent vehicle (the initial housing condition report).
4 Selected an appropriate superordinate (his immediate supervisor).

5 Spoke directly with the supervisor and explained the role.
6 Gained the supervisor's agreement to his carrying out of this role (verbal consensus).
7 Exercised the role (prepared a data-based housing report).
8 Circulated this report to external organizations (HUD, State Housing Authority).
9 Received approval from these agencies regarding the quality of the report.

This was a fairly common and direct way of proceeding, particularly in a situation without complications (opposition by any of the relevant actors or groups). One additional factor to consider is the degree to which the practitioner is able to pursue the role with existing skills and information. In several cases practitioners had to seek additional knowledge before undertaking the new role, such as policies of other agencies, insurance policy provisions, and agency service data.

2 Legitimation or Support ⟶ Agreement ⟶ Exercising the Role.

A crucial factor in the pattern of implementation is the degree to which the relevant superordinate is initially sympathetic to the role the practitioner wishes to fulfill. When there is considerable compatibility of outlook, a simple straightforward discussion and verbal agreement will suffice. In other cases, some prior support or legitimation may be necessary. A practitioner who wished to establish a client-advocate role (for retarded children) in a traditional family service agency first needed to convince her executive director (the critical superordinate) that there was considerable support for such a professional function:

In my case there was no written role description, only a very vague agreement between my agency and the Act 54 Community Mental Health Board. Because my agency is a family counseling type, the executive really saw that as the major aspect of my work with families having a retarded member. I felt that this approach would only be crisis oriented and accomplish little. Rather, I saw a more comprehensive role directed toward broader problem solving on behalf of the mentally retarded citizens of our county, and set out to accomplish this in a variety of ways.

First I attempted to point out (in writing) what "is" and what "should be," then listed the "should be's" in some priority order for action. This really wasn't too difficult to do, but took a lot of time because it was necessary to talk with the executive frequently; to support all statements with accurate factors; and to test out ideas on a number of other agency professionals involved with the retarded. It paid off in a number of ways, the most important of which was the successful completion of the guideline itself! In addition it accomplished the total acceptance of my role as a comprehensive one in planning for all manner of "rights" and services for retarded citizens.

Her pattern of implementation can be outlined as follows:

1 Obtained general support from relevant internal agency actors (casework supervisor, staff opinion leader, and general agency staff), while talking informally with the agency director also.

2 Obtained support from relevant community groups, especially the Association for Retarded Children.

3 Used this support in discussion with agency director to obtain his agreement.

4 Demonstrated role to superordinate (in community education, public relations, socialization, etc.).

5 Formalized role in written report to executive.

6 Further legitimated role by gaining support of Board Priorities Committee on report.

7 Obtained additional formal institutionalization of role by notifying Act 54 Community Mental Health Executive (a substantial portion of her salary came from this source).

8 Obtained additional informal legitimation of role by illustrative discussion with general staff.

Here the worker, a skillful community organizer, gained support for the role both below and above the level of the superordinate, and although the executive director was virtually "boxed in," the guideline was carried out in a congenial, "professional" aura rather than in an acrimonious fashion. Clearly the tone of implementation is influenced by the practitioner's posture toward the "agreement process."

In another instance the practitioner started by having a discussion with the board chairman, with whom she had a personal, informal relationship. With this agreement achieved she spoke to the executive director (who was the relevant superordinate). This encounter failed, whereupon she prevailed upon the board chairman to serve as a surrogate for her in achieving the director's agreement to her role.

Sometimes external community support may be important in winning over a relevant superordinate. A practitioner in a Model Cities "Street Academy" program wished to develop a role as a militant organizer. When a crisis incident occurred in the black community, the worker aided various community groups in articulating their demands. These groups then supported the worker's position regarding the new role.

3	Demonstration → Agreement → Expanded Exercise of the Role.

This approach may be advisable when the role is particularly complex, or unusual in the agency setting, or unexpected because of tradition or the perceived qualifications of the practitioner. Demonstration of the role clarifies what is intended, shows it can be done, and proves competence. The family service worker who wanted to play a client-advocate role in part used this type of "modeling."

The function and importance of demonstration were expressed by a human relations worker in a school system who wanted to serve as a facilitator-resolver in instances of racial conflict:

> *Along with a number of other school personnel, I was asked to go to a high school where serious fights were occurring. My participation in that situation was a kind of turning point. I acted as a mediator between students and staff, and between students and students. Actually demonstrating my competence during and after this very serious situation helped to establish my role as facilitator-resolver.*
>
> *What was most important in the legitimation of my role was the actual demonstration of skills visible to supervisor, clients, community, and peers.*

One of the possible pitfalls is that the worker may demonstrate, but not follow up by obtaining formal approval. A school-community agent performed a community-oriented role, as opposed to functioning mainly within the confines of the building. She felt constrained, however, from going beyond the limited display of her new activities:

> *It seemed better to me not to challenge possible negative reactions by making an issue of it at this time. This proved true. However, it also means that we may have to cover similar ground again in the future.*

When there is significant disagreement regarding the role, the practitioner has two options: biding one's time until an opportunity to move presents itself (this may mean abandoning the role), or carrying it out as above at a level of low public or organizational awareness – that is, in a "low profile" fashion. One caution with this kind of demonstration is that the practitioner may be viewed as insubordinate or defiant for developing a role without prior authorization. Or, the role may fail because of lack of back-up support. One way of mitigating these problems is to select a role aspect initially small enough to avoid such consequences.

4 Agreement → Demonstrating the Role. → Expanded Exercise of the Role.

Because of the complexity and dynamic character of the human service field, official approval of a role does not necessarily mean that it will be accepted by the people who may be involved or affected by it—for example, clients, colleagues, and external organizations. Very frequently the role has to be demonstrated before it can be effectively or widely carried out, even if prior authorization has been secured.

The narrative that follows depicts this process. It was written by the school social worker described earlier. Her principal confined her to work with problem children on a one-to-one basis. She used the guideline to attempt to establish herself as a consultant to the teaching staff with regard to individualizing behavior problems within the normal classroom setting:

> *The principal and I have been continually at odds concerning my services at the school. He has repeatedly told me that the only things he wants me to do involve individual casework with children. Because of this limited role definition I explained that I would only be able to be at the school 1 1/2 days a week, spending a greater proportion of my time at other schools. Initially he agreed to that but later called the coordinator of my department expressing concern about the reduction in service and asking for a meeting between himself, me, the coordinator, and the school psychologist. It seemed to me that he might be willing to negotiate about my job responsibilities in order to gain more of my time at the school. This seemed a good time to specify my role and get agreement on it.*
>
> *At the meeting the principal and I spelled out what we each saw as relevant things for me to be involved in; my list included a pretty clear statement on consulting with teachers. The prin-*

cipal agreed with this generally, but no specifics were outlined. However, after the next faculty meeting he called me aside to say that some teachers had been discussing the whole area of communications with students and that this might offer a lead into the new role I had talked to him about.

The next week he set up a meeting which included himself, the school psychologist, me, and a teacher, for the purpose of brainstorming solutions to problems she was having with youngsters in her class. The meeting went very well. This is a difficult teacher who does not readily accept suggestions and I could see that the principal was pleased to have the suggestions coming from all of us rather than just from him. After the meeting, I suggested we might try this again since it had proved so useful. He was agreeable and said that he would announce it at the next teachers' meeting—he would explain to the teachers that on certain children we would be having meetings from time to time. He wanted to do it this way so that the first few teachers we met with would not feel they had been singled out, but would know this was now a standard procedure. I was pleased to know that he would even consider calling it "standard procedure." During this discussion, we came up with the name, Educational Planning Committee, for the group.

Following these events her new role continued to expand as it was perceived with increased confidence by the principal and the teaching staff. Some of the specific outcomes attained were indicated earlier.

The demonstration may have functions in addition to showing the role and consolidating it. In several of the cases it also served the purpose of allowing the practitioner to test himself for the role, as well as gradually to build up increased proficiency.

QUANTITATIVE FINDINGS FROM PRACTITIONER LOGS

This section is based on the 16 practitioners who were rated as successfully implementing this guideline (out of 20 implementations). The strategy of the guideline involves considerable internal activity within the agency in dealing with the organizational hierarchy. Thirty-eight percent of the practitioners considered no outside groups important in the implementation process and another forty-four percent considered between one and five groups important (Table 5-1). Few voluntary associations were important (19%), although 44 percent found public agencies useful for a variety of different reasons.

Table 5-1
Key Community Groups Contacted[a,b]

Type of Group Contacted	Percent of Practitioners Who Contacted This Group	Major Reasons for Contact
Public agency	44	Variation, no major tendencies
Private agency	50	Immediate participation
Voluntary association	19	Variation, no major tendencies

[a]For Tables 5-1 and 5-2, refer to the logs in the Appendix B for full range of variables from which those cited here are reported.

[b]Number of groups considered important: Range was 0 to 15. Mode (44%) was 1 to 5; 38% indicated no groups.

One half of the practitioners reported contacting important private agencies, frequently to obtain immediate participation.

In all instances contact with individuals was important in implementing the guideline, with considerable variation in the actual numbers considered important.

Agency executives (63%) and peers (56%) were considered important by the largest percentages of successful practitioners. Agency executives were considered important by 100% of the most successful practitioners, indicating that they may be particularly important in the implementation of this guideline.

Table 5-2
Key Individuals Contacted[a]

Types Most Frequently Considered Important	Major Reasons for Contact
Agency executives	Immediate participation Legitimation
Agency peers	Exercise of personal influence Immediate participation
Board members	Legitimation
Community people	No trends
Clients	No trends

[a]Number of individuals considered important: Range was 1 to over 30; with broad dispersion within this range. 63% contacted between 1 and 10.

Immediate participation was sought from agency executives (13%) and peers (16%), and legitimation from executives (31%) and board members (19%). Agency peers were also asked to exercise personal influence (16%).

The practice implications of these data are evident and basically consistent with logical inferences that can be derived from the action principle underlying the guideline.

An examination of Table 5-3 shows that many personal factors may be facilitating in carrying out the guideline. A great deal of per-

Table 5-3
Facilitating and Limiting Factors Scores from Intensity Scale (O=None, 4=Great Deal)

Facilitating Factors (general intensity $\overline{2.7}$)		Limiting Factors (general intensity $\overline{1.6}$)	
	Personal ($\overline{3.3}$)		Personal ($\overline{1.5}$)
1	Position or role	1	Lack of time
2	Commitment to the program	2	Overinvolvement
3	Good relationships with supervisor		
4	Good relationships with board		
5	Good relationships with administrator		
6	Good relationships with staff		
7	Commitment to agency		
8	Commitment to guideline		
9	Knowledge of community		
	Client ($\overline{2.4}$)		Client ($\overline{1.2}$)
1	Interest in program	1	Other activities compete for time and interests
		2	Lack of knowledge
	Agency ($\overline{2.9}$)		Agency ($\overline{2.0}$)
1	Practitioner assignments and tasks consistent with effort	1	Unclear or shifting goals, programs, assignments
2	Supervisor support	2	Lack of power
3	Administration support	3	Lack of resources
4	Administration involvement		
5	Supervisor involvement		
	Community ($\overline{2.3}$)		Community ($\overline{1.5}$)
No trends		No trends	

sonal effort and competency may be necessary in order to clarify ones role and gain consensus with relevant and significant individuals in the agency administrative or policy structure. Careful attention to a range of personal considerations is a must. In terms of specific agency factors, it is well to choose an objective that is compatible with existing organizational assignments, and to foster administrative and supervisory involvement and support. Client and community are of less moment in this particular intervention, although client interest in the programmatic area being addressed may be useful. Here again, choice of a suitable program area should be carefully considered in planning, or time should be set aside to motivating and educating clients.

The limiting section of Table 5-3 reveals that lack of knowledge by clients and competition from other activities must be contended with in winning over the interest of this group. Several other sources of limitation are found within the agency, including unclear goals and assignments and lack of resources. Fuzzy goals, which we will elaborate in the next section, can be turned into an advantage in carrying out this guideline by a sophisticated practitioner. Lack of power is also hindering in attempting to establish or crystallize a role in the agency. Working through other individuals or groups possessing power or forming informal alliances may be a way of dealing with this problem. As usual, lack of time and overinvolvement in the specific area of guideline activity can impede progress. This defines both an endemic environment in human service work as well as an urgent managerial task for human service professionals. Let us hear from practitioners directly on some of these matters.

PRACTITIONERS' VIEWS OF PROBLEMS AND PROSPECTS

This guideline was one of the more difficult ones for our practitioners to cope with cognitively. It contains a number of elements, and it also seems to touch an extremely personal chord (a personal view of self and where one is going professionally). Typical comments include: "I found this guideline confusing," and "Thinking through the guideline and deciding how to use it was difficult for me because of my own haziness about my role." At the same time, there were also expressions of enthusiasm for the guideline's helpfulness in aiding the clarification of important aspects of role definition. For example, the school social worker who broke out of her confining assignment as a counselor to individual children said:

I was really excited about this guideline because my role, for external and internal reasons, has been very cloudy. I am pleased with the direction this strategy has provided.

The average rating for this guideline on the five-point continuum was 4, and 35 percent of the field workers checked the highest point.

The major problems the field workers pointed out concerned the guideline's complexity and the fact that it cannot be applied under certain conditions. While one practitioner asserted that, "For me this guideline was relatively easy and presented no problems," most people reacted more in keeping with the practitioner who commented: "I would caution would-be users that application is not simple. Most situations have a mixture of values and orientations." Another expanded on the theme:

There is a high degree of interpersonal involvement in any conflict resolution situation. Therefore implementation is more difficult than it seems. Theoretically, gaining understanding and support from a superordinate is sensible. In reality the whole situation was a complex web of interpersonal relationships, rivalries, power struggles, and rip-offs.

Another worker warned, "Others may view your move as politically threatening to their status in the agency or system and act to sabotage the effort."

The fact is, of course, that role clarity and consensus are not always functional. Role ambiguity and role dissensus may contribute to workers' autonomy or creativity, or allow the pursuit of multiple incompatible objectives. On the other hand, they may be a means of maintaining control by upper level personnel through keeping workers off balance. When such considerations can be set aside, and the issue presents itself in terms of rational, task-oriented role performance, where the interests and objectives of the practitioner and his superordinates are compatible, then the guideline seems most applicable.

Additional comments from our field staff support and further clarify these assumptions. One stated: "This is a sound technique when the necessary pre-conditions are there—i.e., fundamental consensus among superordinates about relevant goals." An elaboration by another practitioner stated: "The guideline is useful in areas where people agree and the task is obtaining clarification and support. It does not pertain as readily to a situation where agreement on role function does not already implicitly exist or where there is basic conflict. The guideline does not provide a strategy for dealing with such strong conflict over role function."

Thus, if there are irreconcilable differences in outlook or interest, it would not be appropriate to use this guideline in its given form. A union organizer offers these cautions:

> *This guideline is very tricky. The question you have to keep in mind is if I clearly specify my role and tasks, will I be able to foster mutual agreement among relevant superordinates concerning them? This question becomes key if there are fundamental political, ideological, or partisan disagreements held by superordinates. This approach to practice reflects these disagreements, and to specify roles and tasks of that practice may result in an organizational crisis rather than increasing my effectiveness. I am not saying that this guideline is not useful. What I am saying is that you first have to determine the level of disagreement among relevant superordinates if it exists. This may indicate that you must first engage in a preliminary intervention. Where there is sharp disagreement over the goal orientation, the use of this guideline could very well heighten tensions and intensify disagreements and actually reduce the effectiveness of the practitioner and the agency by forcing both to deal with the internal dynamics rather than the function of the agency. Gaining agreement of superordinates depends on the situation; it may be better to keep superordinates uncertain as to moves of the practitioners and of the organization.*

Several other problems were indicated.

1 The concentration on professional role may evoke some very personal reactions: Who am I professionally? What kind of status or influence am I seeking in this agency? Where am I heading in my career? One practitioner put it this way:

> *One element that I think affected my working with this guideline was what we call "theme interference." This means that my own personal dissatisfaction with my lack of control and leverage regarding assigned tasks crept into my use of the guideline. Feelings about my future career goals and ambivalence about graduate school are examples of this. This was the most difficult guideline for me to deal with because of my internal confusion about directions I wanted to go in.*

2 There was an initial tendency for practitioners to think very broadly about roles and, thus, to set objectives that were unattainable or that took too long to achieve. More finite roles (and role aspects) were recommended:

I had trouble with the scope of the guideline. I tried to think of my role and tasks in larger terms, like to institute a half-way house program, or to develop referral programs with unions. I did not think of smaller roles that might have been used. This will be important to get across in the manual.

3 In addition to stimulating personal introspection, the guideline (as indicated in the quantitative findings) may call for a substantial outlay of personal energy, as well as time:

The accomplishment of the guideline was not really difficult but did require a considerable amount of initiative on the part of the worker; much written work and much verbal effort with the executive.

A caution: I undertook this guideline with bright hopes that I would have gained the respect for my role within a few weeks. I forgot about the fact that time is a key respect-building factor.

4 Several practitioners made it a point to emphasize that demonstrating the role in a delimited way was helpful.

My situation was traditional, but it was supposedly moving in a totally new kind of area, and although the philosophy was there, the willingness to accept the new philosophy was not there. I had to proceed to establish that, demonstrate it, and get it legitimized, and therefore the guideline helped me to think through the kinds of things I should try to do.

Other comments included the observation that not only conflict but also agency policies and regulations can lock one into a particular role definition. "I found it difficult to shift to a social change orientation in my community work because agency specifications require that a certain number of staff hours be spent doing social adjustment tasks." Another interesting observation came from a supervisor in the juvenile court who suggested using a mediator in situations of role conflict. This is an especially meaningful suggestion when clashing values exist (such as punitive vs. rehabilitative orientations toward offenders). Mediation can be a means of ensuring that neither side loses out altogether. Or it can preserve both sets of values intact in circumstances where both are desirable or there is uncertainty about which is more effective.

Additional reactions gleaned from experience included:

The guideline is especially helpful when starting a new position or job situation.

This is a good guideline to start with because it may be difficult to carry out the others until basic roles are defined.

Establishing a role as an expert was helpful as a beginning step and facilitated moving into other roles.

GETTING STARTED

In attempting to use this guideline for the first time you might follow a thought-action process roughly as follows:

1. Ask yourself in what way or ways would you like to *improve your effectiveness*—for instance in serving some specific new client group, obtaining more funding for a particular purpose, or having your suggestions accepted to a greater degree by the agency staff (or board).
2. *Think of a role (or role aspect)* that is linked with attainment of this increased effectiveness (client advocate, fund-raiser, a committee chairman).
3. *Specify this role* in more particular form (become a women's rights advocate, a funding proposal drafter, or a chairman of the staff program planning committee).
4. *Determine a relevant superordinate* for authorizing or facilitating the role (a community group, the agency executive, or a board committee). (Is there reasonable agreement or possibility of agreement concerning this role between you and the superordinate?)
5. *Determine a procedure for reaching agreement with the superordinate:* direct discussion, obtaining prior intra- or extra-agency support, working through a surrogate, demonstrating the role in a limited way, etc.
6. *Decide upon the form for agreement* (formal-informal, verbal-written, or public-private, for example), and how you expect it to be manifested. (Determine whether further support or legitimation by other people is necessary to stabilize the role.)
7. *Enact the role.* (This is, of course, a complex phase that is only noted here.)
8. *Assess the degree to which exercising the role improved your effectiveness* as set down in 1. (Are you now serving a specific new client group? How many in number? Are you raising more grant monies and how much? Are your suggestions being accepted to a greater degree and do the staff minutes show it?)

INITIAL LOG FORM

As a further step toward getting started, we suggest that you put down your tentative thoughts on the implementation of the guideline. The Initial Log Form we developed for the field test was helpful to practitioners in that connection. The Initial Log is a tool for organizing your thinking in a systematic way. It is geared especially to helping you think about your goal, ways of operationalizing the guideline, the key individual and community groups to involve, and the facilitating and limiting factors in the situation (personal, agency, client, community).

Following the Log Form you will find illustrations of key sections that were completed by project practitioners.

INITIAL LOG

A Preliminary Guide for Action

1 Date of Preparation of Guide for Action _____________.

2 In relation to using the guideline, what is your goal (some more effective practice outcome based on clarifying and gaining consensus on your role)? Be as specific and concrete as possible. Think in proximate terms and with regard to short-range prospects (something that can be accomplished in a five to 12 week period).

3 Describe the circumstances (conditions, events, assignments, requests, etc.) that led you to use this guideline to achieve the goal above.

4 Look back at the intervention guideline. How would you begin to define or concretize *each* element of the guideline in your immediate practice situation (i.e., how might you operationalize these components)? Keep in mind the proximate goal stated in part 2.

(a) What role (or role aspect) do you intend to establish (that is linked to intended more effective practice outcomes)?

(b) Can you further specify this role with clarity?

(c) What will be the basis for agreement?

(d) What relevant superordinates will you involve?

5 List the *major* steps you anticipate going through in order to utilize this guideline. Describe specific behaviors in the order in which you expect they will occur.

____

____

____

____

____

____

____

6 What *key* community groups will you probably involve (if any)?

Group	Reason for Contact
________________	________________
________________	________________
________________	________________
________________	________________
________________	________________

7 What *key* individuals will you probably involve (if any)?

Individual(s)	Title and/ or Affiliation	Reason for Contact
__________	__________	________________
__________	__________	________________
__________	__________	________________
__________	__________	________________
__________	__________	________________
__________	__________	________________

8 Facilitating and limiting factors in guideline implementation.

As an aid to implementation you should consider factors that will affect your progress. We have provided checklists of common *facilitating factors*, those that will assist you to carry out the guideline, and typical *limiting factors*, those that may inhibit your success. In the checklists we have included conditions that were frequently indicated by practitioners in the field study. Others may be important in your own situation, and space is provided for you to note these.

Following the itemized checklists, you are asked to estimate the relative importance of various facilitating and limiting factors.

Personal Factors

Facilitating

- ☐ Good personal relationships with board/board members
- ☐ Good personal relationship with administrator
- ☐ Good personal relationships with non-staff professional peers or friends
- ☐ Personal knowledge of the programs
- ☐ Personal gain (promotion, job title, etc.)
- ☐ Professional "disinterest"
- ☐ Other: ______________________
- ☐ ______________________
- ☐
- ☐

Limiting

- ☐ Poor personal relationships with community people
- ☐ Personal position or role
- ☐ Professional "disinterest"
- ☐ Fatigue
- ☐ Lack of time
- ☐ Other: ______________________

____

Agency Factors

Facilitating

- ☐ Affiliated organizational support or involvement
- ☐ Board support
- ☐ Administration involvement
- ☐ Supervisor support or involvement
- ☐ Supervisor disinterest
- ☐ Staff involvement
- ☐ Practitioner assignments are consistent with effort
- ☐ Physical facilities aid the effort
- ☐ Other: ______________________________

  ____

Limiting

- ☐ Lack of power and/or authority of organization
- ☐ Lack of support or hindering action of affiliated organizations
- ☐ Lack of support or hindering action of administration
- ☐ Lack of support of staff
- ☐ Other: ______________________________

  ____

Client Factors

Facilitating

- ☐ Client participation in organization or program (voluntary)
- ☐ Client interest in organization generally
- ☐ Client interest in program specifically
- ☐ Client disinterest or dissatisfaction with the agency or program, leading to a desire for change
- ☐ Client support of practitioner
- ☐ Other: ______________________________

  ____

Limiting

- ☐ Client lack of knowledge about the organization, its purpose, programs, or activities
- ☐ Pressure from clients
- ☐ Dissensus among clients
- ☐ Other: ______________________________

  ____

Community Factors

Facilitating

- ☐ Community support of organization generally
- ☐ Support of (influential) community groups for your organization or program
- ☐ Influential or other community groups involved with organization or program
- ☐ External influences making the community support your organization or program
- ☐ Community support of the practitioner
- ☐ Other: ______________________________

____

Limiting

- ☐ Community residents lack other necessary knowledge or skills [editor note: other necessary knowledge or skills than 'lack of knowledge of organization purposes, programs and/or activities']
- ☐ Pressure from community residents
- ☐ Community lacks funds needed to support your organization or program
- ☐ Other: ______________________________

____

9 Facilitating factors—relative importance

In general, to what degree do you think *personal factors related to yourself* may be facilitating in implementing this guideline? (These factors might include good relationships with staff, good relationships with community people, personal knowledge of community, and positive effects of skill, etc.)

Rate the degree of facilitation:

None ______ ______ ______ ______ ______ Great Deal
0 1 2 3 4

In general, to what degree do you think *agency* factors may be facilitating in implementing this guideline? (These factors might include administration support, supervisor support, staff support, and physical facilities aid in effort.)

Rate the degree of facilitation:

None ______ ______ ______ ______ ______ Great Deal
0 1 2 3 4

In general, to what degree do you think *client* factors may be facilitating in implementing this guideline? (These factors might include client participation in organization or program, client receptivity to organization or program, and client support of practitioner.)

Rate the degree of facilitation:

None ______ ______ ______ ______ ______ Great Deal
0 1 2 3 4

In general, to what degree do you think *community* factors may be facilitating in implementing this guideline? (These factors might include community support of organization generally, influential and other community groups support organization or program, changes in community tend to support organization or program, and community support of practitioner.)

Rate the degree of facilitation:

None ______ ______ ______ ______ ______ Great Deal
0 1 2 3 4

10 Limiting factors—relative importance

In general, to what degree do you think *personal factors related to yourself* may be limiting in implementing this guideline? (These factors might include poor relationships with staff, poor relationships with community people, lack of personal knowledge of community, and negative effects of insufficient skills.)

Rate the degree of limitation:

None ______ ______ ______ ______ ______ Great Deal
0 1 2 3 4

In general, to what degree do you think *agency* factors may be limiting in implementing this guideline? (These factors might include unclear or shifting goals, programs, or assignments; lack of funds, facilities, and other resources; lack of support or hindering action of supervisor; and lack of support or hindering action of staff.)

Rate the degree of limitation:

None ______ ______ ______ ______ ______ Great Deal
0 1 2 3 4

In general, to what degree do you think *client* factors may be limiting in implementing this guideline? (These factors might include negative response to organization generally, clients interference with organization activities, and dissensus among clients.)

Rate the degree of limitation:

None ______ ______ ______ ______ ______ Great Deal
0 1 2 3 4

In general, to what degree do you think *community* factors may be limiting in implementing this guideline? (These factors might include negative response to organization generally; lack of knowledge of organization purposes, programs, or activities; influential community groups or leaders that do not support organization or program; competition by other activities with community residents' time and interests.)

Rate the degree of limitation:

None ______ ______ ______ ______ ______ Great Deal
0 1 2 3 4

ILLUSTRATIONS OF INITIAL LOGS COMPLETED BY PRACTITIONERS

I. EXAMPLE OF HOUSING DATA EXPERT IN THE REGIONAL PLANNING COUNCIL

A. Goal Statement

I want to increase my effectiveness by being viewed as a housing data expert by key decision-making housing agencies like the Department of Housing and Urban Development and the State Housing Development Authority. (This should benefit my agency by giving it more influence in the housing field generally.)

B. Concretization (Operationalization) of Guideline Elements

Increase their effectiveness: Being able to influence housing development agencies in the region with regard to their planning.

Establishing a relevant role or role aspect: Becoming an expert in the field of housing.

Clearly specifying this role or role aspect: Delineate my role as a housing data expert through preparing the "Condition of Housing" status report for the Council.

Fostering mutual agreement: Gain a verbal understanding about the validity of my doing a strongly data based "Condition of Housing" report.

Among relevant superordinates: Approach the Deputy Director of the Council (my superior, who could legitimize my role in preparing the report) on this.

II. EXAMPLE OF PLANNING-ADVOCATE ROLE FOR SERVICES TO THE RETARDED (FAMILY AGENCY)

A. Goal Statement

To help provide (through our agency and other organizations) more comprehensive services to the retarded. Specifically to set up a volunteer program that would initially service 100 retardates.

B. Concretization (Operationalization) of Guideline Elements

Increase their effectiveness: Be better able to stimulate and provide comprehensive services to the retarded. Initially set up a voluntary program.

Establishing a relevant role or role aspect: Develop a planning-advocacy role for services to the retarded.

Clearly specifying this role or role aspect: Writing out the details of the tasks and activities that might be associated with the planning-advocacy role.

Fostering mutual agreement: Obtain verbal approval.

Among relevant superordinates: The agency executive (although back-up support was sought from others including the supervisor, peer staff, and board committee).

6

CONCLUSION

In the previous chapters we have discussed each guideline separately and in its own terms. Here we will compare them and make general observations based on viewing them together.

SEQUENCING OF GUIDELINES

While it is possible to conceive of each guideline as a discrete strategy for dealing with a given problem, it is useful also to think of combinations of guidelines that act on multiple-related problems or objectives. Many of the practitioners who participated in the field tests suggested that there were many ways in which guidelines could be used either sequentially or simultaneously. We will offer here a few suggestive possibilities that should stimulate the reader to think of others.

Some practitioners have found use of the innovation guideline to be an excellent precursor to the establishment of a new role. For example, in the second year field test a school social worker was interested in functioning as a consultant to classroom teachers to help them improve their handling of children with behavior problems within the classroom setting. It happened that a helping teacher asked this practitioner for assistance in setting up a volunteer tutor program as an innovation in her school. The practitioner gave advice using the partialization principle as a way of instituting the new program. With the consultation role thus demonstrated, the practitioner was able to branch out and, through clarification and consensus with the school administrator, begin to operate in the desired broader consultation role with classroom teachers.

A regional planner involved in the pilot year productively linked these two interventions in the reverse order. He initially established a new role as a data expert in the housing field, as described in an earlier chapter. This role provided legitimation and a platform for developing an innovation in which he and his organization became agents for screening new housing applications forwarded to HUD by local municipalities.

Another practitioner, in a field report, indicated the utility of using three guidelines sequentially:

> *After working with these guidelines during the last year I feel that three of them can be used in the following order: promoting an innovation, establishing a new role, changing an organization's goals.*
>
> *It appears that a practitioner relatively new in an agency would possibly have considerable success in using the above stated sequence. For example, if a practitioner is capable of implementing an innovation it may facilitate clarification of a role for that practitioner. Often new persons seeking legitimation of roles or ideas may gain that legitimation best by demonstrating their idea, then possibly being responsible for continuing and broadening it after it has been accepted. Carrying out the role in a practical way allows the practitioner both to clarify what is involved for himself as well as to show it in action to other people in the situation. Based on a newly legitimated role, and having already shown competency in setting up an innovative program, the practitioner may be in a good position to tackle the more difficult task of making changes in organizational goals. The acquisition of a new role may put the practitioner in a much better position to implement a shift in organizational goals, especially through the mobilization of a group within the organization, a group to which he or she gains access because of the new role.*

As an alternative, one guideline may be executed *within,* and as an expediting substep in, the implementation of another guideline. Examples are found in the manual chapters. Recall the family service worker who wished to introduce outreach services in a public housing project. To institute the service in the demonstration court the worker developed participation there through the benefits principle. After the service has been instituted in that court, the innovation spread to other parts of the housing project. The participation guideline had serviced the innovation guideline in a supportive way.

It is evident that there are a large variety of possibilities for utilizing these strategies sequentially or simultaneously. Viewed another way, when there is a substantial shift in the practice situation—because of the practitioner, the organization he or she works for, the client population, or the larger community—opportunities for further change are frequently generated. Several studies have shown, for example, that changes in organizations often follow a turnover in leadership, and that new patterns of participation in a community may develop when there are abrupt shifts in the social situation.[1]

The progression in the development of change opportunities may well be geometric rather than arithmetic, in the sense that not only does each change itself create a situation that offers new opportunities for further changes, but also the multiple reactions in the total environmental setting to that change process may also be a stimulant for other changes. Obviously, it is ordinarily impossible to exploit the maximum number of change potentials. However, it makes sense to pause and look carefully at the variety of avenues opened by a particular intervention.

All too often our tunnel vision inclines us to a predetermined long-term effort in a particular direction while other short-term change possibilities remain unexploited. For example, in the rush to include minority oppressed populations in the internal decision-making process of OEO community action programs, practitioners often missed their chance, once the residents were operating effectively on the required boards, to take advantage of that newly gained competence to move residents systematically into participation in any one of several other political, economic, and social organizations.

Just as these guidelines may be variously interconnected in practice, so may they be articulated differentially in the process of study. The order of presentation in this book was not meant to freeze the structure of their interrelationship. The most useful order for training is probably contingent on the availability of relevant practice situations in which to implement them, and such situations may flow naturally and unpredictably as a consequence of any given implementation episode. Student interest and motivation may be still another important factor that should determine the order in which they are taken up. In addition, the past experience and competence of

[1]Richard O. Carlson, "Succession and Performance among School Superintendents," *Administrative Science Quarterly,* 6 (1961) 210-227; F.W. Terrien and D.L. Mills, "The Effect of Changing Size upon Internal Structure of Organization," *American Sociological Review,* 20 (1955), 11-13; Donald R. Trow, "Membership Succession and Team Performance," *Human Relations,* 13 (1960), 259-268.

students and teachers may influence the sequencing; it may be useful to start initially in areas where a base of familiarity or experience already exists.

QUANTITATIVE FINDINGS ACROSS GUIDELINES

In addition to looking at the dynamics of guideline interaction comparatively, it is also instructive to examine the quantitative field test data across guidelines to discover patterns. This may suggest, for example, variables that are common to all these guidelines and, hence, perhaps generalizable to this genre of social intervention. We will also be interested in discerning the variables that are peculiar to specific guidelines.

We do not believe it is advisable to make a comprehensive presentation of findings here. Rather, using simple descriptive statistics we will give selective highlights and trends that can prove useful for the central purpose of the manual. We will focus on information that has fairly clear application potentials for practice-oriented readers. As stated earlier, another book employing a more complex form of analysis will elaborate findings and deal with more formal research aspects of this study.[2]

Contacts with Community Groups

Major reasons for contacting key community groups varied with respect to the guidelines. Among important contacts, private agencies are contacted mainly for participation, regardless of guideline. Contacts with voluntary associations are more specialized according to guidelines. For example, in *Changing Goals* and *Promoting an Innovation,* voluntary associations are contacted for information and guidance or public relations; in *Fostering Participation* these associations are contacted, naturally, for purposes of immediate participation; in the *Role Performance* guideline there were no trends in reason for contact. We find here an interesting pattern of generalized and specialized reasons for dealing with community groups.

[2]However, we do include a note on methodology in Appendix A.

Contacts with Individuals

Contacts with important individuals, according to the data available in this study, were somewhat more specialized than contacts with community groups. Here are some examples:

Agency supervisors were frequently considered important in *Changing an Organization's Goals* for purposes of participation or legitimation;

Agency peers were useful for exercising personal influence and participating in *Changing Organizational Goals* and *Enhancing Role Performance.* They were also considered important in *Promoting an Innovation,* but for no single reason;

Board committee members were considered important in *Changing Organizational Goals* and *Promoting an Innovation,* but no reasons were consistently given for these contacts;

Agency subordinates were found to be important participants in *Changing Organizational Goals;*

Community people were considered important in the implementation of all four guidelines, and particularly for immediate participation in *Fostering Participation* and *Promoting an Innovation;*

Agency peers were contacted generally for participation, however his was combined with personal influence in *Role Performance,* with information and guidance in the *Innovation and Participation guidelines,* and with no other reason in *Changing an Organizations Goals;*

Agency subordinates were generally contacted for participation.

Community people were contacted for participation in the *Fostering Participation* guideline and not contacted in the others;

Clients were contacted for participation in the *Fostering Participation* and the *Goal Change* guidelines and not contacted in the others.[3]

For most of the guidelines contacts with individuals were made for a variety of reasons. In the Role Performance guideline there was greater specialization, most contacts being made for purpose of legitimation.

[3]"Not contacted" in this discussion means not contacted in substantial numbers.

Facilitating and Limiting Conditions

Practitioners consistently gave a considerably higher intensity rating (3.3) to facilitating factors than to limiting factors (1.6) across all guidelines.[4] This is one of the strongest, most persistent results of the field test. There are two related ways of looking at this. First, since we are dealing with successful practice outcomes, the facilitating factors must by definition outweigh the limiting factors—if they did not, such success would not have been achieved. Thus, relative strength of facilitating factors is an inherent component of a successful intervention. Stated another way, successful practitioners give special attention to the facilitating factors in their practice situation. Capability in exploiting or optimizing these facilitating factors may be the mark of a successful practitioner. A further extrapolation would suggest that it is better to give emphasis to the positives in the situation than dwell on the negatives.

This type of interpretation should be evaluated in light of writings by Kurt Lewin and his followers[5] by using a "force field" form of analysis. There it is suggested that reducing resistance (or opposing) forces has a tendency to lower the general level of tension. For certain change objectives, they hypothesize, this may be the most advantageous strategy.

Another major finding was that, for all guidelines, personal factors attached to the practitioner were reported as substantially strongest for facilitation, and sponsoring agency factors were strongest for limitation. How does one explain this predominance of personal and agency considerations?

Personal factors, inhering as they do to the internal realm of the practitioner, are most accessible to his immediate manipulation and control. At least there is no one else to blame if he is not able to discipline himself.[6]

[4]Mean score of an interval scale 0-4.

[5]Kurt Lewin, "Group Decision and Social Change," in *Readings in Social Psychology,* Theordore M. Newcomb and Eugene L. Hartley, *eds.,* (New York: Holt, Rinehart and Winston), 1947, pp. 340-44; David H. Jenkins, "Force Field Analysis Applied to a School Situation," in Warren G. Bennis, Kenneth D. Benne and Robert Chin, *eds., The Planning of Change* (New York: Holt, Rinehart and Winston), 1961, pp. 238-244.

[6]An alternative interpretation is that practitioners tended to "take credit" for success by attributing much of the facilitation to themselves. Or it may be that the personal is simply an area of greater attention and interest. Leaving aside for the moment considerations of bias and distortion, it can be stated that practitioners in their written reports uniformly gave proportionately great weight to personal areas on notations concerning various factors of facilitation (once they got beyond taking them for granted).

One reason for the prominence of agency factors as limitations may be that they are the most immediate structural variables that must be dealt with in the practice environment. Agency policies and regulations functionally have a constraining influence on practitioners' autonomy. Just as the self may be experienced as subject to control, the most proximate social structure may be experienced as externally restricting. Indeed, human service workers, in the experience of the authors, commonly sprinkle their conversations with comments about the ways in which agencies tie their hands and impede their activities and potential. Highly radical or service-oriented practitioners, in particular, feel bogged down by conservative, middle-class policymaking bodies and rigid, maintenance-oriented administrators.

The agency may curtail the practitioner's autonomy, but it also serves as an important locus of resources and legitimation. For this reason the agency was consistently also rated high among facilitating factors, although not predominantly so.

An implication to be drawn from the previous discussion is that it is essential for the practitioner to "get a handle" on himself and his sponsoring agency in order to be effective. It may be exhilarating to talk of broad forces of social change, historical trends, overarching values, and the like but, without a high degree of attentiveness to tangible aspects of self and agency, the impact on close-at-hand realities is likely to be negligible.[7]

We shall now turn to additional, more specific findings about both facilitating and limiting factors.

1 Facilitating Factors

As indicated, personal factors were most facilitating. Among these the *practitioner's commitment to the program* involved in the guideline, *good interpersonal relationships within the agency, com-*

[7]Again, results and implications may be an artifact of the methodology. All findings are based on reports written from the practitioner's perspective. An outside observer—sociologist or anthropologist—bringing either "objectivity" or a particular theoretical orientation related to his discipline, might have discovered a different ordering of influences. For example, community variables might have been given greater weight, or client factors. Nevertheless, for a publication directed to practitioners, material based on how practitioners think and take action may offer extremely useful intelligence. In any social situation there are many different "truths," the well known "Rashomon effect." The "truth" of the practitioner's view of the world is the particular perspective and contribution of this study.

Additionally, the short time frame and modest scale of goals in these interventions preclude broad community targets and involvements and favor change objectives that are close to the agency's boundaries and sphere of operations.

mitment to the guideline, and his *position or role in the agency* were rated highest across all guidelines. The most common agency factor was *consistency with other assignments and tasks*. Among client factors, *interest in the program* was uniformly a salient factor. There were no community factors that were rated high for all guidelines. Because of their importance in all instances these factors appear to be fairly universal sources of facilitation in the types of practice situations examined in this study. Further research to substantiate such tentative assumptions would be useful.

In previous chapters practice implications related to the above were suggested; for example, a practitioner should choose a program to which he has a commitment, interpersonal skills should be applied sensitively, the program should ideally reinforce his position or be reinforced by his position or role in the agency, and the program should be consistent with other assignments and tasks. It should conform to current or potential client interests.

In addition to factors that applied to all guidelines, other patterns appeared. An example of each is given:

Facilitating factors generally present with one exception:

Administrative support applied to all guidelines except Goal Change. (Goal Change may involve conflict rather than cooperation with authority figures.)

Facilitating factors generally absent with one exception:

Board support applied to none of the guidelines except Innovation. (Innovation may involve program changes requiring board approval. Goal Change is more political, sometimes requiring advocacy against board policy. Role Performance and Participation are operations that may be far below the board policy level.)

Facilitating factors variably present and absent:

Administration involvement applied to Role Performance and Innovation. (Both of these guidelines call for superordinate legitimation or release of agency resources. Goal Change may imply in some instances going against or around administrators, while participation is often a legitimate, conventional activity that may be implemented as a matter of course.)

2 Limiting Factors

Several limiting factors were reported for all four guidelines: *personal overinvolvement, lack of time, lack of funds, unclear or shift-*

ing goals, and *competition for client attention.* These factors may reflect certain conditions omnipresent in community work: the impinging of many demands and pressures on practitioners and of many competing programs and interests on clients. These are not likely to be eliminated, but they may perhaps be coped with through more efficient management of the practitioner's time and the design of programs that are attractive and powerful in meeting significant client needs and interests. Varying patterns of other limitations appear:

> Limiting factors generally present but with one exception:
>
> > Competition for community interest applied to all guidelines except Role Performance. (Defining one's organizational role is a more intra-agency task than are tasks involved in other guidelines.)
>
> Limiting factors generally absent but with one exception:
>
> > Lack of commitment to the agency applied as a limitation only in the Innovation guideline. (Commitment to the agency itself may be important in establishing new organizational services and programs. Role Performance may involve personal commitment, Participation client commitments and Goal Change alientation from the agency.)
>
> Limiting factors variably present and absent:
>
> > Lack of staff support applied to Promoting an Innovation and Fostering Participation did not apply to Role Performance or Goal Change. (Promoting an Innovation may require service personnel, and Participation may require aid in motivating people and obtaining and delivering rewards. Role Performance implies shifts in responsibilities, rather than increased staffing, and Goal Change apparently may also entail rearrangements rather than increases in personnel use when viewed in proximate terms.)

Beyond the specifics presented above, which are subject to the limitations of the design and resources of the study, what may be of overriding value is an orientation toward practice that is suggested. These results should serve to alert the practitioner to facilitating or limiting factors that may be invariably present, others that may be frequently present, and some that may be rarely present. A practitioner who assimilates such a point of view based on personal experience in practice may be in a better position to quickly and efficiently diagnose new practice situations.

SOME CONCLUDING COMMENTS

Thus far our discussion has centered on specific recorded behavior, empirical outcomes, and so on. In these closing pages we allow ourselves the luxury of engaging in a bit of prognostication and general professional discussion. Because both nationally, and to a considerable degree locally, political alientation is high and political patterns in flux, it is important to try to note some of the areas in which the strategies we have explored may prove to be particularly useful in the years ahead. Community mental health efforts will probably gain momentum once again and offer a fruitful field for the kinds of change efforts in which these strategies may be applied. The reorganization of health care at the local level, particularly through the emergence of Health Maintenance Organizations, suggests similar opportunities for intervention. The development of the social side of urban planning posits a variety of areas for guideline use. Despite the failure of many highly touted urban educational programs, we believe that new and innovative efforts ranging from comprehensive preschool and day-care centers to special college programs for parolees will give rise to heightened opportunities for the use of this kind of community and organizational level strategic thinking. We would also predict a more vigorous effort to build an integrated and more just society. Intergroup relations has always proved a fruitful area for interventions of the type explored in our research.

If human service professionals are to take a hand in local politics, and several leaders in the human services have suggested that this is necessary, then many of these approaches could clearly support that effort. The development of an effectively participating electorate may in part depend on the use of these and similar change strategies.

While we have oriented this manual toward students, it may be used as well in in-service training to enhance and update the skills of practitioners in operating agencies. Among various unintended consequences of our efforts was the receipt of a number of requests from agency staffs to be introduced to certain guidelines. Typically this occurred because a particular practitioner was utilizing the guidelines in the context of innovative change efforts that were highly regarded by his or her staff colleagues. One agency staff was able to use the material as a vehicle for initiating some long-desired changes in both their in-service training program and their approach to outreach efforts in the community. The project has conducted several continuing education workshops for staffs of agencies, using the manual as the main teaching tool.

The strategies are potentially usable not only by individual practitioners but also by groups of practitioners who want to explore together the most effective ways of initiating changes. One staff group, for example, met on a team basis using the goal change guideline to plan an approach for modifying goals within their own youth development agency.

The procedures incorporated in the manual, particularly in the Getting Started section, represent a general scheme for systematic problem solving—the consideration of particular factors in analyzing practice situations and the laying out of a series of steps and procedures to follow in formulating a plan of action. Through the repeated use of the initial log this type of analytic methodology can become internalized and, subsequently, can be applied automatically or by relying only on informal notes.

The broader research methodology of the study provides a vehicle to foster the development of practice theory and technique. We have demonstrated the specific utility of existing social science research for practice purposes. Furthermore, we hope to have articulated, even if in a preliminary and suggestive way, the potentialities of a research and development model for creating intervention technologies in the human services fields. This model, carried over from the physical sciences and industry, can be employed by other people to construct and operationalize new theory-based practice strategies.

With regard to the manual itself, at this point the center of action has shifted to our readers. This endeavor has not been an academic exercise; we have not attempted to produce a pristine contribution to knowledge that essentially fulfills its purpose by being assigned a place in the library stacks. The "name of the game" in this instance is use, change, and human development.

Our experience with many practitioners and many agencies suggests that this material can help to make the pursuit of humanistic goals more systematic, tangible, and effective, as well as accessible to evaluation. If our effort can be regarded as an invention, then it is an incremental step on which others will need to build; our offerings must not be regarded as a rigid set of final prescriptions. Not only should the material be subjected to review, but we also hope that it will be revised in light of the practical experiences of students, teachers, and a wide variety of practitioners. What does not work should be discarded. We look forward to being updated and corrected. We give a set of tools that must be operationalized with skill. There is no magic in the guidelines, and no source of strength that can be used without the thoughtful application of discerning and committed practitioners. And there is little value in the manual unless that happens.

APPENDICES

APPENDIX A

A NOTE ON THE METHODOLOGY OF THE STUDY

The second-year field study was conducted through use of a field staff of 22 practitioner informant-field researchers[1] who were employed in a range of human service agencies in the southeast Michigan area. The practitioners comprised a purposive sample selected on the basis of such characteristics as being: (1) competent, (2) reliable, and (3) conceptually able.[2] The field staff served as a corps of "social engineers" who had the task of operationalizing general action principles in concrete and functional terms, thus specifying patterns of implementation, ranges of activity in operationalization, and circumstances surrounding implementation. The project, with its action-research design, falls most closely within the research and development school of study.[3] A practitioner staff with special qualifications was considered necessary to fulfill requisite functions. Since there was some attrition during the one-year duration of the main field study, the number of practitioners implementing any given guideline varied.
number of practitioners implementing any given guideline varied.

[1]George J. McCall and J.L. Simmons, *Issues in Participant Observation* (Reading, Massachusetts: Addison-Wesley, 1969).

[2]Claire Selltis, Marie Jahoda, Morton Deutsch, and Stuart W. Cook, *Research Methods in Social Relations* (New York: Holt, Rinehart and Winston, 1959), pp. 520-521.

[3]Richard E. Schutz, "The Nature of Educational Development," *Journal of Research and Development in Education* (Winter 1970), 39-64; National Academy of Sciences, "The Experimental Manpower Laboratory as an R&D Capability," National Research Council, Washington, D.C. (February 1974); Edward B. Roberts, *The Dynamics of Research and Development* (New York: Harper and Row, 1964).

their ongoing activities on log forms, which included close-ended checklists, and items calling for narrative observations. Logs were of three types: (1) the initial log, which was basically a planning tool; (2) periodic logs, which recorded ongoing activities and behavior on a biweekly basis; and (3) summary logs, which were completed after an implementation had been concluded and which were retrospective and evaluative in character. A sample periodic and final log are in Appendix B. Practitioners received an initial orientation and regular supervision and support throughout the field study. Unit coordinators and the central project staff were actively involved in an intensive process of training, monitoring, and quality control. Logs received in the project offices were thoroughly checked, treated for accuracy and completeness, and routed for machine-data processing, as well as qualitative analysis.

The logs covered four general categories: (1) key community groups contacted during implementation (i.e., public agencies, private agencies, voluntary associations); (2) key individuals contacted (i.e., agency staff, staff of other agencies, clients); (3) facilitating factors (personal, organizational, client, and community) in implementation (i.e., personal commitment, support of agency staff, client and community interest); (4) limiting factors (personal, organizational, client, and community) in implementation (i.e., lack of time, lack of goal clarity in the agency, lack of knowledge in the community). These latter factors can be defined as any influences that serve to aid or hinder the practitioner in successfully attaining intended goals.

Results of the field study are reported in both qualitative and quantitative terms. Qualitative data includes general patterns of implementation, problems encountered, and advice offered. These are taken from narrative and open-ended items of the logs. The more quantitative findings are based on standard checklists in the logs that were filled out by practitioners, both during the course of carrying out a guideline, and at the end. These findings include groups and individuals involved in implementation and facilitating and limiting factors. The presentation in the manual emphasizes the results of "successful" practice—instances where intended outcomes were substantially attained.

The rating instrument used to evaluate the implementation process (outcome) was a five-point continuum ranging from no to complete attainment, framed in wording specific to each guideline. These continuum points were assigned a numeric value, ranging from 1 (none) to 5 (complete), indicating the raters' judgment of the practitioner's success in implementation of a strategy. The rating continuum for each guideline is presented below.

Guideline Four

Innovation carried out (or accepted by) none of proximate general target system	Innovation carried out (or accepted by) a few members of proximate general target system	Innovation carried out (or accepted by) about half of proximate general target system	Innovation carried out (or accepted by) most of proximate general target system	Innovation carried out (or accepted by) all of proximate general target system

Guideline One

No change at all toward intended new organizational goals	Slight attainment of intended new organizational goals	Partial attainment of intended new organizational goals	Considerable attainment of intended new organizational goals	Complete attainment of intended new organizational goals

Guideline Two

Dropoff or no increase in participation	Slight increase toward intended participation	Partial increase toward intended participation	Considerable increase toward intended participation	Complete attainment of intended participation

Guideline Five

Practitioner achieved none of intended increase in effectiveness	Practitioner slightly achieved intended increase in effectiveness	Practitioner partially achieved intended increase in effectiveness	Practitioner considerably achieved intended increase in effectiveness	Practitioner completely achieved intended increase in effectiveness

The rating continuum is not intended to be an interval scale; the numeric values were assigned for convenience in dividing practitioners into broad categories. Successful practitioners for purposes of our profile of successful practice were judged as obtaining a level of "considerable" (4) or "complete" (5) goal attainment. In the comparative analysis the more successful practitioner had a rating of five (complete attainment) and the less successful a rating from one to four (all others). Three raters with varying backgrounds and relationships to the project were used in this process, and standardized procedures were employed. The interrater reliability by guideline was .98, .90, .98, and .73, respectively. The discussion of the manual concentrates on the profiles of successful practitioners (rated 4 and 5), although occasional references will be made when pertinent to differences between more successful and less successful practitioners.

The presentation descriptively highlights general tendencies in our practitioner sample. For purposes of this manual, the findings of the field study are abbreviated. We have found that a fuller presentation interferes with the reader's ability to focus on the application thrust of the manual. Fuller treatment of methods and findings will be found in other places.[4] In addition, Appendix B presents a full set of data tables on a sample guideline (innovation) for illustrative purposes.

Some qualifying remarks need to be made here about the data from the field study. First, these are aggregated data for all the practitioners who participated, viewed as a total group. This causes some important limitations and problems. There were quite different circumstances surrounding the interventions of different practitioners. Furthermore, the practitioners held different positions in their agencies: line workers, middle management supervisors, and administrative personnel. Some of these agencies were large, formal bureaucracies; some were small, informal associations. Certainly it can be assumed that the specifics of intervention have varied among these different types of settings and according to certain background characteristics of the practitioners themselves.

Second, our sample is relatively small, although it is as large as could be managed with limited resources in a complex field study. When we present a profile of successful practice, we use only those cases in which complete or nearly complete attainment of the intended outcomes was achieved, according to ratings by our judges. For any one guideline, the number of cases is between 13 and 16. Dividing this relatively small number into subcategories for further treatment is unsound statistically, although it would be desirable to make such more refined analyses.

What is offered is a composite, suggestive picture of performance for a varied sample of practitioners. (The sample was selected to optimize a wide range of existing categories of people and set-

[4]Jack Rothman, Joseph Teresa, John L. Erlich, "The Community Intervention Study: Reviving Action Research," presented at the American Sociological Association Annual Meeting, New York, New York, August 1973. A full research report will be published by the University of Michigan Press (tentative).

tings.) This overview provides a preliminary general frame of reference for describing and analyzing patterns of practice. We hope that other researchers will be encouraged to do more detailed investigations so that the specific practice approaches of different types of practitioners in different situations will be given sharper focus. The set of summary tables of findings presented in Appendix C permit the reader to interpret and assess for himself the nature of the data and the use he wishes to make of it. (Space precludes similar detail on other guidelines.)

We have emphasized that in a study concerned with both research and the creation of practical tools and products an inevitable tension is present.

> *One question of strategy appears to loom larger than all the others. This question is.*
>
> **What should be the relative balance in an R&D program between research and evaluation on one hand and development on the other.**
>
> *This balance is extremely critical if we are to develop products that offer any chance of real [practice] improvement.*[5]

We keenly felt this duality. We might have tried to write a book that would have equally interested both the practitioner and the social scientist. After some experimentation that course was abandoned. We are reminded of the comment of a colleague who discovered a great diversity of student ability and interest in his class. The solution he formulated was to aim for the middle. His lamentful evaluation of that route was that "nobody was there."

Our solution in this instance has been to gear this manual to a primarily practitioner audience and to prepare a separate technical report for social scientists and researchers. Just as researchers may find the manual lacking in important ways, and perhaps of low interest professionally, so may most practitioners find the companion methdological volume of little interest and of less use. A balance has been sought through different publications for different relevant audiences.

Litwak and Meyer, sociologists who have been our associates at the University of Michigan, have produced an analogous practitioner's manual. In their work they attempted to apply a set of sociological theories to the tasks of school community agents. Their observations concerning their own situation have also much relevance to ours. Litwak and Meyer also chose to emphasize intervention approaches that

[5]Walter R. Borg, "The Balance Between Educational Research and Development: A Question of Strategy," *Education Technology. IX (7) (July 1969), 6.*

would be of practical utility to operators in the field. The manual, they say, "is intended primarily to offer guidelines to practitioners concerned with local school-community relations of educational institutions. Practical suggestions are offered, sometimes in prescriptive language, as proposals for action rather than as rules....We hope the result will be the posing of significant hypotheses to be tried by the result will be... tried by practice and tested by research."[6] This expresses also the spirit underlying what has been attempted here.

[6]Eugene Litwak and Henry J. Meyer, *School, Family and Neighborhood: The Theory and Practice of School-Community Relations.* (New York: Columbia University Press, 1974), pp. vii-viii.

APPENDIX B

A PRACTITIONER'S FILLED-OUT SET OF LOGS-INNOVATION GUIDELINE

Set of recordings of one implementation of the Innovation Guideline. This is a verbatim reproduction of the practitioner's recording, with slight editorial modifications to disguise the locale for purposes of confidentiality and to aid in clarity of presentation.

COMMUNITY INTERVENTION PROJECT

Initial Log Questionnaire

1 Guideline number 4 (Innovation

2 Practitioner Jane Jones

3 Agency Human Services Association

4 Date of report 12/9/72 5 Date of decision to use guideline 12/9/72

- -

6 At this point, in relation to the guideline, what is your overall goal?

Overall goal: To set up three Community Councils in communities where I am working. At the present time the agency has no councils functioning.

7 Look back at the intervention guideline. How would you begin to define or concretize *each* element of the guideline in your immediate practice situation (that is to say, how might you operationalize these components)?

School of Social Work
University of Michigan
REVILQ 10/72

Promote acceptance:

A. Talk to interested community members. B. Notify supervisor. C. Notify director. D. Present the idea to various community groups, formal organizations, and public bodies.

Of an innovation:

Innovation: To set up Community Councils in Hudson Township, Baldwin Township, and Newton.

Formulate it in such a way that the total innovation can be experienced initially by a limited portion of the target system:

Partialization: A model will be set up in Hudson Township, the limited portion of the target system and will be expanded to Baldwin Township, and Newton.

8 Please describe the circumstances (conditions, facts, events, requests, assignments, etc.) that led you to decide to use the guideline.

Circumstances: The director sent out a memo during the summer emphasizing the importance of Advisory Councils and Community Councils in fall plans.

The director reiterated the emphasis at a staff mixer in October 1972.

The director of community schools in the Hudson school district indicated his interest in having a community council for the Hudson area at an interview I had with him in November 1972.

9 Describe the *major* steps you anticipate going through in order to utilize this guideline. List specific behaviors in the order in which you expect they will occur. (Use the boxes to indicate this order, repeating numbers for simultaneous events.)

[2] I will talk to interested community members in the Hudson area. I will talk to indigenous community members in Hudson, particularly the senior citizen group that I work with already.

[3] I will contact the Hudson Committee, an indigenous volunteer group.

4	I will call a small meeting including representatives from the aforementioned organizations, plus the director of the community schools to begin to discuss which agencies and groups should be included in the council.
1	I will inform my immediate supervisor and director of my plan.
5	Begin contacting other agencies and organizations for their support and representation.
5	Announce the plan at public meetings such as the school board and city council (in Hudson, board of trustees).
5	Call a meeting of the council.
6	At the meeting I will state some of the goals that I see and suggest that a workshop be set up for the purpose of explaining some of the reasons for having an area advisory council.
7	Discussion of major community problems at the same meeting.
6	Set up an organizational structure: steering committee, task force subcommittee, secretary, and chairman.
6	Set up another open meeting for the council.
7	Get started in establishing similar councils in Baldwin and Newton by meeting with selected community groups, leaders, etc. (The specifics about how to proceed will depend on the success of the experience in Hudson.)

10 What key community groups will you probably involve?

Group	Reasons for Contact
Hudson Health Committee	Powerful, cohesive, well-organized indigenous organization
Senior Citizens	Well-organized, includes power figures
Community School and School Bd.	By-laws demand a community council
Churches	Community contacts
Township	Power over funds

11 What key individuals will you probably involve?

Individual(s) (initials)	Title and/ or Affiliation	Reasons for Contact
P.R.	President of Hudson Health Committee	Interest and hard working
R.N.	Member of Hudson Health Committee	Interest and motivation
B.P.	Director of Community Schools	Interest and resources
Rev. N. and Rev. R.	Reverends of Protestant churches	Interest, influence, and human resources
Father P.	Father of church	Interest, cooperation, influence, and human resources
V.I.	Supervisor of township	Power

12 Facilitating factors:

In general, to what degree do you feel *community* factors may be facilitating in implementing the guideline? (These factors might include community support of organization generally, influential and other community groups support organization or program, changes in community tend to support organization or program, and community support of practitioner, etc.)

Please rate the degree of facilitation:

None	0	1	2	3	4	Great Deal
					X	

In general, to what degree do you feel *client* factors may be facilitating in implementing the guideline? (These factors might include client participation in organization or program, client receptivity to organization or program, and client support of practitioner.)

Please rate the degree of facilitation:

None	0	1	2	3	4	Great Deal
				X		

In general, to what degree do you feel *agency* factors may be facilitating in implementing the guideline? (These factors might include administration support, supervisor support, staff support, and physical facilities aid in effort.)

Please rate the degree of facilitation:

None ______ __X__ ______ ______ ______ Great Deal
0 1 2 3 4

In general, to what degree do you feel *personal factors related to yourself* may be facilitating in implementing the guideline? (These factors might include good relationships with staff, good relationships with community people, personal knowledge of community, and positive effects of skill.)

Please rate the degree of facilitation:

None ______ ______ __X__ ______ ______ Great Deal
0 1 2 3 4

13 *Limiting factors:*

In general, to what degree do you feel *community* factors may be limiting in implementing the guideline? (These factors might include negative response to organization generally; lack of knowledge of organization purposes, programs, or activities; influential community groups or leaders do not support organization or program; and competition by other activities with community residents' time and interests.)

Please rate the degree of limitation:

None ______ __X__ ______ ______ ______ Great Deal
0 1 2 3 4

In general, to what degree do you feel *client* factors may be limiting in implementing the guideline? (These factors might include negative response to organization generally, clients interfere with organization activities, and dissensus among clients.)

Please rate the degree of limitation:

None ______ __X__ ______ ______ ______ Great Deal
0 1 2 3 4

In general, to what degree do you feel *agency* factors may be limiting in implementing the guideline? (These factors might include unclear or shifting goals, programs or assignments; lack of funds, facilities, and other resources; lack of support or hindering action of supervisor; and lack of support or hindering action of staff.)

Please rate the degree of limitation:

None ______ ___X___ ______ ______ ______ Great Deal
0 1 2 3 4

In general, to what degree do you feel *personal factors related to yourself* may be limiting in implementing the guideline? (These factors might include poor relationships with staff, poor relationships with community people, lack of personal knowledge of community, and negative effects of insufficient skills.)

Please rate the degree of limitation:

None ___X___ ______ ______ ______ ______ Great Deal
0 1 2 3 4

DEMOGRAPHIC DATA ON DELIMITED CLIENT POPULATION

Name Jane Jones

Guideline 4 Date 1/28/73

1 Geographic location of intended client beneficiaries of your intervention:

Hudson, Baldwin, and Newton

2 Approximate number of intended client beneficiaries of your intervention:

24,000 (if projects transpire)

3 Distribution of the intended client beneficiary population as you are able to describe it:

A *Age* (%)
10 (1) 0-9 years
10 (2) 10-17 years
20 (3) 18-29 years
20 (4) 30-39 years
10 (5) 40-64 years
10 (6) 65 + years

B *Sex* (%)
45 (1) Male
55 (2) Female

C *Race* (%)
10 (1) Black
83 (2) White
5 (3) Other (specify) Latino
2 (4) Other (specify) Other races

D *General Educational Attainment* (those age 25 and over) (%)

_20_ (1) 0-8 years completed
_20_ (2) 1-3 years high school
_50_ (3) High school diploma
_10_ (4) 1 or more years college

E *Family Income* (%)

____ (1) $0 to $3,999
_25_ (2) $4,000 to $9,999
_75_ (3) $10,000 to $29,999
____ (4) $30,000 and over

F *Occupation of Dwelling Units* (%)

_75_ (1) % owner occupied
_25_ (2) % renter occupied

G *Families with Children Below 18 Years of Age* (%)

_70_ (1) % with children below 18 years of age

4 Characterize the intended beneficiaries in regard to mobility:

Very mobile	1	2	3	4	5	Very stable
				✓		

5 Characterize the intended beneficiaries in regard to homogeneity:

Homogeneous	1	2	3	4	5	Heterogeneous
		✓				

COMMUNITY INTERVENTION PROJECT

Periodic Log Questionnaire

1 Guideline number 4 (Innovation)

2 Practitioner Jane Jones

3 Agency Human Services Association

4 Date of Report 12/23/72 5 Time period covered by report 12/9-12/23/72

- -

6 In your own words, please describe what happened as you carried out the guideline during the time period covered by this log. If you need more space, please use the reverse side of this page.

I informed my immediate supervisor and director of my plan by submitting an outline. At the time I submitted the outline, I sat down with the director and my immediate supervisor and discussed the rationale for such a council. I then began talking to people in the community that I feel would have an interest in the community council. I contacted the Hudson Health Committee to find out what agencies and community persons they feel important. I also contacted the director of community schools who knows the community quite well. I talked to some of the senior citizens

School of Social Work
University of Michigan
REVPLQ 10/72

in order to find out who they feel should be on the council (lay people and representatives from their organization).

My activity thus far has involved talking about the council and informing my agency of my intention to create this new body. I have comprised a list of about thirty-six persons representing various organizations, agencies, and community persons.

7 Has (Have) there been any change(s) (refinements, additions, deletions, etc.) in your overall goal?

There have been no revisions in the overall goal.

8 Look back at the intervention guideline. Was there any change in how you defined or concretized *each* element of the guideline in your practice (that is, how you operationalized these components)?

Promote acceptance:

To promote, I will proceed with all items mentioned: talk to interested community members, notify supervisor, formal organizations, and public bodies. I will not necessarily find it mandatory to publicize this activity to my agency board.

Of an innovation:

Formulate it in such a way that the total innovation can be experienced initially by a limited portion of the target system:

9 Describe the *major* steps you went through as you continued to use this guideline. List specific behaviors in the order in which they occurred. (Use the boxes to indicate this order, repeating numbers for simultaneous events.)

[1] I informed my supervisor and agency director during a staff conference.

[2] I talked to interested community members in the Hudson area, senior citizens, Hudson Health Committee, director of Hudson Community Schools.

[3] I had a meeting with the director of Hudson Community Schools and drew up my list of 36 (approximately) representatives based on this series of discussions.

☐

☐

10 *Instructions:* In your answer to question 10 we are interested in the number of key community groups involved in each category and the *key* reason(s) for contact. Put the total number of key community groups involved in any given category in the spaces provided at the left. The *key* reason(s) for contact category should be recorded in the space to the right. Please indicate *no more* than *2* reasons for each type of key community group.

10 What key community groups did you involve?

Total Number Involved	Type of Group	Reason for Contact (Select from List at Right)		Reason for Contact
4	1 Public agency or organization	1	2	1 Seeking exercise of influence by contact 2 Seeking financial support
6	2 Quasi-public or private agency or organization	1	6	3 Seeking non-financial material resources
4	3 Informal association and single issue group	1	6	4 Public relations (seeking goodwill or general approval) 5 Seeking information and guidance
____	4 None	____	____	6 Seeking to prepare the contact for future participation

(10 continued)

Total Number Involved	Title and/or Affiliation	Reason for Contact (Select from List at Right)	Reason for Contact
			7 Seeking immediate participation
			8 Seeking legitimation or formally expressed approval
			9 Other (specify)_____
			10 _____
			11 _____

11 Instructions: In your answer to question 11 we are interested in the number of key individuals involved in each category and the *key* reason(s) for contact. Put the total number of key individuals involved in any given category in the spaces provided at the left.

The *key* reason(s) for contact category should be recorded in the space to the right. Please indicate *no more* than *2* reasons for each type of key individual.

11 What key individuals did you involve?

Total Number Involved	Title and/or Affiliation	Reason for Contact (Select from List at Right)		Reason for Contact
2	1 Board officers and members	1	8	1 Seeking exercise of personal influence by contact
_____	2 Board committee members	_____	_____	2 Seeking financial assistance
1	3 Staff committee members	5	6	3 Seeking nonfinancial

1	4	Agency director, assistant director	8	____
____	5	Agency supervisors	____	____
____	6	Agency peers (colleagues)	____	____
____	7	Agency subordinates	____	____
2	8	External governmental officials	2	1
____	9	External nongovernmental organization administrative and supervisory staff	____	____
1	10	External nongovernmental organization line and operating staff	5	____
10	11	Voluntary association external to agency—chairman and members	6	4
____	12	Professional peers and friends	____	____
6	13	Community leaders	1	5
10	14	Other community people	5	6
3	15	Clients	____	____
____	16	None	____	____
____	17	Other (specify)____ ________________	____	____
____	18	________________	____	____
____	19	________________	____	____

material resources
4 Public relations (seeking good will or general approval)
5 Seeking information and guidance
6 Seeking to prepare the contact for future participation
7 Seeking immediate participation
8 Seeking legitimation or formally expressed approval
9 Other (specify)_____
10 ________________
11 ________________

12 Were there facilitating conditions as you implemented the guideline? Please check the degree of facilitation for *each* condition listed.

12A	Community Factor	None 0	1	2	3	Great Deal 4
		Degree of Facilitation				
1	Community participation in organization or program (voluntary)				X	
2	Community participation in organization or program (through legal or administrative ruling)		X			
3	Community support of organization generally				X	
4	Community interest in program specifically				X	
5	Influential and other community groups support organization or program				X	
6	Influential or other community groups involved with organization or program			X		
7	Community receptivity to organization or program				X	
8	Community disinterest in, or dissatisfaction with, organization or program (leading to a desire for change)	X				
9	Changes in community tend to support organization or program		X			
10	External influences make community supportive of organization or program		X			
11	Community support of clients		X			
12	Community support of practitioner				X	
13	Other (specify)________					
14	________					
15	________					

12B Please indicate the number(s) given above for the three most important community facilitating conditions.

6 ; 4 ; 1

12C Client Factor	None 0	1	2	3	Great Deal 4
		Degree of Facilitation			
1 Client participation in organization or program (voluntary)		X			
2 Client participation in organization or program (through legal or administrative ruling)	X				
3 Client interest in organization generally		X			
4 Client interest in program specifically			X		
5 Client receptivity to organization or program			X		
6 Disinterest in or dissatisfaction with agency or program (leading to a desire for change		X			
7 Client support of other clients			X		
8 Client support of practitioner				X	
9 Other (specify)______					
10					
11					

12D Please indicate the number(s) given above of the three most important client facilitating conditions.

4 ; 5 ; 8

12E Agency Factor	None 0	1	2	3	Great Deal 4
		Degree of Facilitation			
1 External authority requirements of organization support effort			X		

(12E continued)

2	Affiliated organizational support	X				
3	Affiliated organizational involvement	X				
4	Board support	X				
5	Board involvement	X				
6	Administration support		X			
7	Administration involvement	X				
8	Administration disinterest	X				
9	Supervisor support			X		
10	Supervisor involvement	X				
11	Supervisor disinterest	X				
12	Staff support	X				
13	Staff involvement	X				
14	Practitioner assignments and	X				
	tasks are consistent with effort		X			
15	Physical facilities aid in effort		X			
16	Other (specify)__________					
17	__________					
18	__________					

12F Please indicate the number(s) given above of the three most important agency facilitating conditions.

1 ; 6 ; 7

		Degree of Facilitation				
		None				Great Deal
12G	Personal Factor	0	1	2	3	4

A Personal Relations and Commitments

Good relationships with:

I Within Agency

		0	1	2	3	4
1	Board/Board members	X				
2	Administrator				X	
3	Supervisor			X		
4	Staff				X	
5	Clients				X	

II <u>Outside Agency</u>					
6 Community leaders				X	
7 Community people				X	
8 Other organizations					X
9 Nonstaff professional peers or friends					X

Positive effects of:

III <u>Commitment</u>					
10 Commitment to agency				X	
11 Commitment to program				X	
12 Commitment to guideline				X	

B <u>Personal Knowledge and Attributes</u>

Knowledge of:

I <u>Personal Knowledge</u>					
13 Community				X	
14 Clients			X		
15 Programs			X		
16 Relevant ideology (and theory)					X

Positive effects of:

II <u>Personal Attributes</u>					
17 Position or role				X	
18 Good reputation			X		
19 Personal gain (promotion, job title, etc.)		X			
20 Prior experiences			X		
21 Self-confidence			X		
22 Skill				X	
23 Professional "disinterest"		X			
24 Enjoyment of job				X	
25 Patience			X		

(12G continued)

		Degree of Facilitation				
		None 0	1	2	3	Great Deal 4
C	Other (specify)					
26	______					
27	______					
28	______					

12H Please indicate the number(s) given above of the three most important personal facilitating conditions.

8 ; 9 ; 16

13 Please rate the overall importance of the facilitating factors below.

	Degree of Importance				
	None 0	1	2	3	Great Deal 4
Community					X
Client			X		
Agency				X	
Personal				X	

14 Were there limiting conditions as you implemented the guideline? Please check the Degree of Limitation for *each* condition listed.

		Degree of Limitation				
14A	Community Factor	None 0	1	2	3	Great Deal 4
1	Negative response to organization generally	X				
2	Disinterest in or dissatisfaction with organization or program	X				

3	Lack of knowledge of organization purposes, programs, or activities				X	
4	Community residents lack other necessary knowledge or skills			X		
5	Community residents interfere with organization activities		X			
6	Pressure from community residents		X			
7	Influential community groups and/or leaders do not support organization or program		X			
8	External influences make community unsupportive of organization or program	X				
9	Community residents not interested in program specifically	X				
10	Dissensus among community residents	X				
11	Other activities compete with community residents' time and interests				X	
12	Community lacks funds needed to support organization or program		X			
13	Differences in life-styles between staff (including practitioner) and community residents		X			
14	Other (specify)________					
15	________					
16	________					

14B Please indicate the number(s) given above of the three most important community limiting conditions.

3 ; 4 ; 11

14C Clients	None 0	1	2	3	Great Deal 4
1 Negative response to organization generally	X				
2 Disinterest in or dissatisfaction with organization or program			X		
3 Lack of knowledge of organization purposes, programs, or activities				X	
4 Clients lack other knowledge or skills			X		
5 Clients interfere with organization activities		X			
6 Pressure from clients	X				
7 Clients not interested in program specifically			X		
8 Dissensus among clients	X				
9 Other activities compete with clients' time and interests				X	
10 Other (specify)______					
11 ______					
12					

Degree of Limitation applies to columns 0–4.

14D Please indicate the number(s) given above of the three most important client limiting conditions.

3 ; 7 ; 9

14E Agency	None 0	1	2	3	Great Deal 4
1 External authority requirements hamper efforts	X				
2 Lack of power or authority of organization		X			

Degree of Limitation applies to columns 0–4.

(14E continued)

		Degree of Limitation				
		None 0	1	2	3	Great Deal 4
3	Unclear or shifting goals, programs, or assignments			X		
4	Hindering structure of organization		X			
5	Negative attitudes or actions toward clients or community		X			
6	Lack of knowledge of clients or community				X	
7	Practitioner-organization conflict		X			
8	Lack of staff (both adequate numbers or staff with specialized knowledge, training, etc.)					X
9	Lack of funds, facilities, and other resources					X
10	Lack of support or hindering action of affiliated organizations			X		
11	Lack of support or hindering action of board		X			
12	Lack of support or hindering action of administration	X				
13	Lack of support or hindering action of supervisor	X				
14	Lack of support or hindering action of staff	X				
15	Other (specify) ______					
16	______					
17	______					

14F Please indicate the number(s) given above of the three most important agency limiting conditions.

6 ; 8 ; 9

14G Personal Factor	Degree of Limitation None 0	1	2	3	Great Deal 4
A Personal Relations and Commitments					
Poor relationships with:					
I Within Agency					
1 Board/Board members	X				
2 Administration	X				
3 Supervisor	X				
4 Staff	X				
5 Clients	X				
II Outside Agency					
6 Community leaders		X			
7 Community people		X			
8 Other organizations		X			
9 Nonstaff professional peers or friends	X				
Negative effects of:					
III Commitment					
10 Lack of commitment to agency	X				
11 Lack of commitment to program	X				
12 Lack of commitment to guideline	X				
B Personal Knowledge and Attributes					
Lack of personal knowledge of:					
I Personal Knowledge					
13 Community					X
14 Clients				X	
15 Programs			X		
16 Relevant ideology (and theory)	X				

Negative effects of:

II Personal Attributes

17	Position or role	X				
18	Poor reputation	X				
19	Personal loss (demotion, job title, etc.)			X		
20	Lack of self-confidence		X			
21	Insufficient skills		X			
22	Professional "disinterest"			X		
23	Overinvolvement		X			
24	Do not enjoy job	X				
25	Impatience	X				
26	Fatigue		X			
27	Lack of time				X	

C Other (specify)

28						
29						
30						

14H Please indicate the number(s) given above of the three most important personal limiting conditions.

13 ; 2 ; 27

15 Please rate the overall importance of the limiting factors below.

	Degree of Importance				
	None 0	1	2	3	Great Deal 4
Community		X			
Client	X				
Agency			X		
Personal			X		

COMMUNITY INTERVENTION PROJECT

Periodic Log Questionnaire

1 Guideline number 4 (Innovation)

2 Practitioner Jane Jones

3 Agency Human Services Association

4 Date of Report Jan. 6 5 Time period covered by report 12/23-1/6/73

- -

6 In your own words, please describe what happened as you carried out the guideline during the time period covered by this log. If you need more space, please use the reverse side of this page.

I prepared a cover letter, designating the first meeting date and giving an outline of the goals and objectives of a community council. The mailing has been sent out. Whenever possible I tried to request certain known persons in the agencies and organizations to be members based on their interest and potential contributions to such an effort. There were a few agencies that I simply requested a representative to attend the meeting. I have continued to talk to people in the community about the council and have attended several community meetings where I have publicized the concept of a community council.

I have started to discuss the concept of forming a community council in the Newton and Baldwin areas. I am forming similar lists of possible community membership on a council in those areas.

School of Social Work
University of Michigan
REVPLQ 10/72

7 Has (Have) there been any change(s) (refinements, additions, deletions, etc.) in your overall goal?

There have been no refinements, additions or deletions in my overall goal.

8 Look back at the intervention guideline. Was there any change in how you defined or concretized *each* element of the guideline in your practice (that is, how you operationalized these components)?

Promote acceptance:

To promote acceptance, I am discussing the concept, possibilities and the need for community councils to coordinate and facilitate community planning.

Of an innovation:

Formulate it in such a way that the total innovation can be experienced initially by a limited portion of the target system:

I am now beginning to use parallel methods in setting up community councils in the target area at large. The first council will serve as a model for the formation of other councils in my target area.

9 Describe the *major* steps you went through as you continued to use this guideline. List specific behaviors in the order in which they occurred. (Use the boxes to indicate this order, repeating numbers for simultaneous events.)

[1] I wrote a letter to agencies, organizations, and individuals that I would like to serve on a community council.

[1] I explained the goals and possible objectives of such a council.

[1] I addressed the board of trustees and the supervisor in the township concerning the creation of the community council.

[2] I continued to discuss the council with concerned community members.

[1] I have addressed groups that I work with regularly and have requested their designee to be a part of the council. (I

usually try to make my own selection, but have found it 'politically' impossible when there is interpersonal power rivalry within the group).

10 *Instructions:* In your answer to question 10 we are interested in the number of key community groups involved in each category and the *key* reason(s) for contact. Put the total number of key community groups involved in any given category in the spaces provided at the left. The *key* reason(s) for contact category should be recorded in the space to the right. Please indicate *no more* than *2* reasons for each type of key community group.

10 What key community groups did you involve?

Total Number Involved	Type of Group	Reason for Contact (Select from List at Right)	
4	1 Public agency or organization	1	2
6	2 Quasi-public or private agency or organization	1	6
4	3 Informal association and single issue group	1	6
	4 None		

Reason for Contact

1 Seeking exercise of influence by contact
2 Seeking financial support
3 Seeking nonfinancial material resources
4 Public relations (seeking goodwill or general approval)
5 Seeking information and guidance
6 Seeking to prepare the contact for future participation
7 Seeking immediate participation
8 Seeking legitimation or formally expressed approval

(10 continued)

Total Number Involved	Type of Group	Reason for Contact (Select from List at Right)	Reason for Contact
			9 Other (specify)______
			______
			10 ______
			11 ______

11 *Instructions:* In your answer to question 11 we are interested in the number of key individuals involved in each category and the *key* reason(s) for contact. Put the total number of key individuals involved in any given category in the spaces provided at the left.

The key reason(s) for contact category should be recorded in the space to the right. Please indicate *no more* than *2* reasons for each type of key individual.

11 What key individual did you involve?

Total Number Involved	Title and/or Affiliation	Reason for Contact (Select from List at Right)		Reason for Contact
2	1 Board officers and members	1	8	1 Seeking exercise of personal influence by contact
____	2 Board committee members	____	____	2 Seeking financial assistance
1	3 Staff committee members	5	6	3 Seeking nonfinancial material resources
1	4 Agency director, assistant director	8	____	4 Public relations (seeking goodwill or general approval)

____	5	Agency supervisors	____	____
____	6	Agency peers (colleagues)	____	____
____	7	Agency subordinates	____	____
2	8	External governmental officials	2	1
____	9	External nongovernmental organization administrative and supervisory staff	____	____
1	10	External nongovernmental organization line and operating staff	5	____
10	11	Voluntary association external to agency—chairman and members	6	4
____	12	Professional peers and friends	____	____
10	13	Community leaders	1	5
10	14	Other community people	5	6
3	15	Clients	5	6
____	16	None	____	____
____	17	Other (specify)____ ____________	____	____
____	18	____________	____	____
____	19	____________	____	____

5 Seeking information and guidance
6 Seeking to prepare the contact for future participation
7 Seeking immediate participation
8 Seeking legitimation or formally expressed approval
9 Other (specify)____
10 ____________
11 ____________

12 Were there facilitating conditions as you implemented the guideline? Please check the Degree of Facilitation for *each* condition listed.

12A	Community Factor	None 0	1	2	3	Great Deal 4
		Degree of Facilitation				
1	Community participation in organization or program (voluntary)				X	
2	Community participation in organization or program (through legal or administrative ruling)		X			
3	Community support of organization generally				X	
4	Community interest in program specifically				X	
5	Influential and other community groups support organization or program				X	
6	Influential or other community groups involved with organization or program			X		
7	Community receptivity to organization or program				X	
8	Community disinterest in, or dissatisfaction with, organization or program (leading to a desire for change)		X			
9	Changes in community tend to support organization or program		X			
10	External influences make community supportive of organization or program		X			
11	Community support of clients			X		
12	Community support of practitioner			X		
13	Other (specify)________					
14	________					
15	________					

12B Please indicate the number(s) given above of the three most important community facilitating conditions.

1 ; 6 ; 7

12C	Client Factor	None 0	1	2	3	Great Deal 4
		Degree of Facilitation				
1	Client participation in organization or program (voluntary)		X			
2	Client participation in organization or program (through legal or administrative ruling)	X				
3	Client interest in organization generally		X			
4	Client interest in program specifically			X		
5	Client receptivity to organization or program			X		
6	Disinterest in or dissatisfaction with agency or program (leading to a desire for change		X			
7	Client support of other clients			X		
8	Client support of practitioner				X	
9	Other (specify)					
10						
11						

12D Please indicate the number(s) given above of the three most important client facilitating conditions.

4 ; 5 ; 8

12E	Agency Factor	None 0	1	2	3	Great Deal 4
		Degree of Facilitation				
1	External authority requirements of organization support effort			X		

(12E continued)

		Degree of Facilitation: None 0	1	2	3	Great Deal 4
2	Affiliated organizational support	X				
3	Affiliated organizational involvement	X				
4	Board support	X				
5	Board involvement	X				
6	Administration support		X			
7	Administration involvement	X				
8	Administration disinterest	X				
9	Supervisor support		X			
10	Supervisor involvement	X				
11	Supervisor disinterest	X				
12	Staff support	X				
13	Staff involvement	X				
14	Practitioner assignments and tasks are consistent with effort		X			
15	Physical facilities aid in effort		X			
16	Other (specify)________					
17	________					
18	________					

12F Please indicate the number(s) given above of the three most important agency facilitating conditions.

1 ; 6 ; 7

12G	Personal Factor	Degree of Facilitation: None 0	1	2	3	Great Deal 4
A	Personal Relations and Commitments					
	Good relationships with:					
I	Within Agency					
1	Board/Board members	X				
2	Administrator				X	
3	Supervisor			X		
4	Staff				X	

		Degree of Facilitation				
		None 0	1	2	3	Great Deal 4
	5 Clients				X	
II	Outside Agency					
	6 Community leaders				X	
	7 Community people				X	
	8 Other organizations					X
	9 Nonstaff professional peers or friends					X
Positive effects of:						
III	Commitment					
	10 Commitment to agency				X	
	11 Commitment to program				X	
	12 Commitment to guideline				X	
B	Personal Knowledge and Attributes					
Knowledge of:						
I	Personal Knowledge					
	13 Community			X		
	14 Clients			X		
	15 Programs			X		
	16 Relevant ideology (and theory)					X
Positive effects of:						
II	Personal Attributes					
	17 Position or role				X	
	18 Good reputation			X		
	19 Personal gain (promotion, job title, etc.)		X			
	20 Prior experiences			X		
	21 Self-confidence			X		
	22 Skill				X	
	23 Professional "disinterest"			X		
	24 Enjoyment of job				X	
	25 Patience			X		

(12G continued)

	Degree of Facilitation				
	None 0	1	2	3	Great Deal 4
C Other (specify)					
26 ______					
27 ______					
28 ______					

12H Please indicate the number(s) given above of the three most important personal facilitating conditions.

8; 9; 16

13 Please rate the overall importance of the facilitating factors below.

	Degree of Importance				
	None 0	1	2	3	Great Deal 4
Community					X
Client			X		
Agency				X	
Personal				X	

14 Were there limiting conditions as you implemented the guideline? Please check the Degree of Limitation for *each* condition listed.

	Degree of Limitation				
14A Community Factor	None 0	1	2	3	Great Deal 4
1 Negative response to organization generally	X				
2 Disinterest in or dissatisfaction with organization or program	X				

3	Lack of knowledge of organization purposes, programs, or activities				X	
4	Community residents lack other necessary knowledge or skills			X		
5	Community residents interfere with organization activities		X			
6	Pressure from community residents		X			
7	Influential community groups or leaders do not support organization or program		X			
8	External influences make community unsupportive of organization or program	X				
9	Community residents not interested in program specifically	X				
10	Dissensus among community residents	X				
11	Other activities compete with community residents' time and interests				X	
12	Community lacks funds needed to support organization or program		X			
13	Differences in life-styles between staff (including practitioner) and community residents		X			
14	Other (specify)______					
15	______					
16	______					

14B Please indicate the number(s) given above of the three most important community limiting conditions.

__3__; __4__; __11__

14C Clients	Degree of Limitation: None 0	1	2	3	Great Deal 4
1 Negative response to organization generally	X				
2 Disinterest in or dissatisfaction with organization or program			X		
3 Lack of knowledge of organization purposes, programs, or activities				X	
4 Clients lack other knowledge or skills			X		
5 Clients interfere with organization activities		X			
6 Pressure from clients	X				
7 Clients not interested in program specifically			X		
8 Dissensus among clients	X				
9 Other activities compete with clients' time and interests				X	
10 Other (specify)________					
11 ________					
12 ________					

14D Please indicate the number(s) given above of the three most important client limiting conditions.

3 ; 7 ; 9

14E Agency	Degree of Limitation: None 0	1	2	3	Great Deal 4
1 External authority requirements hamper efforts	X				
2 Lack of power or authority of organization		X			
3 Unclear or shifting goals, programs, or assignments			X		
4 Hindering structure of organization		X			

5	Negative attitudes or actions toward clients or community		X			
6	Lack of knowledge of clients and/or community				X	
7	Practitioner-organization conflict		X			
8	Lack of staff (both adequate numbers or staff with specialized knowledge, training, etc.)					X
9	Lack of funds, facilities, and other resources					X
10	Lack of support or hindering action of affiliated organizations			X		
11	Lack of support or hindering action of board		X			
12	Lack of support or hindering action of administration	X				
13	Lack of support or hindering action of supervisor	X				
14	Lack of support or hindering action of staff	X				
15	Other (specify) ________					
16	________					
17	________					

14F Please indicate the number(s) given above of the three most important agency limiting conditions.

6 ; 8 ; 9

		Degree of Limitation				
		None				Great Deal
14G	Personal Factor	0	1	2	3	4
A	Personal Relations and Commitments					
	Poor relationships with:					
	I Within Agency					
	1 Board/Board members	X				

(14G continued)

	Degree of Limitation: None 0	1	2	3	Great Deal 4
2 Administration	X				
3 Supervisor	X				
4 Staff	X				
5 Clients	X				
II Outside Agency					
6 Community leaders		X			
7 Community people		X			
8 Other organizations		X			
9 Nonstaff professional peers or friends	X				
Negative effects of:					
III Commitment					
10 Lack of commitment to agency	X				
11 Lack of commitment to program	X				
12 Lack of commitment to guideline	X				
B Personal Knowledge and Attributes					
Lack of personal knowledge of:					
I Personal Knowledge					
13 Community					X
14 Clients				X	
15 Programs			X		
16 Relevant ideology (and theory)	X				
Negative effects of:					
II Personal Attributes					
17 Position or role	X				
18 Poor reputation	X				
19 Personal loss (demotion, job title, etc.)	X				
20 Lack of self-confidence		X			

21	Insufficient skills		X			
22	Professional "disinterest"			X		
23	Overinvolvement				X	
24	Do not enjoy job	X				
25	Impatience		X			
26	Fatigue			X		
27	Lack of time				X	

C Other (specify)

28						
29						
30						

14H Please indicate the number(s) given above of the three most important personal limiting conditions.

13 ; 23 ; 27

15 Please rate the overall importance of the limiting factors below.

	Degree of Importance				
	None 0	1	2	3	Great Deal 4
Community		X			
Client	X				
Agency			X		
Personal			X		

COMMUNITY INTERVENTION PROJECT

Periodic Log Questionnaire

1 Guideline number 4 (Innovation)

2 Practitioner Jane Jones

3 Agency Human Services Association

4 Date of report 1/28/73 5 Time period covered by report 1/6-1/30/73

- -

6 In your own words, please describe what happened as you carried out the guideline during the time period covered by this log. If you need more space, please use the reverse side of this page.

I have prepared the list of agencies, organizations, and community persons to be involved in community councils in Baldwin and Newton. I have talked personally to interested community members and to organizational leadership in order to mobilize support and interested in the program. I have addressed several public meetings. I have sent out a mailing announcing the meeeting date and rationale for the council in the two areas. My description of activities and progress in Hudson has evoked interest and encouraged people in these other areas to proceed along similar lines.

School of Social Work
University of Michigan
REVPLQ 10/72

7 Has (Have) there been any change(s) (refinements, additions, deletions, etc.) in your overall goal?

There have been no refinements, additions or deletions in my overall goal.

8 Look back at the intervention guideline. Was there any change in how you defined or concretized *each* element of the guideline in your practice (that is, how you operationalized these components)?

Promote acceptance:

I find that I get a better response and understanding if I discuss the plan personally with key community people before operationalizing the guideline. Community people then feel more a part of the decision-making and planning process.

Of an innovation:

None

Formulate it in such a way that the total innovation can be experienced initially by a limited portion of the target system:

The model used in Hudson Township is now being replicated actively in Newton and Baldwin.

9 Describe the *major* steps you went through as you continued to use this guideline. List specific behaviors in the order in which they occurred. (Use the boxes to indicate this order, repeating numbers for simultaneous events.)

[1] I talked to interested community members in Newton and Baldwin (township supervisor, mayor and city council, the schools, senior citizens groups, civic association, and others).

[2] I have prepared a set of mailing lists for Baldwin and Newton and have completed the mailing to appropriate agencies, organizations, and lay people announcing meeting date and purpose of the council.

[3] I have prepared agendas for both meetings based on my conversations in these areas, as well as my previous experience in Hudson.

10 *Instructions:* In your answer to question 10 we are interested in the number of key community groups involved in each category and the *key* reason(s) for contact. Put the total number of key community groups involved in any given category in the spaces provided at the left. The *key* reason(s) for contact category should be recorded in the space to the right. Please indicate *no more* than *2* reasons for each type of key community group.

10 What key community groups did you involve?

Total Number Involved	Type of Group	Reason for Contact (Select from List at Right)	
5	1 Public agency or organization	1	2
4	2 Quasi-public or private agency or organization	1	6
8	3 Informal association and single issue group	1	6
	4 None		

Reason for Contact

1 Seeking exercise of influence by contact
2 Seeking financial support
3 Seeking non-financial material resources
4 Public relations (seeking good will or general approval)
5 Seeking information and guidance
6 Seeking to prepare the contact for future participation
7 Seeking immediate participation
8 Seeking legitimation or formally expressed approval
9 Other (specify)_____
10 _____
11 _____

11 *Instructions:* In your answer to Question 11 we are interested in the number of key individuals involved in each category and the *key* reason(s) for contact. Put the total number of key individuals involved in any given category in the spaces provided at the left.

The *key* reason(s) for contact category should be recorded in the space to the right. Please indicate *no more* than *2* reasons for each type of key individual.

11 What key individuals did you involve?

Total Number Involved	Title and/or Affiliation	Reason for Contact (Select from List at Right)	
6	1 Board officers and members	1	8
	2 Board committee members		
3	3 Staff committee members	8	4
3	4 Agency director, assistant director	8	4
4	5 Agency supervisors	5	6
	6 Agency peers (colleagues)		
	7 Agency subordinates		
4	8 External governmental officials	1	2

Reason for Contact

1 Seeking exercise of personal influence by contact
2 Seeking financial assistance
3 Seeking non-financial material resources
4 Public relations (seeking good will or general approval)
5 Seeking information and guidance
6 Seeking to prepare the contact for future participation
7 Seeking immediate participation

____	9	External non-governmental organization administrative and supervisory staff	____	____
2	10	External non-governmental organization line and operating staff	5	6
14	11	Voluntary association external to agency—chairman and members	6	4
____	12	Professional peers and friends	____	____
6	13	Community leaders	1	5
22	14	Other community people	5	6
8	15	Clients	5	6
____	16	None	____	____
____	17	Other (specify)____ ____________	____	____
____	18	____________	____	____
____	19	____________	____	____

8 Seeking legitimation or formally expressed approval
9 Other (specify)____
10 ____________
11 ____________

12 Were there facilitating conditions as you implemented the guideline? Please check the Degree of Facilitation for *each* condition listed.

		Degree of Facilitation				
		None				Great Deal
12A	Community Factor	0	1	2	3	4
1	Community participation in organization or program (voluntary)	____	____	____	X	____

(12A continued)

		Degree of Facilitation: None 0	1	2	3	Great Deal 4
2	Community participation in organization or program (through legal or administrative ruling)	X				
3	Community support of organization generally				X	
4	Community interest in program specifically					X
5	Influential and other community groups support organization or program				X	
6	Influential or other community groups involved with organization or program			X		
7	Community receptivity to organization or program					X
8	Community disinterest in, or dissatisfaction with, organization or program (leading to a desire for change)		X			
9	Changes in community tend to support organization or program		X			
10	External influences make community supportive of organization or program		X			
11	Community support of clients			X		
12	Community support of practitioner			X		
13	Other (specify) ______					
14	______					
15	______					

12B Please indicate the number(s) given above of the three most important community facilitating conditions.

___3___; ___4___; ___7___

12C	Client Factor	None 0	1	2	3	Great Deal 4
		Degree of Facilitation				
1	Client participation in organization or program (voluntary)			X		
2	Client participation in organization or program (through legal or administrative ruling)	X				
3	Client interest in organization generally		X			
4	Client interest in program specifically				X	
5	Client receptivity to organization or program				X	
6	Disinterest in or dissatisfaction with agency or program (leading to a desire for change)		X			
7	Client support of other clients			X		
8	Client support of practitioner			X		
9	Other (specify)________					
10	________					
11	________					

12D Please indicate the number(s) given above of the three most important client facilitating conditions.

___4___; ___5___; ___1___

12E	Agency Factor	None 0	1	2	3	Great Deal 4
		Degree of Facilitation				
1	External authority requirements of organization support effort			X		
2	Affiliated organizational support				X	
3	Affiliated organizational involvement				X	

(12E continued)

		Degree of Facilitation				
		None 0	1	2	3	Great Deal 4
4	Board support	X				
5	Board involvement	X				
6	Administration support			X		
7	Administration involvement	X				
8	Administration disinterest	X				
9	Supervisor support			X		
10	Supervisor involvement		X			
11	Supervisor disinterest		X			
12	Staff support			X		
13	Staff involvement		X			
14	Practitioner assignments and tasks are consistent with effort	X				
15	Physical facilities aid in effort		X			
16	Other (specify)________					
17						
18						

12F Please indicate the number(s) given above of the three most important agency facilitating conditions.

2 ; 3 ; 6

12G Personal Factor	Degree of Facilitation				
	None 0	1	2	3	Great Deal 4
A Personal Relations and Commitments					
Good relationships with:					
I Within Agency					
1 Board/Board members	X				
2 Administrator				X	
3 Supervisor			X		
4 Staff				X	
5 Clients				X	

II	Outside Agency					
6	Community leaders				X	
7	Community people				X	
8	Other organizations					X
9	Nonstaff professional peers or friends					X
	Positive effects of:					
III	Commitment					
10	Commitment to agency				X	
11	Commitment to program				X	
12	Commitment to guideline				X	
B	Personal Knowledge and Attributes					
	Knowledge of:					
I	Personal Knowledge					
13	Community			X		
14	Clients			X		
15	Programs				X	
16	Relevant ideology (and theory)				X	
	Positive effects of:					
II	Personal Attributes					
17	Position or role				X	
18	Good reputation			X		
19	Personal gain (promotion, job title, etc.)		X			
20	Prior experiences					X
21	Self-confidence			X		
22	Skill			X		
23	Professional "disinterest"		X			
24	Enjoyment of job				X	
25	Patience			X		
C	Other (specify)					
26	____					
27	____					
28	____					

12H Please indicate the number(s) given above of the three most important personal facilitating conditions.

8 ; 9 ; 20

13 Please rate the overall importance of the facilitating factors below.

	Degree of Importance				
	None 0	1	2	3	Great Deal 4
Community					X
Client			X		
Agency				X	
Personal				X	

14 Were there limiting conditions as you implemented the guideline? Please check the Degree of Limitation for *each* condition listed.

14A Community Factor	Degree of Limitation				
	None 0	1	2	3	Great Deal 4
1 Negative response to organization generally		X			
2 Disinterest in or dissatisfaction with organization or program		X			
3 Lack of knowledge of organization purposes, programs, and/or activities					X
4 Community residents lack other necessary knowledge or skills			X		
5 Community residents interfere with organization activities				X	
6 Pressure from community residents			X		

7	Influential community groups and/or leaders do not support organization or program			X		
8	External influences make community unsupportive of organization or program		X			
9	Community residents not interested in program specifically		X			
10	Dissensus among community residents		X			
11	Other activities compete with community residents' time and interests					X
12	Community lacks funds needed to support organization and/or program			X		
13	Differences in life styles between staff (including practitioner) and community residents		X			
14	Other (specify)________					
15	________					
16	________					

14B Please indicate the number(s) given above of the three most important community limiting conditions.

3 ; 4 ; 11

14C	Clients	None 0	1	2	3	Great Deal 4
			Degree of Limitation			
1	Negative response to organization generally		X			
2	Disinterest in or dissatisfaction with organization or program			X		
3	Lack of knowledge of organization purposes, programs, or activities					X
4	Clients lack other knowledge or skills				X	

(14C continued)

		Degree of Limitation				
		None 0	1	2	3	Great Deal 4
5	Clients interfere with organization activities		X			
6	Pressure from clients			X		
7	Clients not interested in program specifically		X			
8	Dissensus among clients				X	
9	Other activities compete with clients' time and interests					X
10	Other (specify)________					
11	________					
12	________					

14D Please indicate the number(s) given above of the three most important client limiting conditions.

___3___; ___8___; ___9___

14E	Agency	Degree of Limitation				
		None 0	1	2	3	Great Deal 4
1	External authority requirements hamper efforts		X			
2	Lack of power or authority of organization					X
3	Unclear or shifting goals, programs, or assignments			X		
4	Hindering structure of organization		X			
5	Negative attitudes or actions toward clients and/or community		X			
6	Lack of knowledge of clients or community				X	
7	Practitioner-organization conflict		X			
8	Lack of staff (both adequate numbers or staff with specialized knowledge, training, etc.)					X

9	Lack of funds, facilities, and other resources					X
10	Lack of support or hindering action of affiliated organizations			X		
11	Lack of support or hindering action of board		X			
12	Lack of support or hindering action of administration	X				
13	Lack of support or hindering action of supervisor	X				
14	Lack of support or hindering action of staff	X				
15	Other (specify) ______					
16	______					
17	______					

14F Please indicate the number(s) given above of the three most important agency limiting conditions.

2 ; 8 ; 9

		Degree of Limitation				
		None				Great Deal
14G	Personal Factor	0	1	2	3	4

A Personal Relations and Commitments

Poor relationships with:

I Within Agency

		0	1	2	3	4
1	Board/Board members	X				
2	Administration	X				
3	Supervisor		X			
4	Staff	X				
5	Clients	X				

(14G continued)

		Degree of Limitation: None 0	1	2	3	Great Deal 4
II	**Outside Agency**					
6	Community leaders		X			
7	Community people		X			
8	Other organizations		X			
9	Nonstaff professional peers or friends	X				
	Negative effects of:					
III	**Commitment**					
10	Lack of commitment to agency	X				
11	Lack of commitment to program	X				
12	Lack of commitment to guideline	X				
B	**Personal Knowledge and Attributes**					
	Lack of personal knowledge of:					
I	**Personal Knowledge**					
13	Community					X
14	Clients				X	
15	Programs		X			
16	Relevant ideology (and theory)	X				
	Negative effects of:					
II	**Personal Attributes**					
17	Position or role	X				
18	Poor reputation	X				
19	Personal loss (demotion, job title, etc.)	X				
20	Lack of self-confidence		X			
21	Insufficient skills		X			
22	Professional "disinterest"			X		
23	Overinvolvement				X	

24	Do not enjoy job		X			
25	Impatience		X			
26	Fatigue			X		
27	Lack of time					X

C Other (specify)

28						
29						
30						

14H Please indicate the number(s) given above of the three most important personal limiting conditions.

13 ; 23 ; 27

15 Please rate the overall importance of the limiting factors below.

	Degree of Importance				
	None 0	1	2	3	Great Deal 4
Community			X		
Client		X			
Agency			X		
Personal			X		

COMMUNITY INTERVENTION PROJECT

Final Summary Log Questionnaire

1 Guideline number 4 (Innovation)

2 Practitioner Jane Jones

3 Agency Human Services Association

4 Date of summary report 2/1/73

- -

5 In your own words, please summarize your use of the guideline as you experienced it. If you need more space, please use the reverse side of this page.

The Human Services Association agency flow chart specifies that citizen advisory councils be set up in all of its service areas. Lip service has been paid to the notion, but no councils have actually been set up. I decided to develop an organizational model in one of the areas assigned to me and then expand that model to some of the other communities. While my agency formally approved this innovation, it had made no progress in bringing it about.

The first community council was set up in Hudson Township, a limited portion of the target population. I informed my immediate supervisor and director of my plan by submitting an outline. I began talking to people in the community that I felt would be interested in the council. The director of Hudson community schools was particularly

School of Social Work
University of Michigan
REVFSLQ 10/72

helpful in assisting me draw up a list of appropriate community contacts. I sent out a mailing and addressed public meetings in order to publicize the new group.

The first community council meeting in Hudson was a big success. The meeting was designed to assist community members to get to know one another and to identify community problems. Everyone had a name tag and was instructed to talk to three people they did not already know. After a short talk session, everyone reported on the people they talked to, specifying what those persons had to offer a community council. Groups of ten were formed to do community problem identification. Each group was instructed to come up with eight community problems. When all problems were compiled, the entire group chose three major problem areas and formed three committees to deal with those problems. The committees are functioning and a second meeting has been called.

Lists of appropriate community contacts from Baldwin and Newton have been compiled. A mailing has been sent out announcing the formation of the community council and the first meeting date. Public forums like the city council and the school board meetings have been addressed regarding the creation of the new council. Hopefully the replication of the model will be as successful in the other communities as it was in Hudson Township. I plan to use the same meeting format.

I have held preliminary meetings with the Baldwin Supervisor (city manager), Baldwin Health Council and the Newton Civic Association and School-Community Advisory Committee. (In addition, I will be contacting many people in Baldwin and Newton in positions which I found useful in Hudson—like school-community director (or continuing education director in the high schools), director of state and federal programs for the schools and OEO community development staff.)

6 What was your overall goal (as you would generally characterize it) in using this guideline?

The overall goal is to set up three community councils in communities that I am responsible to for providing service (Hudson, Baldwin and Newton community).

6A To what degree was this goal attained?

1 Not at all	2 Little	3 Some	4 Much	5 Complete
			X	

6B Give some concrete empirical indicators of goal attainment.

(1) The council has met once in Hudson, working committees have been set up and a second meeting has been called by the existing group.

(2) Under the aegis of the council, task forces have been set up to plan a comprehensive service program for senior citizens.

* (3) In Baldwin mailings have been sent out to appropriate community "influentials" and community organizations. Preliminary meetings have been held with Baldwin Supervisor and Baldwin Health Council. I have set a target date for an initial Baldwin Council meeting (2/12/73).

* (4) In Newton, mailings have been sent out to appropriate community "influentials" and community organizations. Preliminary meetings have been held with the Newton Civic Association and School-Community Advisory Committee. I am aiming for an initial meeting of the Newton Council in March or April.

- -

1 The initial meeting was held in Newton in March, organized after the model used in Hudson Township.

The Newton council met monthly during March, April, and May. It has recessed for the summer with plans to resume monthly meetings in the fall.

The Newton council has been functioning effectively and has addressed some of the housing problems in that area.

2 The meeting for Baldwin was not held as scheduled. The Practitioner does not anticipate setting up a council there now until fall (because of numerous other time commitments).

*Update on empirical indicators (5/21/73 K.K., evaluation research assistant).

7 Look back at the intervention guideline. How did you finally define or concretize the elements of the guideline in your practice (that is, how you finally operationalized these components)? To what degree do you feel that you have successfully operationalized each element?

Promote acceptance (define):

I talked to interested community members, notified my supervisor, and presented the idea to various community groups. (See narrative.)

Unsuccessful						Successful
					X	
	1	2	3	4	5	

Of an innovation (define):

Innovation: To set up Community Councils in Hudson Township, Baldwin Township, and Newton community.

Unsuccessful						Successful
			X			
	1	2	3	4	5	

Formulate it in such a way that the total innovation can be experienced initially by a limited portion of the target system (define):

The model was first set up in Hudson Township, the limited portion of the target system and was then expanded to Baldwin and Newton.

Unsuccessful						Successful
				X		
	1	2	3	4	5	

8 In terms of the overall process describe the *major* steps you went through while using this guideline. List the most important behaviors in the order in which they occurred. (Use the boxes to indicate this order, repeating numbers for simultaneous events.)

[1] I decided to set up community councils in some of my assigned service areas and submitted an outline to my supervisor.

[2] I drew up the mailing lists and talked to interested community members in one township.

[3] I publicized the creation of the community council at public forums prior to the first meeting.

[4] I held the meeting in Hudson Township and scheduled a second.

[4] A discussion of community problems was conducted and problem solving committees were formed.

[4] A date was set for an educational workshop involving service coordination and community problem solving.

[5] The model proved successful in Hudson, so I repeated the same process in Baldwin and Newton, pointing to the previous success as a way of encouraging and motivating participants.

9 *Instructions:* In your answer to question 9 we are interested in the number of key community groups involved in each category and the *key* reason(s) for contact. Put the total number of key community groups involved in any given category in the spaces provided at the left. The *key* reason(s) for contact category should be recorded in the space to the right. Please indicate *no more* than *2* reasons for each type of key community group.

9 Of all key community groups you involved while using this guideline, which do you consider, on the whole, to have been most important?

Total Number Involved	Type of Group	Reason for Contact (Select from List at Right		Reason for Contact
10	1 Public agency or organization	1	2	1 Seeking exercise of influence by contact 2 Seeking financial support
14	2 Quasi-public or private agency or organization	1	6	3 Seeking nonfinancial material resources
12	3 Informal association and single issue group	1	6	4 Public relations (seeking goodwill or general approval) 5 Seeking information and guidance
	4 None			

(9 continued)

Total Number Involved	Type of Group	Reason for Contact (Select from List at Right)	Reason for Contact
			6 Seeking to prepare the contact for future participation
			7 Seeking immediate participation
			8 Seeking legitimation or formally expressed approval
			9 Other (specify)_____
			10 _____
			11 _____

10 *Instructions:* In your answer to question 10 we are interested in the number of key individuals involved in each category and the *key* reason(s) for contact. Put the total number of key individuals involved in any category in the spaces provided at the left.

The *key* reason(s) for contact category should be recorded in the space to the right. Please indicate *no more* than *2* reasons for each type of key individual.

10A Of all key individuals you involved while using this guideline, who do you consider on the whole to have been most important?

Total Number Involved	Title and/or Affiliation	Reason for Contact (Select from List at Right)		Reason for Contact
2	1 Board officers and members	1	8	1 Seeking exercise of personal influence by contact
____	2 Board committee members	____	____	2 Seeking financial assistance
2	3 Staff committee members	5	6	3 Seeking nonfinancial material resources

6	4	Agency director, assistant director	8	7
2	5	Agency supervisors	5	6
10	6	Agency peers (colleagues)	5	6
____	7	Agency subordinates	____	____
6	8	External governmental officials	1	2
____	9	External nongovernmental organization administrative and supervisory staff	____	____
11	10	External nongovernmental organization line and operating staff	5	6
7	11	Voluntary association external to agency—chairman and members	6	4
____	12	Professional peers and friends	____	____
15	13	Community leaders	1	5
26	14	Other community people	5	6
9	15	Clients	5	6
____	16	None	____	____
____	17	Other (specify)____ ____________	____	____
____	18	____________	____	____
____	19	____________	____	____

4 Public relations (seeking goodwill or general approval)
5 Seeking information and guidance
6 Seeking to prepare the contact for future participation
7 Seeking immediate participation
8 Seeking legitimation or formally expressed approval
9 Other (specify)____
10 ____________
11 ____________

11 Overall, what were the most important facilitating conditions while you were using the guideline? Please check the Degree of Facilitation for *each* condition listed.

11A	Community Factor	None 0	1	2	3	Great Deal 4
		Degree of Facilitation				
1	Community participation in organization or program (voluntary)				X	
2	Community participation in organization or program (through legal or administrative ruling)		X			
3	Community support of organization generally				X	
4	Community interest in program specifically				X	
5	Influential and other community groups support organization or program				X	
6	Influential or other community groups involved with organization or program			X		
7	Community receptivity to organization or program				X	
8	Community disinterest in, or dissatisfaction with, organization or program (leading to a desire for change)		X			
9	Changes in community tend to support organization or program			X		
10	External influences make community supportive of organization or program		X			
11	Community support of clients				X	
12	Community support of practitioner			X		
13	Other (specify) ________					

14	____________	____	____	____	____	____
15	____________	____	____	____	____	____

11B Please indicate the number(s) given above of the three most important community facilitating conditions.

1 ; 4 ; 7

		Degree of Facilitation				
		None				Great Deal
11C	Client Factor	0	1	2	3	4
1	Client participation in organization or program (voluntary)		X			
2	Client participation in organization or program (through legal or administrative ruling)	X				
3	Client interest in organization generally			X		
4	Client interest in program specifically				X	
5	Client receptivity to organization or program			X		
6	Disinterest in or dissatisfaction with agency or program (leading to a desire for change		X			
7	Client support of other clients				X	
8	Client support of practitioner			X		
9	Other (specify)____________					
10	____________					
11	____________					

11D Please indicate the number(s) given above of the three most important client facilitating conditions.

4 ; 8 ; 7

11E Agency Factor	Degree of Facilitation: None 0	1	2	3	Great Deal 4
1 External authority requirements of organization support effort			X		
2 Affiliated organizational support				X	
3 Affiliated organizational involvement				X	
4 Board support	X				
5 Board involvement	X				
6 Administration support		X			
7 Administration involvement	X				
8 Administration disinterest	X				
9 Supervisor support		X			
10 Supervisor involvement	X				
11 Supervisor disinterest	X				
12 Staff support	X				
13 Staff involvement	X				
14 Practitioner assignments and tasks are consistent with effort			X		
15 Physical facilities aid in effort		X			
16 Other (specify)________					
17 ________					
18 ________					

11F Please indicate the number(s) given above of the three most important agency facilitating conditions.

2 ; 3 ; 14

11G Personal Factor	Degree of Facilitation: None 0	1	2	3	Great Deal 4
A Personal Relations and Commitments					
Good relationships with:					
I Within Agency					
1 Board/Board members	X				

	2	Administrator				X	
	3	Supervisor			X		
	4	Staff		X			
	5	Clients				X	
II	Outside Agency						
	6	Community leaders				X	
	7	Community people				X	
	8	Other organizations					X
	9	Nonstaff professional peers or friends				X	

Positive effects of:

III	Commitment						
	10	Commitment to agency				X	
	11	Commitment to program				X	
	12	Commitment to guideline				X	

B Personal Knowledge and Attributes

Knowledge of:

I	Personal Knowledge						
	13	Community			X		
	14	Clients			X		
	15	Programs				X	
	16	Relevant ideology (and theory)				X	

Positive effects of:

II	Personal Attributes						
	17	Position or role				X	
	18	Good reputation			X		
	19	Personal gain (promotion, job title, etc.)	X				
	20	Prior experiences			X		
	21	Self-confidence			X		
	22	Skill			X		
	23	Professional "disinterest"				X	

(11G continued)

		Degree of Facilitation				
		None 0	1	2	3	Great Deal 4
24	Enjoyment of job				X	
25	Patience				X	

C Other (specify)

26						
27						
28						

11H Please indicate the number(s) given above of the three most important personal facilitating conditions.

6 ; 8 ; 14

12 In retrospect, please rate the overall importance of each facilitating factor below.

	Degree of Importance				
	None 0	1	2	3	Great Deal 4
Community					X
Client				X	
Agency			X		
Personal				X	

13 Overall, what were the most important limiting conditions while you were using the guideline? Please check the Degree of Limitation for *each* condition listed.

13A Community Factor	Degree of Limitation None 0	1	2	3	Great Deal 4
1 Negative response to organization generally		X			
2 Disinterest in or dissatisfaction with organization or program		X			

3	Lack of knowledge of organization purposes, programs, or activities					X
4	Community residents lack other necessary knowledge or skills				X	
5	Community residents interfere with organization activities			X		
6	Pressure from community residents		X			
7	Influential community groups or leaders do not support organization or program		X			
8	External influences make community unsupportive of organization or program		X			
9	Community residents not interested in program specifically		X			
10	Dissensus among community residents					X
11	Other activities compete with community residents' time and interests				X	
12	Community lacks funds needed to support organization or program				X	
13	Differences in life-styles between staff (including practitioner) and community residents		X			
14	Other (specify)________					
15						
16						

13B Please indicate the number(s) given above of the three most important community limiting conditions.

3 ; 10 , 12

13C	Client Factor	None 0	1	2	3	Great Deal 4
		Degree of Limitation				
1	Negative response to organization generally		X			
2	Disinterest in or dissatisfaction with organization or program		X			
3	Lack of knowledge of organization purposes, programs, or activities					X
4	Clients lack other knowledge or skills				X	
5	Clients interfere with organization activities		X			
6	Pressure from clients		X			
7	Clients not interested in program specifically			X		
8	Dissensus among clients				X	
9	Other activities compete with clients' time and interests					X
10	Other (specify)______					
11	______					
12	______					

13D Please indicate the number(s) given above of the three most important client limiting conditions.

3 ; 8 ; 9

13E	Agency Factor	Degree of Limitation: None 0	1	2	3	Great Deal 4
1	External authority requirements hamper efforts		X			
2	Lack of power or authority of organization					X
3	Unclear or shifting goals, programs, or assignments		X			
4	Hindering structure of organization	X				
5	Negative attitudes or actions toward clients or community	X				
6	Lack of knowledge of clients or community				X	
7	Practitioner-organization conflict		X			
8	Lack of staff (both adequate numbers or staff with specialized knowledge, training, etc.)					X
9	Lack of funds, facilities, and other resources					X
10	Lack of support or hindering action of affiliated organizations		X			
11	Lack of support or hindering action of board		X			
12	Lack of support or hindering action of administration	X				
13	Lack of support or hindering action of supervisor	X				
14	Lack of support or hindering action of staff	X				
15	Other (specify) ______					
16	______					
17	______					

13F Please indicate the number(s) given above of the three most important agency limiting conditions.

2 ; 8 ; 9

			Degree of Limitation				
13G	**Personal Factor**		None 0	1	2	3	Great Deal 4
A	**Personal Relations and Commitments**						
	Poor relationships with:						
	I Within Agency						
	1	Board/Board members	X				
	2	Administration	X				
	3	Supervisor		X			
	4	Staff	X				
	5	Clients	X				
	II Outside Agency						
	6	Community leaders	X				
	7	Community people	X				
	8	Other organizations	X				
	9	Nonstaff professional peers or friends	X				
	Negative effects of:						
	III Commitment						
	10	Lack of commitment to agency	X				
	11	Lack of commitment to program	X				
	12	Lack of commitment to guideline	X				
B	**Personal Knowledge and Attributes**						
	Lack of personal knowledge of:						
	I Personal Knowledge						
	13	Community				X	
	14	Clients					X
	15	Programs			X		
	16	Relevant ideology (and theory)	X				

Negative effects of:

II Personal Attributes

17	Position or role		X			
18	Poor reputation	X				
19	Personal loss (demotion, job title, etc.)	X				
20	Lack of self-confidence		X			
21	Insufficient skills			X		
22	Professional "disinterest"				X	
23	Overinvolvement				X	
24	Do not enjoy job		X			
25	Impatience			X		
26	Fatigue				X	
27	Lack of time					X

C Other (specify)

28						
29						
30						

13H Please indicate the number(s) given above of the three most important personal limiting conditions.

13 ; 14 ; 27

14 In retrospect, rate the overall importance of each limiting factor below.

	Degree of Importance				
	None 0	1	2	3	Great Deal 4
Community				X	
Client		X			

(14 continued)

	Degree of Importance				
	None 0	1	2	3	Great Deal 4
Agency				X	
Personal			X		

15 Were there any factors, other than the intervention, which may have caused (partially or totally) the outcome which resulted from use of the guideline? In other words, what intruding circumstances or unforeseen events may have affected the outcome? Be as specific as possible in your answer.

The guideline was probably easier to operationalize in Hudson than in the other two communities because the director of community schools and the Hudson Health Committee were interested in having such a body organized to advise their programs. The chances for success were much better in the partial target system.

16 How useful do you feel this particular guideline can be to other practitioners?

Not useful	1	2	3	4	5	Useful
				X		

Explain:

I feel that the concept is valid and ideologically sound (leading to democratic participation, citizen advice to service program). I also feel that the methods employed are functional.

17 How likely are you to use this guideline again in your practice?

Unlikely	1	2	3	4	5	Likely
				X		

Explain:

I will use a similar procedure soon when setting up a senior citizens planning committee. I may also use it in other service areas as time permits.

18 On the whole, what did you find to be the most problematic aspects of the use of the guideline?

The most problematic aspects were lack of staff to do the necessary community profiles prior to setting up the councils. I did not feel that I knew enough about Baldwin to be as effective there as I was in Hudson.

19 What modifications of the guideline, if any, are suggested as a result of your experience?

I would not advise one person to try to work in as many communities as I have attempted to do. It's too much of a workload if responsibilities are not substantially delegated to other leaders and organizations.

APPENDIX C

ILLUSTRATIVE DATA TABLES FOR INNOVATION GUIDELINE

Illustrative tables for guideline. The discussion in the text is based primarily on tabulations of the "profile of successful practice" (scores of 4-5 on outcome; complete or almost complete success). An attempt was made to "tease out" further variables associated with success by comparing complete success (score of 5) with all other implementations (scores of 1-4). This is viewed as a preliminary type of analysis that may prove suggestive of areas for further exploration, both in research and practice. Data given for periodic logs in aggregate, and for the final summary log. Total sample sizes are as follows: successful profile 15, more successful 11, less successful 9.

Figures in boldface indicate variables referred to in quantitative findings discussion of manual as suggesting tendencies in the data.

The retrospective summary log data were the primary basis of analysis. A tendency was noted when 10 percent or more of the responses fell in a given cell or, for facilitating conditions, when an intensity of 3.0 was indicated or for limiting conditions when an intensity of 2.5 or more was indicated on the intensity scale.

The difference in discrimination level intensity for facilitating and limiting conditions is based on the fact that facilitating factors were generally given higher intensity ratings by respondents. Therefore, there are clearer differences between high and low ratings for facilitation. The lower discriminating intensity level for limiting conditions signifies at the outset that the data is more clustered at the lower portion of the scale, and more "lenient" criteria were applied in order to indicate relatively higher ratings or "tendencies" within rather homogeneous data. The reader should take into account this basic difference in distribution between facilitating and limiting conditions, and keep these criteria in mind when considering tendencies in limiting conditions.

Table 1
Number of Key Community Groups Contacted

Percent of Practitioners Who Checked:		Number of Groups								
		0	1–5	6–10	11–15	16–20	21–25	26–30	>30	Total
Successful outcome (score of 4-5) n = 15	Periodic Log	26.7	60.0	6.7	6.7					100
	Summary Log	**26.7**	**46.7**	13.4	6.7	6.7				100
More successful (score of 5) n = 11	Periodic Log	27.3	63.7	9.1						100
	Summary Log	27.3	45.5	18.2		9.1				100
Less successful (score of 1-4) n = 9	Periodic Log	22.2	55.5		11.1	11.1				100
	Summary Log	22.2	44.4	11.1	11.1				11.1	100

Table 2
Types of Key Community Groups

Percent of Practitioners Who Checked:		Type of Group: Public	Private	Voluntary
Successful outcome (score of 4-5)	Periodic Log	60	26.7	46.7
	Summary Log	**53.3**	33.3	40
More successful (score of 5)	Periodic Log	54.5	18.2	45.5
	Summary Log	45.5	27.3	45.5
Less successful (score of 1-4)	Periodic Log	66.7	55.6	55.6
	Summary Log	55.6	66.7	44.4

Table 3
Reasons for Contacting Key Community Groups (Periodic Log)

	Percent of Practitioners Who Checked								
	Successful Outcome (Score of 4-5)			More Successful (Score of 5)			Less Successful (Score of 1-4)		
Type of Agency	Public	Private	Voluntary	Public	Private	Voluntary	Public	Private	Voluntary
Reason for Contact									
1 Seeking exercise of influence	3.4		6.7	4.5		9.1	5.6	5.6	11.1
2 Financial support	3.4	6.7		4.5	4.5		5.6	11.1	
3 Nonfinancial material resources		3.4	3.4		4.5	4.5	11.1		
4 Public relations	6.7	6.7	13.4	4.5	4.5	9.1	11.1	11.1	11.1
5 Information and guidance	3.4		13.3			13.7	5.6		5.6
6 Future participation	6.7	3.4		4.5			16.7	16.7	5.6
7 Immediate participation	13.4	3.4	10.0	13.7		13.7	11.1	11.1	11.1
8 Legitimation	16.7			13.7			11.1	5.6	
9 Other									
Missing <1	46.7	76.7	53.3	54.6	86.4	50.1	22.2	38.9	55.5
Total	100	100	100	100	100	100	100	100	100

Table 4
Reasons for Contacting Key Community Groups (Summary Log)

	Percent of Practitioners Who Checked								
	Successful Outcome (Score of 4-5)			More Successful (Score of 5)			Less Successful (Score of 1-4)		
Type of Agency	Public	Private	Voluntary	Public	Private	Voluntary	Public	Private	Voluntary
Reason for Contact									
1 Seeking exercise of influence	3.4			4.6			5.6	11.1	5.6
2 Financial support		3.4	3.4			4.6	5.6	5.6	
3 Nonfinancial material resources		3.4	3.4		4.6	4.6	5.6		
4 Public relations	3.4	3.4	**10.0**		4.6	9.1	5.6	5.6	5.6
5 Information and guidance	6.7	3.4	**13.3**	4.6	4.6	13.7	5.6	5.6	11.1
6 Future participation	**10.0**	3.4	3.4	13.7		4.6		11.1	11.1
7 Immediate participation	**13.3**	**10.0**	3.4	13.7	9.1	4.6	11.1	11.1	5.6
8 Legitimation	**13.3**			9.1			11.1		
9 Other									
Missing <1	50.1	73.4	63.4	54.5	77.3	59.1	50.0	50.0	61.2
Total	100	100	100	100	100	100	100	100	100

Table 5
Number of Key Individuals Contacted

Percent of Practitioners Who Checked:		0	1-5	6–10	11–15	16–20	21–25	26–30	>30	Total
		Number of Individuals								
Successful outcome (score 4-5)	Periodic Log		20.0	40.0	6.7	33.3				100
	Summary Log		6.7	13.4	33.4	13.4	6.7		**26.7**	100
More successful (score of 5)	Periodic Log		27.3	45.5		27.3				100
	Summary Log		9.1	18.2	36.4	18.2			18.2	100
Less successful (score of 1-4)	Periodic Log		22.2	11.1	11.1	33.3	11.1		11.1	100
	Summary Log			22.2	11.1		11.1		55.6	100

Table 6
Types of Individuals Contacted

	Periodic Log						Summary Log					
	Successful Outcome (Score of 4–5)		More Successful (Score of 5)		Less Successful (Score of 1–4)		Successful Outcome (Score of 4–5)		More Successful (Score of 5)		Less Successful (Score of 1–4)	
	Percent of Practitioners	Average Number Used	Percent of Practitioners	Average Number Used	Percent of Practitioners	Average Number Used	Percent of Practitioners	Average Number Used	Percent of Practitioners	Average Number Used	Percent of Practitioners	Average Number Used
1. Board officers and members	40.0	2.7	36.4	1.8	55.6	4.8	33.3	**7.6**	27.3	3.3	55.6	9.8
2. Board committee members	20.1	5.7	9.1	8	22.2	4.5	26.7	**8.3**	18.2	5	33.3	9.7
3. Staff committee members	13.3	1	18.2	1	22.2	3.5	6.7	1	9.1	1	22.2	2.5
4. Agency director, assistant director	53.3	2.4	63.6	1.4	44.4	3.5	**66.7**	3.2	63.6	3.1	66.7	3.7
5. Agency supervisors	40.0	1.2	36.4	1.3	44.4	1.3	40	1.3	36.4	1.5	44.4	1.3
6. Agency peers	66.7	2.6	81.9	2.1	33.3	3	33.3	**6.2**	36.4	2.8	44.4	10.3
7. Agency subordinates	46.8	3.0	45.5	2.4	55.6	2.4	33.3	3.3	27.3	3.7	44.4	2
8. External government officials	13.3	1	9.1	1	44.4	1.5	13.3	1.5	9.1	2	33.3	2.7
9. External nongovernment administrators and supervisors	26.7	1.8	18.2	2	44.4	1.3	26.7	2	18.2	2.5	33.3	1.3
10. External nongovernment staff	13.3	1	9.1	1	44.4	1.3	13.3	3.5	9.1	5	33.3	4.7
11. Voluntary association members	20	1.3	27.3	1.3	11.1	12	33.3	2.4	45.5	2.4	11.1	7
12. Professional peers and friends	33.3	3.2	45.5	3.2	0	0	20	3	27.3	3	22.2	1
13. Community leaders	13.3	1	18.2	1	33.3	3	6.7	1	9.1	1	22.2	8
14. Community people	26.7	2	27.3	2.3	22.2	8.5	20	**6.7**	18.2	9.5	44.4	9.7
15. Clients	20.1	3	9.1	3	66.7	5.8	26.7	**14.8**	18.2	7	66.7	16.2
16. Other	6.7	1	9.1	1	0	0	6.7	2	9.1	2	0	0

Table 7a
Reasons for Contacting Key Individuals (Successful)[a]

			1	2	3	4	5	6	7	8	9	Missing	<1	Total
Board officers and members	Percent of practitioners who checked:	Periodic Log	10.0				6.7	3.4		16.7		63.4		100
		Summary Log	6.7				3.4		3.4	**16.7**		66.7	3.4	100
Board committee members	Percent of practitioners who checked:	Periodic Log	6.7				3.4	6.7	3.4	13.4		66.7		100
		Summary Log	3.4			3.4	3.4	3.4	3.4	3.4		73.3	6.7	100
Staff committee members	Percent of practitioners who checked:	Periodic Log	6.7			3.4				3.4		86.7		100
		Summary Log	3.4			3.4						93.3		100
Agency director, assistant director	Percent of practitioners who checked:	Periodic Log	6.7					6.7	20.0	16.7	3.4	26.7	20.0	100
		Summary Log	3.4			3.4		**10.0**	**16.7**	**16.7**	3.4	33.3	13.4	100
Agency supervisors	Percent of practitioners who checked:	Periodic Log	6.7		3.4		6.7	6.7	6.7	3.4	3.4	60.0	3.4	100
		Summary Log				3.4	3.4	10.0	10.0	6.7		60.0	6.7	100
Agency peers	Percent of practitioners who checked:	Periodic Log				16.7	13.3	10.0	6.7	3.4	3.4	43.4	3.4	100
		Summary Log	3.4			3.4	6.7	6.7	6.7			66.7	6.7	100

Agency subordinates	Percent of practitioners who checked:	Periodic Log	3.4		3.4	3.4	6.7	6.7	16.7	3.4	3.4	40.0	13.4	100
		Summary Log				3.4	3.4	6.7	10.0		3.4	66.7	6.7	100
External government officials	Percent of practitioners who checked:	Periodic Log	6.7				6.7		3.4	3.4		80.0		100
		Summary Log					3.4		3.4	3.4		86.7	3.4	100
External nongovernmental administration and supervisory staff	Percent of practitioners who checked:	Periodic Log				6.7	10.0	6.7	3.4			60.0	13.4	100
		Summary Log	3.4	3.4		3.4	3.4	6.7	6.7			73.3		100
External nongovernmental line and operating staff	Percent of practitioners who checked:	Periodic Log	3.4			3.4	3.4		3.4			86.7		100
		Summary Log				6.7	3.4		3.4	3.4		80.0	3.4	100
Voluntary association members	Percent of practitioners who checked:	Periodic Log	3.4		3.4	6.7	10.0	3.4				66.7	6.7	100
		Summary Log	3.4		3.4	3.4	10.0	6.7				73.3		100

Table 7a
Reasons for Contacting Key Individuals (Successful)[a]
(Continued)

			1	2	3	4	5	6	7	8	9	Missing	<1	Total
Professional peers and friends	Percent of practitioners who checked:	Periodic Log	6.7			6.7	6.7	3.4		3.4	3.4	60.0	10.0	100
		Summary Log	3.4	3.4		3.4	10.0					80.0		100
Community leaders	Percent of practitioners who checked:	Periodic Log				6.7		6.7				73.3	13.4	100
		Summary Log	3.4				3.4					93.3		100
Other community people	Percent of practitioners who checked:	Periodic Log	6.7		3.4		3.4		6.7			73.3	6.7	100
		Summary Log	3.4		3.4		3.4		**10.0**			80.0		100
Clients	Percent of practitioners who checked:	Periodic Log	3.4					3.4	6.7			80.0	6.7	100
		Summary Log	3.4			3.4	3.4	6.7	6.7			73.3	3.4	100
Other (1)	Percent of practitioners who checked:	Periodic Log					3.4	3.4				93.3		100
		Summary Log										100		100

Other (2)	Percent of practitioners who checked:	Periodic Log										100		100
		Summary Log										100		100

[a]Reason for Contact

1 Seeking exercise of personal influence by contact
2 Seeking financial assistance
3 Seeking nonfinancial material resources
4 Public relations (seeking good will or general approval)
5 Seeking information and guidance
6 Seeking to prepare the contact for future participation
7 Seeking immediate participation
8 Seeking legitimation or formal expressed approval
9 Other (specify) ____________________

Table 7b
Reasons for Contacting Key Individuals (More Successful)[a]

			1	2	3	4	5	6	7	8	9	Missing	<1	Total
Board officers and members	Percent of practitioners who checked:	Periodic Log	9.1				4.6	4.6		13.7		68.2		100
		Summary Log	9.1							13.7		72.7	4.6	100
Board committee members	Percent of practitioners who checked:	Periodic Log	4.6					4.6	4.6	13.7		72.7		100
		Summary Log				4.6			4.6	4.6		81.8	4.6	100
Staff committee members	Percent of practitioners who checked:	Periodic Log	9.1			4.6				4.6		81.8		100
		Summary Log	4.6			4.6						90.9		100
Agency director, assistant director	Percent of practitioners who checked:	Periodic Log	9.1					9.1	22.8	18.2		27.3	13.7	100
		Summary Log	4.6			4.6		13.7	18.2	18.2		36.4	4.6	100
Agency supervisors	Percent of practitioners who checked:	Periodic Log	9.1				4.6	9.1	4.6	4.6		63.6	4.6	100
		Summary Log				4.6		13.7	9.1	4.6		63.6	4.6	100
Agency peers	Percent of practitioners who checked:	Periodic Log				22.8	18.2	13.7	4.6	4.6		31.9	4.6	100
		Summary Log	4.6			4.6	9.1	9.1	4.6			63.6	4.6	100

Agency subordinates	Percent of practitioners who checked:	Periodic Log	4.6		4.6	4.6	4.6	4.6	13.7	4.6	4.6	36.4	18.2	100
		Summary Log				4.6		9.1	4.6		4.6	72.7	4.6	100
External government officials	Percent of practitioners who checked:	Periodic Log	9.1				4.6		4.6			81.8		100
		Summary Log							4.6			90.9	4.6	100
External nongovernment administration and supervisory staff	Percent of practitioners who checked:	Periodic Log				4.6	9.1	4.6	4.6			63.6	13.7	100
		Summary Log	4.6					4.6	9.1			81.8		100
External nongovernmental line and operating staff	Percent of practitioners who checked:	Periodic Log	4.6				4.6					90.9		100
		Summary Log				4.6	4.6		4.6			81.8	4.6	100
Voluntary association members	Percent of practitioners who checked:	Periodic Log	4.6		4.6	4.6	13.7					63.6	9.1	100
		Summary Log	4.6		4.6	4.6	13.7	9.1				63.6		100

[a]Reason for Contact

1 Seeking exercise of personal influence by contact
2 Seeking financial assistance
3 Seeking nonfinancial material resources
4 Public relations (seeking good will or general approval)
5 Seeking information and guidance
6 Seeking to prepare the contact for future participation
7 Seeking immediate participation
8 Seeking legitimation or formal expressed approval
9 Other (specify) ________________

Table 7c
Reasons for Contacting Key Individuals (Less Successful)[a]
(Continued)

			1	2	3	4	5	6	7	8	9	Missing	<1	Total
Professional peers and friends	Percent of practitioners who checked:	Periodic Log	9.1			9.1	9.1	4.6		4.6	4.6	45.5	13.7	100
		Summary Log	4.6	4.6		4.6	13.7					72.7		100
Community leaders	Percent of practitioners who checked:	Periodic Log				4.6		9.1				72.7	13.7	100
		Summary Log	4.6				4.6					90.9		100
Other community people	Percent of practitioners who checked:	Periodic Log	9.1				4.6		4.6			72.7	9.1	100
		Summary Log	4.6				4.6		9.1			81.8		100
Clients	Percent of practitioners who checked:	Periodic Log	4.6						4.6			90.9		100
		Summary Log	4.6				4.6	4.6	4.6			81.8		100
Other (1)	Percent of practitioners who checked:	Periodic Log					4.6	4.6				90.9		100
		Summary Log										100		100
Other (2)	Percent of practitioners who checked:	Periodic Log										100		100
		Summary Log										100		100

Board officers and members	Percent of practitioners who checked:	Periodic Log	16.7			5.6	11.1	5.6	5.6	11.1		44.4		100
		Summary Log	11.1			5.6	5.6	5.6	5.6	22.2		44.4		100
Board committee members	Percent of practitioners who checked:	Periodic Log	5.6				5.6	5.6		5.6		77.8		100
		Summary Log	5.6				11.1	11.1				66.7	5.6	100
Staff committee members	Percent of practitioners who checked:	Periodic Log	5.6					5.6				77.8	11.1	100
		Summary Log					11.1	11.1				77.8		100
Agency director, assistant director	Percent of practitioners who checked:	Periodic Log	5.6		5.6				22.2	16.7	5.6	22.2	22.2	100
		Summary Log	5.6		5.6				11.1	22.2	5.6	33.3	16.7	100
Agency supervisors	Percent of practitioners who checked:	Periodic Log			5.6	5.6	16.7	5.6	5.6	5.6	5.6	44.4	5.6	100
		Summary Log					16.7	5.6	5.6	11.1		55.6	5.6	100
Agency peers	Percent of practitioners who checked:	Periodic Log					5.6	5.6	16.7		5.6	66.7		100
		Summary Log	5.6		5.6		11.1	5.6	11.1			55.6	5.6	100

Table 7c
Reasons for Contacting Key Individuals (Less Successful)[a] (Continued)

			1	2	3	4	5	6	7	8	9	Missing	<1	Total
Agency subordinates	Percent of practitioners who checked:	Periodic Log	5.6				5.6	16.7	22.2		5.6	44.4		100
		Summary Log					11.1	5.6	22.2			55.6	5.6	100
External government officials	Percent of practitioners who checked:	Periodic Log	5.6	5.6	5.6		16.7	5.6		5.6		55.6		100
		Summary Log	5.6	5.6			11.1			5.6		66.7	5.6	100
External nongovernmental administration and supervisory staff	Percent of practitioners who checked:	Periodic Log			11.1	5.6	5.6	11.1				55.6	11.1	100
		Summary Log		5.6	5.6	5.6	5.6	5.6				66.7	5.6	100
External nongovernmental line and operating staff	Percent of practitioners who checked:	Periodic Log			5.6	5.6	11.1	5.6	11.1			55.6	5.6	100
		Summary Log			5.6	5.6	5.6	5.6		5.6		66.7	5.6	100

Voluntary association	Percent of practitioners who checked:	Periodic Log			5.6	11.1		11.1	5.6			66.7		100
		Summary Log				5.6		5.6				88.9		100
Professional peers and friends	Percent of practitioners who checked:	Periodic Log					5.6		5.6			88.9		100
		Summary Log				5.6	5.6	5.6				77.8	5.6	100
Community leaders	Percent of practitioners who checked:	Periodic Log	5.6			5.6	11.1		11.1			55.6	11.1	100
		Summary Log	5.6				11.1	5.6				77.8		100
Other community people	Percent of practitioners who checked:	Periodic Log			5.6		5.6	5.6	5.6			77.8		100
		Summary Log			5.6	5.6	11.1	11.1	5.6			55.6	5.6	100
Clients	Percent of practitioners who checked:	Periodic Log	5.6				22.2	11.1	16.7			33.3	11.1	100
		Summary Log				5.6	16.7	16.7	16.7			33.3	11.1	100
Other (1)	Percent of practitioners who checked:	Periodic Log										100		100
		Summary Log										100		100
Other (2)	Percent of practitioners who checked:	Periodic Log										100		100
		Summary Log										100		100

Table 8
Relative Importance of Different Sectors in Facilitation and Limitation

Successful Outcome Mean Scores			
		Facilitation	Limitation
Community	Periodic Log	2.4	1.3
	Summary Log	**2.7**	**1.1**
Client	Periodic Log	2.1	0.9
	Summary Log	**2.5**	**1.1**
Agency	Periodic Log	2.7	1.8
	Summary Log	**2.7**	**1.8**
Personal	Periodic Log	3.4	1.5
	Summary Log	**3.6**	**1.6**
$\overline{X}$	Periodic Log	2.7	1.4
	Summary Log	**2.9**	**1.4**

More Successful Mean Scores			
		Facilitation	Limitation
Community	Periodic Log	2.3	1.3
	Summary Log	2.6	1.2
Client	Periodic Log	1.9	1.2
	Summary Log	2.3	1.3
Agency	Periodic Log	2.5	2.1
	Summary Log	2.6	2.2

More Successful Mean Scores (Continued)			
		Facilitation	Limitation
Personal	Periodic Log	3.4	1.8
	Summary Log	3.5	2.0
$\overline{X}$	Periodic Log	2.5	1.6
	Summary Log	2.8	1.7
Less Successful Mean Scores			
		Facilitation	Limitation
Community	Periodic Log	2.6	1.7
	Summary Log	3.0	1.7
Client	Periodic Log	2.3	1.7
	Summary Log	2.7	1.7
Agency	Periodic Log	2.9	1.9
	Summary Log	2.4	1.9
Personal	Periodic Log	3.0	1.7
	Summary Log	3.5	1.5
$\overline{X}$	Periodic Log	2.7	1.8
	Summary Log	2.9	1.7

Table 9
Personal Facilitating Variables

		Periodic Log					
		Successful Outcome (Score of 4–5)		More Successful (Score of 5)		Less Successful (Score of 1–4)	
		Percent of Practitioners	Intensity	Percent of Practitioners	Intensity	Percent of Practitioners	Intensity
Good Relationships Within Agency	1. Board/Board Members		2.6		3.0		2.3
	2. Administrator		3.0		2.8	3.7	2.9
	3. Supervisor	2.2	3.5	3.0	3.2	3.7	2.9
	4. Staff	11.1	2.3	12.1	3.2	11.1	2.8
	5. Clients	2.2	2.6		2.5	3.7	2.5
Good Relationships Outside Agency	6. Community leaders		2.2		2.3	3.7	2.3
	7. Community people		2.1		2.1		2.0
	8. Other Organizations		2.1		2.0	3.7	2.3
	9. Nonstaff professional peers		2.3		2.3		2.4
	or friends	2.2	3.0	3.0	2.8	3.7	2.9
Commitment	10. Commitment to agency	13.3	3.5	9.1	3.5	14.8	2.9
	11. Commitment to program	2.2	3.1	3.0	3.1		2.4
	12. Commitment to guideline	8.9	3.3	12.1	3.1		2.9
Personal Knowledge of:	13. Community	2.2	3.0	3.0	3.0		2.4
	14. Clients	4.5	3.3	6.1	3.3		2.9
	15. Programs	2.2	3.2	3.0	3.3		2.7
	16. Relevant ideology and theory	15.6	3.2	15.2	3.3	11.1	2.8

		Summary Log					
		Successful Outcome (Score of 4–5)		More Successful (Score of 5)		Less Successful (Score of 1–4)	
		Percent of Practitioners	Intensity	Percent of Practitioners	Intensity	Percent of Practitioners	Intensity
	1. Board/Board Members	4.5	**3.5**	3.0	3.5	3.7	2.4
Good	2. Administrator	4.5	**3.2**	6.1	3.5	7.4	2.6
Relationships	3. Supervisor	2.3	2.7		2.4	3.7	2.7
Within	4. Staff	8.9	**3.5**	9.1	3.6	3.7	2.5
Agency	5. Clients	6.7	2.4	3.0	2.3	7.4	2.4
Good	6. Community leaders		2.6		2.7	3.7	2.4
Relationships	7. Community people	2.3	2.9		3.0	3.7	2.6
Outside	8. Other Organizations		2.3		2.3	7.4	2.4
Agency	9. Nonstaff professional peers	2.3	2.7	3.0	2.9		2.5
	or friends		**3.0**		2.8	3.7	3.0
	10. Commitment to agency	**15.6**	**3.4**	12.1	3.4	14.8	3.0
Commitment	11. Commitment to program		**3.2**		3.2		2.6
	12. Commitment to guideline	4.5	**3.6**	6.1	3.8	3.7	2.9
	13. Community	2.3	**3.3**	3.0	3.6	3.7	2.6
Personal	14. Clients	2.3	**3.2**	3.0	3.2		3.0
Knowledge	15. Programs		**3.4**		3.5		2.9
of:	16. Relevant ideology and theory	**20.0**	**3.3**	24.3	3.5	14.8	2.9

Table 9
Personal Facilitating Variables (Continued)

		Periodic Log					
		Successful Outcome (Score of 4–5)		More Successful (Score of 5)		Less Successful (Score of 1–4)	
		Percent of Practitioners	**Intensity**	Percent of Practitioners	Intensity	Percent of Practitioners	Intensity
Personal Attributes	17. Position or role	2.2	2.8	3.0	2.7		2.6
	18. Good reputation		1.7		1.7		1.7
	19. Personal gain (promotion, etc.)	8.9	2.5	6.1	2.5	14.8	2.4
	20. Prior experiences	4.5	3.0	6.1	3.2		2.3
	21. Self-confidence		2.8		3.0		2.4
	22. Skill		1.3		1.3		1.7
	23. Professional "disinterest"		2.7		2.6		2.8
	24. Enjoyment of job	2.2	2.3		2.2	7.4	2.3
	25. Patience						
	26. Other	15.6		15.2		18.5	
	27. Missing <1						

		Summary Log					
		Successful Outcome (Score of 4–5)		More Successful (Score of 5)		Less Successful (Score of 1–4)	
		Percent of Practitioners	Intensity	Percent of Practitioners	Intensity	Percent of Practitioners	Intensity
	17. Position or role	4.5	**3.0**	6.1	3.0	3.7	2.6
	18. Good reputation		1.6		1.3		1.8
	19. Personal gain (promotion, etc.)	**11.1**	**3.1**	12.1	3.1	7.4	2.8
Personal Attributes	20. Prior experiences	6.7	**3.1**	6.1	3.2	3.7	2.8
	21. Self-confidence		2.9		3.0		2.8
	22. Skill		1.8		1.8		2.5
	23. Professional "disinterest"	2.3	2.8	3.0	2.7		2.9
	24. Enjoyment of job		2.5		2.3	3.7	3.0
	25. Patience						
	26. Other						
	27. Missing <1						

Table 10
Agency Facilitating Variables

	Periodic Log					
	Successful Outcome (Score of 4–5)		More Successful (Score of 5)		Less Successful (Score of 1–4)	
	Percent of Practitioners	Intensity	Percent of Practitioners	Intensity	Percent of Practitioners	Intensity
1. External Authority Requirements of Organizational Support Effort	8.9	2.2	6.1	2.0	7.4	2.1
2. Affiliated organizational support	8.9	2.0	9.1	2.0	7.4	2.0
3. Affiliated organizational involvement	4.5	2.1	6.1	2.1	3.7	2.0
4. Board support	4.4	2.4	3.0	2.2	3.7	2.2
5. Board involvement	4.4	2.2	3.0	2.0	3.7	1.8
6. Administration support	17.8	3.5	18.7	3.4	14.8	3.0
7. Administration involvement	6.7	2.9	9.1	2.8	3.7	2.4
8. Administration disinterest		1.0		1.0	3.7	1.0
9. Supervisor support	11.1	2.8	9.1	2.4	14.8	2.8
10. Supervisor involvement	2.2	2.4	3.0	2.3		2.2
11. Supervisor disinterest		1.0		1.0		1.0
12. Staff support	2.2	2.6		2.4	14.8	2.5
13. Staff involvement	2.2	2.5	3.0	2.3	11.1	2.5
14. Practitioner assignments and tasks are consistent with effort	8.9	2.9	9.1	2.8	3.7	2.6
15. Physical facilities aid in effort		2.0		1.8		2.0
16. Other	2.2	2.0	3.0	2.0		
17. Missing <1	15.6		18.2		7.4	

	Summary Log					
	Successful Outcome (Score of 4–5)		More Successful (Score of 5)		Less Successful (Score of 1–4)	
	Percent of Practitioners	Intensity	Percent of Practitioners	Intensity	Percent of Practitioners	Intensity
1. External Authority Requirements of Organizational Support Effort	4.5	2.9	6.1	2.8		2.7
2. Affiliated organizational support	2.2	2.1	3.0	2.6	7.4	1.8
3. Affiliated organizational involvement	6.7	2.1	9.1	2.5	11.1	1.9
4. Board support	**11.1**	**3.2**	9.1	3.0	7.4	2.4
5. Board involvement	6.7	2.6	6.1	2.4	3.7	2.2
6. Administration support	**15.5**	**3.3**	15.2	3.4	11.1	2.4
7. Administration involvement	4.5	**3.1**	6.1	3.3	3.7	2.2
8. Administration disinterest		2.5		2.5		2.0
9. Supervisor support	**11.1**	2.8	9.1	2.5	11.1	2.7
10. Supervisor involvement	4.5	**3.0**	3.0	3.3	7.4	2.3
11. Supervisor disinterest		1.7		1.0		2.5
12. Staff support	**13.8**	2.9	12.1	2.9	11.1	2.7
13. Staff involvement	8.7	**3.2**	9.1	3.4	11.1	2.4
14. Practitioner assignments and tasks are consistent with effort	6.7	**3.2**	6.1	3.1	14.8	2.8
15. Physical facilities aid in effort		2.3		2.6		1.5
16. Other						
17. Missing <1	4.5		6.1			

Table 11
Client Facilitating Variables

	Periodic Log					
	Successful Outcome (Score of 4–5)		More Successful (Score of 5)		Less Successful (Score of 1–4)	
	Percent of Practitioners	Intensity	Percent of Practitioners	Intensity	Percent of Practitioners	Intensity
1. Client participation in organization or program (voluntary)	11.1	2.6	9.1	2.6	14.8	2.3
2. Client participation in organization or program (through legal or administrative ruling)	4.4	1.2	6.1	1.2	11.1	1.3
3. Client interest in organization generally	6.7	1.8	9.1	1.7	7.4	1.7
4. Client interest in program specifically	20.0	2.1	18.2	2.0	18.5	2.4
5. Client receptivity to organization or program	8.9	1.9	9.1	1.7	18.5	2.0
6. Disinterest in or dissatisfaction with agency or program (leading to a desire for a change)	4.5	1.8	6.1	1.7	3.7	1.7
7. Client support of other clients	4.5	1.8	3.0	1.6	3.7	1.7
8. Client support of practitioner	11.1	2.0	12.1	1.8	3.7	2.0
9. Other						
10. Missing <1	28.9		27.3		18.5	

	Summary Log					
	Successful Outcome (Score of 4–5)		More Successful (Score of 5)		Less Successful (Score of 1–4)	
	Percent of Practitioners	Intensity	Percent of Practitioners	Intensity	Percent of Practitioners	Intensity
1. Client participation in organization or program (voluntary)	**20.0**	2.8	24.2	3.0	11.1	2.2
2. Client participation in organization or program (through legal or administrative ruling)		2.0		2.0	3.7	1.7
3. Client interest in organization generally	4.5	2.1	3.0	2.3	7.4	2.2
4. Client interest in program specifically	**13.3**	2.3	12.1	2.3	14.8	2.3
5. Client receptivity to organization or program	**13.3**	2.3	9.1	2.3	22.2	2.0
6. Disinterest in or dissatisfaction with agency or program (leading to a desire for a change)		1.8		2.0	3.7	1.8
7. Client support of other clients	6.7	2.3	6.1	2.3	11.1	2.2
8. Client support of practitioner	8.9	2.4	9.1	2.5	3.7	2.3
9. Other						
10. Missing < 1	33.3		36.4		22.2	

Table 12
Community Facilitating Variables

	Periodic Log					
	Successful Outcome (Score of 4–5)		More Successful (Score of 5)		Less Successful (Score of 1–4)	
	Percent of Practitioners	Intensity	Percent of Practitioners	Intensity	Percent of Practitioners	Intensity
1. Community participation in organization or program (voluntary)	6.7	2.1	9.1	2.2	3.7	1.9
2. Community participation in organization of program (through legal or administrative ruling)		1.2		1.0	3.7	1.3
3. Community support of organization generally	11.1	1.8	9.1	1.7	11.1	1.9
4. Community interest in program specifically	8.9	1.8	9.1	1.8	11.1	2.1
5. Influential and other community groups support organization or program	13.4	1.9	15.2	1.6	7.4	2.5
6. Influential or other community groups involved with organization or program	6.7	1.6	6.1	1.5	7.4	2.0
7. Community receptivity to organization or program	6.7	1.9	6.1	1.8	11.1	2.1
8. Community disinterest in or dissatisfaction with organization or program (leading to a desire for change)	2.2	1.6	3.0	1.6	3.7	1.6
9. Changes in community tend to support organization or program	4.4	1.8	3.0	1.7	3.7	1.5
10. External influences make community supportive of organization or program	2.2	1.4	3.0	1.5		1.3
11. Community support of clients	8.9	1.7	9.1	1.4	7.4	2.2
12. Community support of practitioner	2.2	1.8	3.0	1.6		2.4
13. Other				1.0		1.0
14. Missing <1	26.7		24.3		29.6	

	Summary Log					
	Successful Outcome (Score of 4–5)		More Successful (Score of 5)		Less Successful (Score of 1–4)	
	Percent of Practitioners	Intensity	Percent of Practitioners	Intensity	Percent of Practitioners	Intensity
1. Community participation in organization or program (voluntary)	8.9	2.9	12.1	2.9	11.1	2.6
2. Community participation in organization of program (through legal or administrative ruling)	2.2	1.6	3.0	1.5	3.7	1.8
3. Community support of organization generally	**11.1**	2.0	12.1	2.0	7.4	2.3
4. Community interest in program specifically	8.9	2.3	9.1	2.3	14.8	2.5
5. Influential and other community groups support organization or program	8.9	2.2	9.1	2.0	7.4	2.3
6. Influential or other community groups involved with organization or program		1.6		1.4	3.7	1.8
7. Community receptivity to organization or program	8.9	2.1	9.1	2.0	7.4	2.1
8. Community disinterest in or dissatisfaction with organization or program (leading to a desire for change)		1.7		2.0	3.7	1.6
9. Changes in community tend to support organization or program	6.7	2.0	3.0	2.0	7.4	1.9
10. External influences make community supportive of organization or program	2.2	1.8	3.0	2.0		1.3
11. Community support of clients	4.5	2.1	3.0	2.0	7.4	2.4
12. Community support of practitioner	**11.1**	2.4	9.1	2.2	14.8	2.7
13. Other						
14. Missing <1	26.7		27.3		11.1	

Table 13
Agency Limiting Variables

	Periodic Log					
	Successful Outcome (Score of 4–5)		More Successful (Score of 5)		Less Successful (Score of 1–4)	
	Percent of Practitioners	Intensity	Percent of Practitioners	Intensity	Percent of Practitioners	Intensity
1. External authority requirements hamper efforts	4.4	2.0	6.1	2.3		1.3
2. Lack of power and/or authority of organization	11.1	2.1	12.1	2.4	3.7	1.8
3. Unclear or shifting goals, programs, or assignments	11.1	2.2	9.1	2.6	14.8	1.9
4. Hindering structure of organization	17.8	2.4	21.2	2.8	7.4	1.4
5. Negative attitudes and/or actions toward clients and/or community		1.4		1.5		1.8
6. Lack of knowledge of clients and/or community		1.3		1.4		2.0
7. Practitioner-organizational conflict	2.2	1.6	3.0	1.7		1.4
8. Lack of staff (both adequate numbers or staff with specialized knowledge, training, etc.)	11.1	2.4	9.1	2.4	22.2	2.6
9. Lack of funds, facilities, and other resources	11.1	2.0	9.1	2.2	22.2	2.4
10. Lack of support or hindering action of affiliated organizations	6.7	1.2	3.0	1.3	7.4	1.4
11. Lack of support or hindering action of board		1.5		1.5	3.7	2.0
12. Lack of support or hindering action of administration	2.2	1.2	3.0	1.2		1.0
13. Lack of supporter hindering action of supervisor	2.2	1.2	3.0	1.2		1.0
14. Lack of support or hindering action of staff		1.5		1.5	3.7	1.7
15. Other	2.2	1.0		1.0	3.7	1.5
16. Missing <1	17.8		21.2		11.1	

	Summary Log					
	Successful Outcome (Score of 4–5)		More Successful (Score of 5)		Less Successful (Score of 1–4)	
	Percent of Practitioners	Intensity	Percent of Practitioners	Intensity	Percent of Practitioners	Intensity
1. External authority requirements hamper efforts	4.5	1.8	6.1	2.0		1.3
2. Lack of power and/or authority of organization	**13.3**	2.2	15.2	2.4	7.4	2.2
3. Unclear or shifting goals, programs, or assignments	**13.3**	2.2	12.1	2.6	22.2	2.3
4. Hindering structure of organization	**13.3**	**2.6**	15.2	3.2	11.1	2.2
5. Negative attitudes and/or actions toward clients and/or community		1.3		1.3		1.8
6. Lack of knowledge of clients and/or community	4.5	1.3	3.0	1.5	3.7	1.8
7. Practitioner-organizational conflict	4.5	1.8	6.1	2.0	3.7	1.9
8. Lack of staff (both adequate numbers or staff with specialized knowledge, training, etc.)	**11.1**	2.0	9.1	2.0	14.8	2.5
9. Lack of funds, facilities, and other resources	**13.3**	2.0	9.1	2.0	14.8	2.5
10. Lack of support or hindering action of affiliated organizations	4.5	1.2		1.5	7.4	1.2
11. Lack of support or hindering action of board		1.0		1.0	3.7	2.3
12. Lack of support or hindering action of administration	2.2	1.0	3.0	1.0	3.7	2.5
13. Lack of supporter hindering action of supervisor	2.2	1.7	3.0	1.7		2.0
14. Lack of support or hindering action of staff		1.3		1.3	7.4	2.7
15. Other						
16. Missing <1	13.3		18.2			

Table 14
Personal Limiting Variables

			Periodic Log					
			Successful Outcome (Score of 4–5)		More Successful (Score of 5)		Less Successful (Score of 1–4)	
			Percent of Practitioners	Intensity	Percent of Practitioners	Intensity	Percent of Practitioners	Intensity
Poor Relationships Within Agency	1.	Board/board members		1.0		1.0		1.5
	2.	Administration		1.0		1.0		1.0
	3.	Supervisor		1.7		1.7		1.0
	4.	Staff	2.2	1.0	3.0	1.0	3.7	1.7
	5.	Clients		1.0		1.0		1.3
Poor Relationships Outside Agency	6.	Community leaders		1.1		1.3		1.2
	7.	Community people		1.3		1.3		1.2
	8.	Other organizations	2.2	1.3		1.3	3.7	1.3
	9.	Nonstaff professional peers or friends		1.3		1.5		1.0
Commitment	10.	Lack of commitment to agency		1.8		1.8		2.0
	11.	Lack of commitment to program	2.2	1.0	3.0	1.0		1.0
	12.	Lack of commitment to guideline		1.4		1.3		1.5
Lack of Personal Knowledge of:	13.	Community		1.3		1.3	3.7	1.6
	14.	Clients	4.4	1.6	6.1	1.8		1.6
	15.	Programs	2.2	1.3	3.0	1.4		1.3
	16.	Relevant ideology (and theory)		1.0		1.0		1.3

		Periodic Log					
		Successful Outcome (Score of 4–5)		More Successful (Score of 5)		Less Successful (Score of 1–4)	
		Percent of Practitioners	Intensity	Percent of Practitioners	Intensity	Percent of Practitioners	Intensity
	17. Position or role	8.9	1.9	12.1	2.0		1.4
	18. Poor reputation		1.5		1.5		1.0
	19. Personal loss (demotion, job title, etc.)		1.0		1.0		1.5
Personal Attributes	20. Lack of self-confidence	2.2	1.0		1.0	3.7	1.3
	21. Insufficient skill		1.0		1.0		1.2
	22. Professional "disinterest"		1.0		1.0		1.5
	23. Overinvolvement	15.6	1.1	12.1	1.6	25.9	2.0
	24. Do not enjoy job		1.0		1.0		1.3
	25. Impatience	6.7	1.5	6.1	1.7	7.4	1.1
	26. Fatigue	6.7	2.5	9.1	2.5	3.7	2.3
	27. Lack of time	26.6	2.2	27.3	2.4	25.9	2.5
	28. Other	4.4	1.5	3.0	2.0	3.7	1.0
	29. Missing <1	15.6		15.2		18.5	

		Summary Log					
		Successful Outcome (Score of 4–5)		More Successful (Score of 5)		Less Successful (Score of 1–4)	
		Percent of Practitioners	Intensity	Percent of Practitioners	Intensity	Percent of Practitioners	Intensity
Poor Relationships Within Agency	1. Board/board members		1.0		1.0	3.7	2.3
	2. Administration		1.3		1.3	3.7	3.0
	3. Supervisor	4.5	1.3	6.1	1.3		1.0
	4. Staff	2.2	1.7	3.0	1.7	7.4	2.5
	5. Clients		1.0		1.0		2.0
Poor Relationships Outside Agency	6. Community leaders		1.2		1.3		1.3
	7. Community people		1.0		1.0		1.0
	8. Other organizations		1.0		1.0		1.3
	9. Nonstaff professional peers or friends	2.2	1.3	3.0	1.4		1.3
Commitment	10. Lack of commitment to agency	2.2	2.5	3.0	2.5		2.0
	11. Lack of commitment to program		1.0		1.0		2.0
	12: Lack of commitment to guideline		1.3		1.3		3.0
Lack of Personal Attributes of:	13. Community		1.0		1.0	3.7	1.5
	14. Clients	2.2	1.3	3.0	1.5	3.7	2.0
	15. Programs		1.0		1.0		1.2
	16. Relevant ideology (and theory)	4.5	1.3	6.1	1.3		1.3

		Summary Log					
		Successful Outcome (Score of 4–5)		More Successful (Score of 5)		Less Successful (Score of 1–4)	
		Percent of Practitioners	Intensity	Percent of Practitioners	Intensity	Percent of Practitioners	Intensity
	17. Position or role	4.5	1.7	6.1	1.8	3.7	1.8
	18. Poor reputation	2.2	1.5	3.0	1.5		1.5
	19. Personal loss (demotion, job title, etc.)		1.0		1.0		2.0
Personal Attributes	20. Lack of self-confidence	4.5	1.3	3.0	1.5	3.7	1.5
	21. Insufficient skill		1.0		1.0		1.5
	22. Professional "disinterest"		1.0		1.0		2.5
	23. Overinvolvement	**17.8**	1.9	15.2	2.0	22.2	2.3
	24. Do not enjoy job		1.0		1.0		1.3
	25. Impatience	6.7	1.0	6.1	1.0	3.7	1.4
	26. Fatigue	8.7	2.3	9.1	2.6	7.4	2.0
	27. Lack of time	**20.0**	**2.8**	18.2	2.9	25.9	3.0
	28. Other						
	29. Missing <1	17.8		15.2		11.1	

Table 15
Client Limiting Variables

	Periodic Log					
	Successful Outcome (Score of 4–5)		More Successful (Score of 5)		Less Successful (Score of 1–4)	
	Percent of Practitioners	Intensity	Percent of Practitioners	Intensity	Percent of Practitioners	Intensity
1. Negative response to organization generally	4.4	1.8	6.1	2.0	3.7	1.4
2. Disinterest in or dissatisfaction with organization or program	4.5	1.7	6.1	2.0	7.4	1.6
3. Lack of knowledge of organization purposes, programs, and/or activities	17.8	2.0	12.1	2.5	25.9	1.8
4. Clients lack other knowledge or skills	8.9	2.7	6.1	2.8	7.4	2.2
5. Clients interfere with organization activities	2.2	1.3	3.0	1.3		1.3
6. Pressure from clients	6.7	1.4	3.0	1.7	7.4	1.3
7. Clients not interested in program specifically	8.9	1.4	9.1	1.3	7.4	1.8
8. Dissensus among clients	4.5	1.2	6.1	1.3	7.4	1.8
9. Other interests compete with clients' time and interest	15.5	1.8	15.2	2.1	25.9	2.0
10. Other	2.2		3.0			
11. Missing <1	24.4		30.3		7.4	

	Summary Log					
	Successful Outcome (Score of 4–5)		More Successful (Score of 5)		Less Successful (Score of 1–4)	
	Percent of Practitioners	Intensity	Percent of Practitioners	Intensity	Percent of Practitioners	Intensity
1. Negative response to organization generally	2.2	1.0	3.0	1.0	7.4	1.2
2. Disinterest in or dissatisfaction with organization or program	2.2	2.0	3.0	4.0	3.7	1.2
3. Lack of knowledge of organization purposes, programs, and/or activities	**15.6**	2.3	12.1	2.5	18.5	2.1
4. Clients lack other knowledge or skills	**11.1**	**3.0**	6.1	4.0	14.8	2.3
5. Clients interfere with organization activities	2.2	1.0		1.0	3.7	1.3
6. Pressure from clients	2.2	1.5		2.0	3.7	1.3
7. Clients not interested in program specifically	6.7	1.7	9.1	1.7	7.4	2.0
8. Dissensus among clients	2.2	1.0	3.0	1.0	7.4	2.3
9. Other interests compete with clients' time and interest	**13.3**	2.4	12.1	2.4	14.8	2.1
10. Other						
11. Missing <1	42.2		51.5		18.5	

Table 16
Community Limiting Variables

	Periodic Log					
	Successful Outcome (Score of 4–5)		More Successful (Score of 5)		Less Successful (Score of 1–4)	
	Percent of Practitioners	Intensity	Percent of Practitioners	Intensity	Percent of Practitioners	Intensity
1. Negative response to organization generally	6.7	1.6	9.1	1.6		1.8
2. Disinterest in or dissatisfaction with organization or program	6.7	1.4	9.1	1.3	3.7	1.6
3. Lack of knowledge of organizational purposes, program, and/or activities	11.1	1.7	12.1	1.8	7.4	1.9
4. Community residents lack other necessary knowledge or skills	4.4	1.8	3.0	1.7	11.1	1.8
5. Community residents interfere with organization activities		1.0		1.0		1.4
6. Pressure from community residents		1.2		1.3		1.3
7. Influential community groups and/or leaders do not support organization or program	2.2	1.3	3.0	1.5		1.3
8. External influences make community unsupportive of organization or program	2.2	1.5	3.0	1.5		1.5
9. Community residents not interested in program specifically	2.2	1.9	3.0	2.2		1.2
10. Dissensus among community residents	8.9	1.6	9.1	1.4	11.1	1.8
11. Other activities compete with community residents' time and interests	13.3	1.9	12.1	1.8	18.5	2.4

	Periodic Log					
	Successful Outcome (Score of 4–5)		More Successful (Score of 5)		Less Successful (Score of 1–4)	
	Percent of Practitioners	Intensity	Percent of Practitioners	Intensity	Percent of Practitioners	Intensity
12. Communtiy lacks funds needed to support organization and/or program	6.7	2.2	6.1	2.7	14.8	2.2
13. Differences in lifestyles between staff (including practitioner) and community residents		1.8		1.5		1.8
14. Other						
15. Missing <1	37.8		39.4		18.5	

Table 16
Community Limiting Variables (Continued)

	Summary Log					
	Successful Outcome (Score of 4–5)		More Successful (Score of 5)		Less Successful (Score of 1–4)	
	Percent of Practitioners	Intensity	Percent of Practitioners	Intensity	Percent of Practitioners	Intensity
1. Negative response to organization generally.	2.2	1.3	3.0	1.5	3.7	1.4
2. Disinterest in or dissatisfaction with organization or program	6.7	1.5	6.1	1.5	7.4	1.5
3. Lack of knowledge of organizational purposes, program, and/or activities	8.9	2.8	9.1	3.0	11.1	2.1
4. Community residents lack other necessary knowledge or skills	8.9	3.3	3.0	4.0	14.8	2.6
5. Community residents interfere with organization activities		1.3		1.0		1.8
6. Pressure from community residents		1.3		2.0		1.3
7. Influential community groups and/or leaders do not support organization or program	2.2	1.3	3.0	1.5	3.7	1.2
8. External influences make community unsupportive of organization or program		1.0		1.0		1.3
9. Community residents not interested in program specifically	4.5	1.1	6.1	1.2	3.7	1.3
10. Dissensus among community residents	6.7	1.2	9.1	1.0	7.4	2.5
11. Other activities compete with community residents' time and interests	15.6	1.9	15.2	1.5	14.8	2.5

	Summary Log					
	Successful Outcome (Score of 4–5)		More Successful (Score of 5)		Less Successful (Score of 1–4)	
	Percent of Practitioners	Intensity	Percent of Practitioners	Intensity	Percent of Practitioners	Intensity
12. Communtiy lacks funds needed to support organization and/or program	6.7	1.5	6.1	1.8	14.8	1.7
13. Differences in lifestyles between staff (including practitioner) and community residents	2.2	1.2		1.0	7.4	1.5
14. Other		1.0		1.0		
15. Missing <1	33.4		30.3		25.9	

INDEX

* Names are of main authors whose ideas are drawn up or who are quoted in the text